HOLT SOCIAL STUDIES

REGIONS

JoAnn Cangemi
General Editor

HOLT, RINEHART AND WINSTON, PUBLISHERS
New York • Toronto • Mexico City • London • Sydney • Tokyo

General Editor

JoAnn Cangemi

is Professor of Education and Director of Graduate Studies in Education at Nicholls State University, Thibodaux, Louisiana. She received her Ph.D. in elementary education from Louisiana State University. Prior to her university work, Dr. Cangemi taught in the public elementary schools for ten years. She has served as a consultant in social studies curriculum development to numerous public and private school systems. She is the author of a number of articles in professional journals. For ten summers she taught in Europe as part of a foreign exchange program. She was a 1981 recipient of the Merit Teacher Awards given by the National Council for Geographic Education.

Contributing Writers

Pat Cuthbertson

is a writer who lives in Santa Cruz, California. She received a B.A. in English literature from the University of California at Santa Cruz, graduating with General College Honors. She has written material for Language Arts and Social Studies texts. She has two sons in whose classes she has worked as a volunteer for several years.

Tom Cuthbertson

is a writer of "how to" books who lives in Santa Cruz, California. He received a B.A. in literature from the University of California at Santa Cruz and an M.A. in writing from San Francisco State. He has written a number of technical manuals, as well as material for Language Arts and Social Studies texts. He has done volunteer work in his sons' elementary school classrooms.

James A. Harris

is an elementary principal in the D.C. Everest Area School District, Schofield, Wisconsin. He graduated from Miami University, Oxford, Ohio, and received his Master's degree in Curriculum and Instruction from the University of Wisconsin. Mr. Harris began his teaching career while a VISTA volunteer and later served in the Wisconsin Native American Teacher Corps. For ten years he taught kindergarten and primary grades in Wisconsin schools. Mr. Harris is a frequent consultant to school systems and educational corporations. He has published many articles in professional magazines and journals.

James J. Rawls

is a native of Washington, D.C. He received a B.A. from Stanford University and a Ph.D. from the University of California, Berkeley. Since 1975, Rawls has been a history instructor at Diablo Valley College. His articles and reviews have appeared in such publications as *The Journal of American History, The Wilson Quarterly, The American West,* and *California History.* He is the author of *Indians of California: The Changing Image,* and coauthor of *California: An Interpretative History* and *Land of Liberty.* Rawls has served as an historical consultant on numerous films and on a series of television programs funded by the National Endowment for the Humanities.

"Oak Street Beach," ©Laura Lynch/Jay Johnson Gallery

Photo and art credits begin on page 383.

ISBN: 0-03-001793-9
5678 039 987654321

Teacher Consultants

Linda R. Aucoin
Teacher
Thibodaux Elementary School
Thibodaux, Louisiana

Sister Eileen Frances M. Cooke
Teacher
Saint Helena School
Philadelphia, Pennsylvania

Patricia F. Ho
Teacher
Thomas J. Watson, Sr., Elementary School
Endicott, New York

Janet A. Kaiser
Teacher
Hawthorne School—District U205
Elmhurst, Illinois

Thomas J. Ladouceur
Teacher
Stone Valley Intermediate School
Alamo, California

Dr. JoAnn B. Seghini
Director of Curriculum Development
Jordan School District
Sandy, Utah

Ramona H. Simpson, M.A.
Teacher
Saffell Elementary
Lawrenceburg, Kentucky

James Robert Warren
Teacher
Tileston School
Wilmington, North Carolina

Content Consultants

Joseph D. Baca
Social Studies Education Specialist
New Mexico Department of Education
Santa Fe, New Mexico

Sam F. Dennard, Ph.D.
Social Studies Coordinator
Clayton County Schools
Jonesboro, Georgia

Dr. George Gregory
Curriculum Consultant
Albany, New York

David M. Helgren, Ph.D.
Assistant Professor
University of Miami
Coral Gables, Florida

Betty Jo Johnson
Coordinator, Social Studies Services
Wake County Public School System
Raleigh, North Carolina

Dr. Helen E. Jones
Associate Professor of Education
Fairmont State College
Fairmont, West Virginia

Diane Lindstrom
Associate Professor of History
University of Wisconsin
Madison, Wisconsin

Eveleen Lorton
Professor of Education
University of Miami
Coral Gables, Florida

Norman McRae
Director of Social Studies Department
Detroit Public Schools
Detroit, Michigan

Thomas H. Pagenhart
Associate Professor of Geography
California State University
Hayward, California

Clyde P. Patton
Professor of Geography
University of Oregon
Eugene, Oregon

Daniel H. Ryan
Professor
College of Lake County
Grayslake, Illinois

Mary Jo Wagner
Director, Women's Studies Program
University of Oregon
Eugene, Oregon

Philip Weeks
Department of History
The University of Akron
Akron, Ohio

Susan A. White
Senior Economics Consultant
Adult Performance Level Project:
The University of Texas at Austin
Austin, Texas

Readability Consultant

Paul Greenfield
Associate Professor
English and Humanities
Dutchess Community College
Poughkeepsie, New York

TABLE OF CONTENTS

UNIT 8

UNIT 9

MAPS AND GLOBES

CHARTS, GRAPHS, AND DIAGRAMS

reviewing GEOGRAPHY skills

If you visited a new city, how would you find your way around? You might use a street **map.** A street map shows street names. It also shows the locations of important places.

A street map is only one of the many kinds of maps that can help you learn about places on the earth. In this book, you will find both **globes** and maps. Most are easy to use once you learn about them.

Using a Globe

You know that the earth is like a big ball or sphere. A globe is a model of the earth. A globe shows the shape of all the earth's land and water areas.

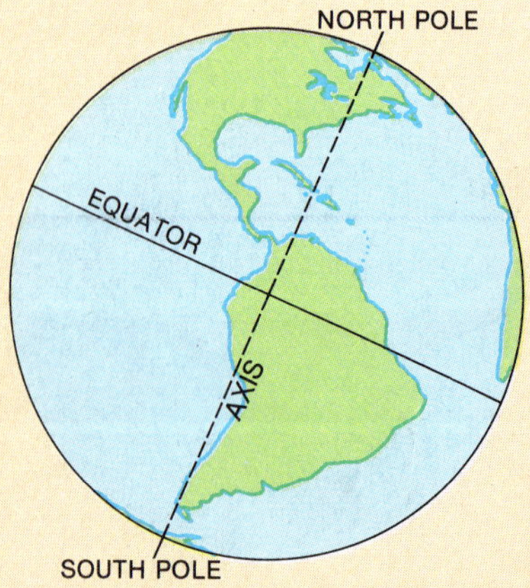

Look at the drawing of the globe at the left. See the lines drawn on it. The top of the globe shows where the **North Pole** is. The North Pole is the most northern place on a globe. The direction north is always toward the North Pole. The bottom of the globe shows the **South Pole.** The South Pole is the most southern place on the globe. The direction south is always toward the South Pole.

The dotted line on the drawing of the globe is called an **axis.** The axis is an imaginary line. It goes through the center of the earth from one pole to the other. The earth makes one turn on this axis every 24 hours. This creates day and night.

Another imaginary line on a globe is the **equator.** The equator divides the earth into two halves, or **hemispheres.** (*Hemi-* means "half," so "hemisphere" means "half of the sphere.") Above the equator is the Northern Hemisphere. Below the equator is the Southern Hemisphere. Look at the drawing of the globe at the left. In which hemisphere is the United States?

The earth can also be divided along another imaginary line. This imaginary line runs from the North Pole to the South Pole. It divides the world into the Western and Eastern hemispheres. Look at the drawing of the globe at the right. In which of these hemispheres is the United States?

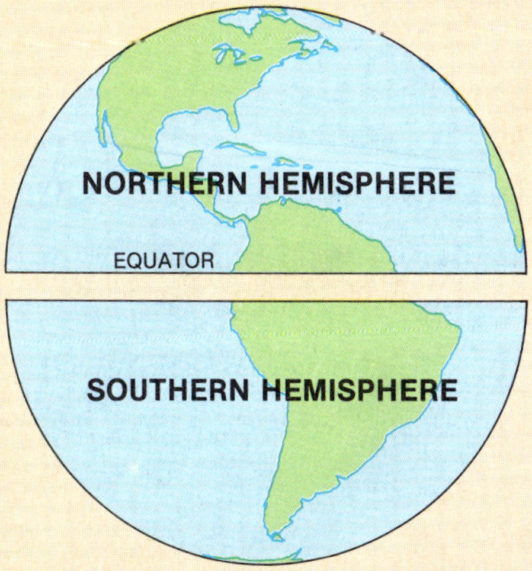

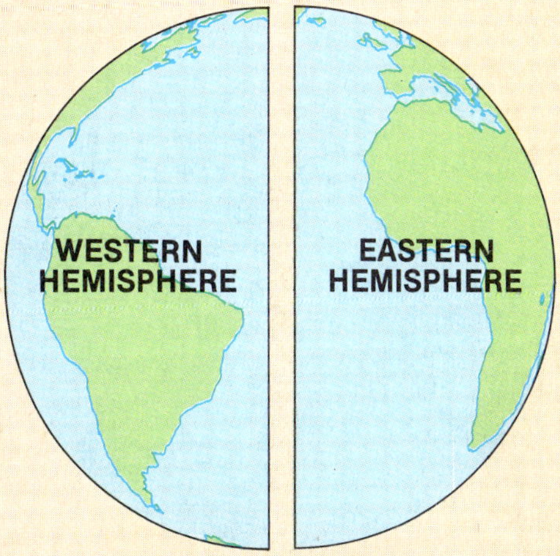

On a globe, you can see that most of the earth is covered by water. The largest bodies of water are called **oceans.** The rest of the earth is land. The largest areas of land are called **continents.** There are four oceans and seven continents. Find the names of the continents and oceans on the globes on this page. Which continents are in the Eastern Hemisphere? Which are in the Western Hemisphere? Which is in both hemispheres? Which ocean is only in the Eastern Hemisphere?

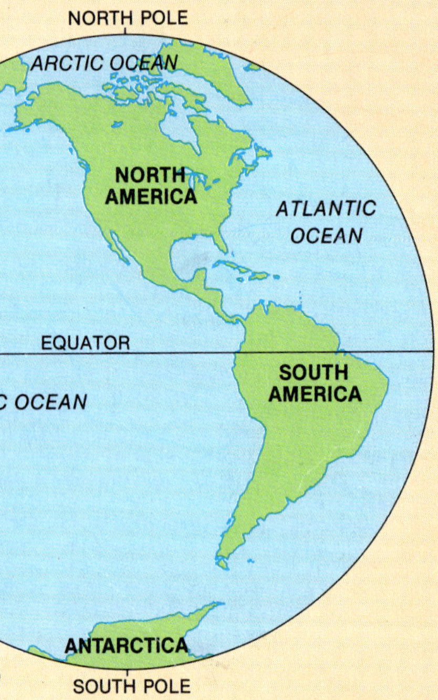

Western Hemisphere

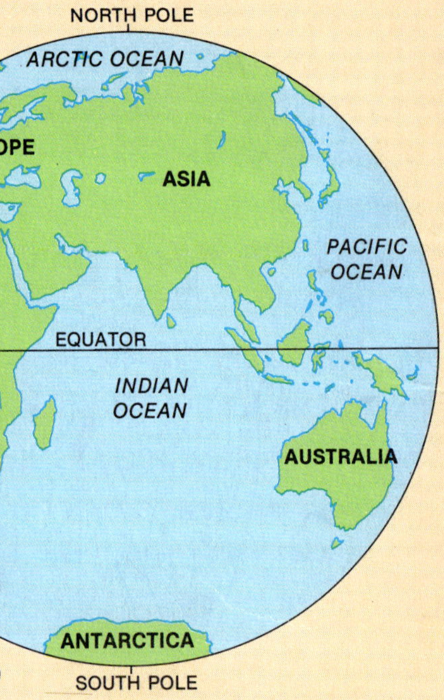

Eastern Hemisphere

Using a Flat Map

On a globe, you cannot see all the continents at once. To see all of the earth, you use a flat map. Imagine that the outside of the earth could be peeled off and flattened out. It might look like the drawing on page 13. Now you can see all the continents.

A flat map can show the whole earth or part of it. The map on page 13 shows the continent of North America.

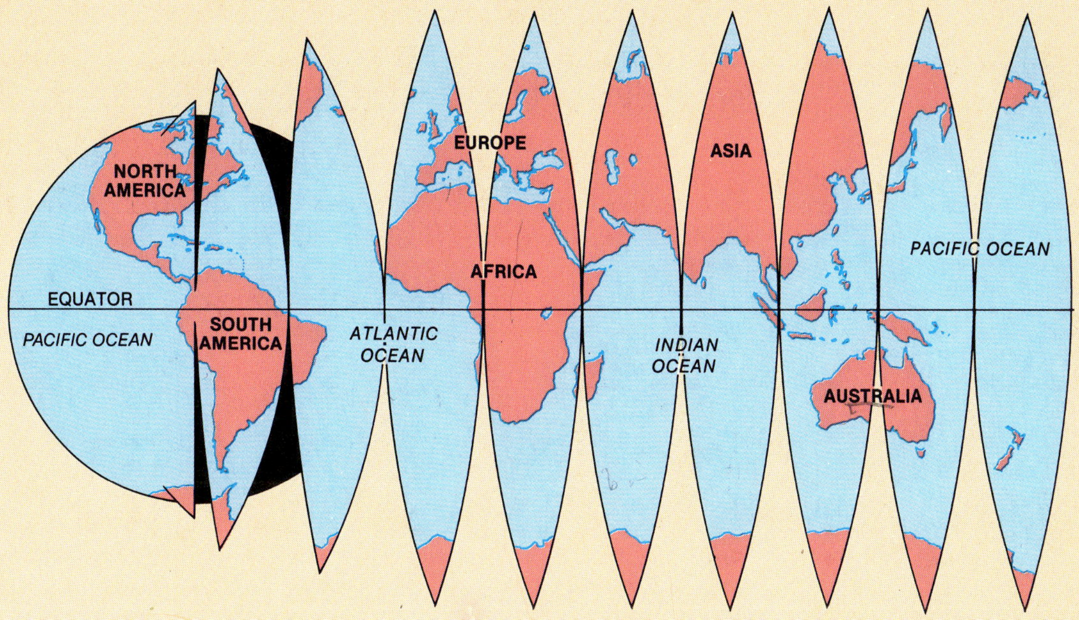

Using Symbols

Symbols are used on maps to stand for real things. Symbols can be colors, shapes, or designs. On most maps, blue is the symbol for water. Brown or green is the symbol for land. A dot might stand for a city.

Map symbols are on a **map key.** The map key tells what the symbols on a map mean. Look at the key on the map of North America. This symbol ⊛ means national capital. What does this ——— mean?

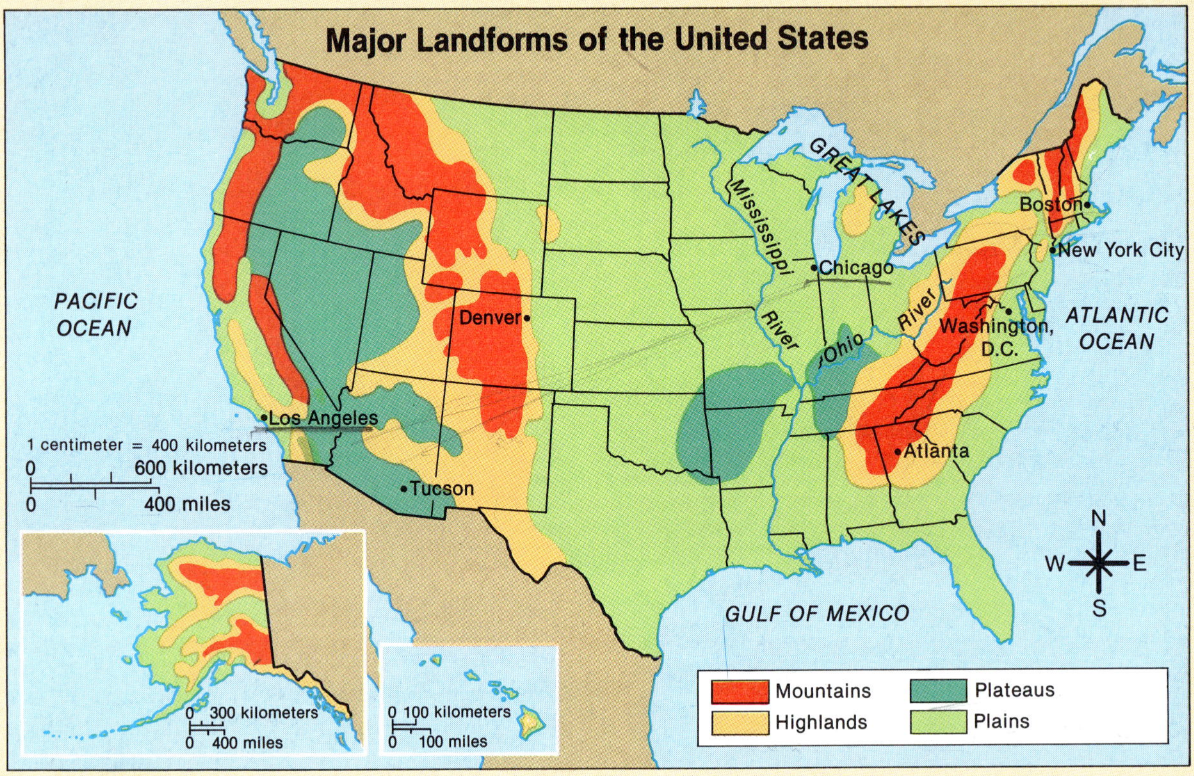

The map on this page is a **landforms map** of the United States. A landforms map uses colors to show the height and form of the land. The map key above lists four landforms. They are mountains, highlands, plateaus, and plains. What colors show mountains? plains? plateaus? highlands?

You can see that there are many plains in the center of the United States. And the country has two mountain regions. There is one in the East and one in the West.

Finding Directions

You know that north, south, east, and west are the main directions. In between the four main directions are northwest, southwest, northeast, and southeast. On a globe, north is the direction of the North Pole. South is the direction of the South Pole. On flat maps, directions are shown with a **compass rose.**

Find the compass rose on the landforms map on page 14. Notice that Boston is northeast of New York City. In which direction is Los Angeles from Chicago?

Finding Distance

A map is a very small picture of the land it shows. A **distance scale** shows how close or how far apart things are on a map. On a distance scale centimeters or inches stand for kilometers or miles. Look at the distance scale on the right. How many kilometers does each centimeter stand for?

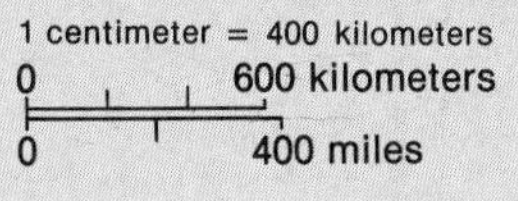

This is how you find distance on a map. You can use a ruler to measure the number of centimeters or inches between points. Then you multiply this distance by the kilometers or miles each centimeter or inch stands for.

Look at the distance scale on the landforms map. Notice how many kilometers each centimeter stands for. Now use a ruler to measure the distance between Tucson, Arizona and Los Angeles, California on the map. The distance on the map is 2 centimeters. What, then, is the distance between Tucson and Los Angeles?

On the next page is a map of the United States. The map has all the tools you will need to read it. It has a map key, a compass rose, and a distance scale. Which will you use to tell how far Miami is from New Orleans?

THE UNITED STATES OF AMERICA
PACIFIC OCEAN
WASHINGTON
Seattle
Olympia
Portland
Columbia R.
Toledo
Salem
OREGON
MONTANA
Helena
Butte
Yellowstone R.
Snake R.
Boise
IDAHO
WYOMING
North Platte R.
Cheyenne
Sacramento R.
Sacramento
San Francisco
NEVADA
Carson City
Great Salt Lake
Salt Lake City
UTAH
Denver
COLORADO
CALIFORNIA
Colorado R.
ARIZONA
Phoenix
Gila R.
Los Angeles
San Diego
Santa Fe
NEW MEXICO
Vaughn
Pecos R.
Rio Grande
MEXICO
HAWAII
PACIFIC OCEAN
Honolulu
0 100 200 km
0 100 200 miles
ASIA
ARCTIC OCEAN
Yukon R.
ALASKA
CANADA
Juneau
PACIFIC OCEAN
0 200 400 km
0 100 200 300 miles
N
S
E
W

CANADA
NORTH DAKOTA
Bismarck
MINNESOTA
St. Paul
Minneapolis
Lake Superior
MICHIGAN
Lake Huron
Lake Michigan
Lake Ontario
Lake Erie
St. Lawrence R.
MAINE
Augusta
Montpelier
Hudson R.
NEW HAMPSHIRE
VERMONT
Concord
MASSACHUSETTS
Boston
RHODE ISLAND
Providence
Hartford
CONNECTICUT
Albany
Buffalo
NEW YORK
New York City
Newark
Trenton
NEW JERSEY
Philadelphia
PENNSYLVANIA
Harrisburg
Pittsburgh
Baltimore
Dover
DELAWARE
Annapolis
MARYLAND
Washington, D.C.
Pierre
SOUTH DAKOTA
WISCONSIN
Madison
Milwaukee
Lansing
Detroit
Cleveland
NEBRASKA
Lincoln
IOWA
Des Moines
Chicago
Illinois R.
Springfield
ILLINOIS
INDIANA
Indianapolis
OHIO
Columbus
Ohio R.
Cincinnati
WEST VIRGINIA
Charleston
Richmond
VIRGINIA
Kansas City
Topeka
KANSAS
Buhler
Arkansas R.
Missouri R.
Jefferson City
St. Louis
MISSOURI
Frankfort
KENTUCKY
OKLAHOMA
Oklahoma City
Canadian R.
ARKANSAS
Little Rock
Mississippi R.
Tennessee R.
Nashville
TENNESSEE
Raleigh
NORTH CAROLINA
Columbia
SOUTH CAROLINA
Savannah R.
Atlanta
GEORGIA
ALABAMA
Montgomery
MISSISSIPPI
Jackson
LOUISIANA
Red R.
Dallas
Sabine R.
TEXAS
Austin
Houston
San Antonio
Baton Rouge
New Orleans
Tallahassee
FLORIDA
Winter Haven
Miami
ATLANTIC OCEAN
GULF OF MEXICO
100°
95°
90°
85°
80°
75°
70°
45°
35°
30°
25°
0 100 200 300 400 500 kilometers
0 100 200 300 400 500 miles
National capital
State capital
City
Town

THE WORLD
Greenland
ICELAND
Arctic Circle
Alaska
CANADA
GREAT BRITAIN
IRISH REPUBLIC
SWITZ.
PORTUGAL
SPAIN
UNITED STATES
ATLANTIC OCEAN
MOROCCO
MEXICO
CAPE VERDE IS.
Tropic of Cancer
BAHAMAS
Hawaii
CUBA
DOMINICAN REPUBLIC
JAMAICA
HAITI
BELIZE
MAURITANIA
MALI
PACIFIC OCEAN
HONDURAS
GUATEMALA
EL SALVADOR
NICARAGUA
COSTA RICA
PANAMA
ST. LUCIA
GRENADA
DOMINICA
BARBADOS
ST. VINCENT—GRENADINES
TRINIDAD AND TOBAGO
SENEGAL
GAMBIA
GUINEA-BISSAU
GUINEA
SIERRA LEONE
LIBERIA
IVORY COAST
GHANA
VENEZUELA
GUYANA
SURINAME
FRENCH GUIANA
COLOMBIA
Equator
KIRIBATI
ECUADOR
PERU
BRAZIL
BOLIVIA
Tropic of Capricorn
PARAGUAY
CHILE
URUGUAY
ARGENTINA
Antarctic Circle
N
S
E
W

ARCTIC OCEAN
SOVIET UNION
FINLAND
MONGOLIA
CHINA
N. KOREA
S. KOREA
JAPAN
TURKEY
BULGARIA
ROMANIA
HUNGARY
CZECH.
GREECE
CYPRUS
LEBANON
ISRAEL
SYRIA
JORDAN
IRAQ
IRAN
KUWAIT
BAHRAIN
QATAR
U.A.E.
SAUDI ARABIA
OMAN
YEMEN
P.D.R. OF YEMEN
AFGHANISTAN
PAKISTAN
INDIA
NEPAL
BHUTAN
BANGLADESH
BURMA
LAOS
THAILAND
KAMPUCHEA
VIETNAM
TAIWAN
PHILIPPINES
MALAYSIA
SINGAPORE
INDONESIA
SRI LANKA
MALDIVES
EGYPT
SUDAN
ETHIOPIA
DJIBOUTI
SOMALIA
UGANDA
KENYA
RWANDA
BURUNDI
ZAIRE
TANZANIA
ZAMBIA
MALAWI
ZIMBABWE
BOTSWANA
MOZAMBIQUE
SWAZILAND
LESOTHO
SEYCHELLES
COMOROS
MADAGASCAR
MAURITIUS
INDIAN OCEAN
PAPUA NEW GUINEA
NAURU
TUVALU
SOLOMON ISLANDS
WESTERN SAMOA
VANUATU
FIJI
TONGA
AUSTRALIA
NEW ZEALAND
International Date Line
ANTARCTICA

UNIT
1
Our Country

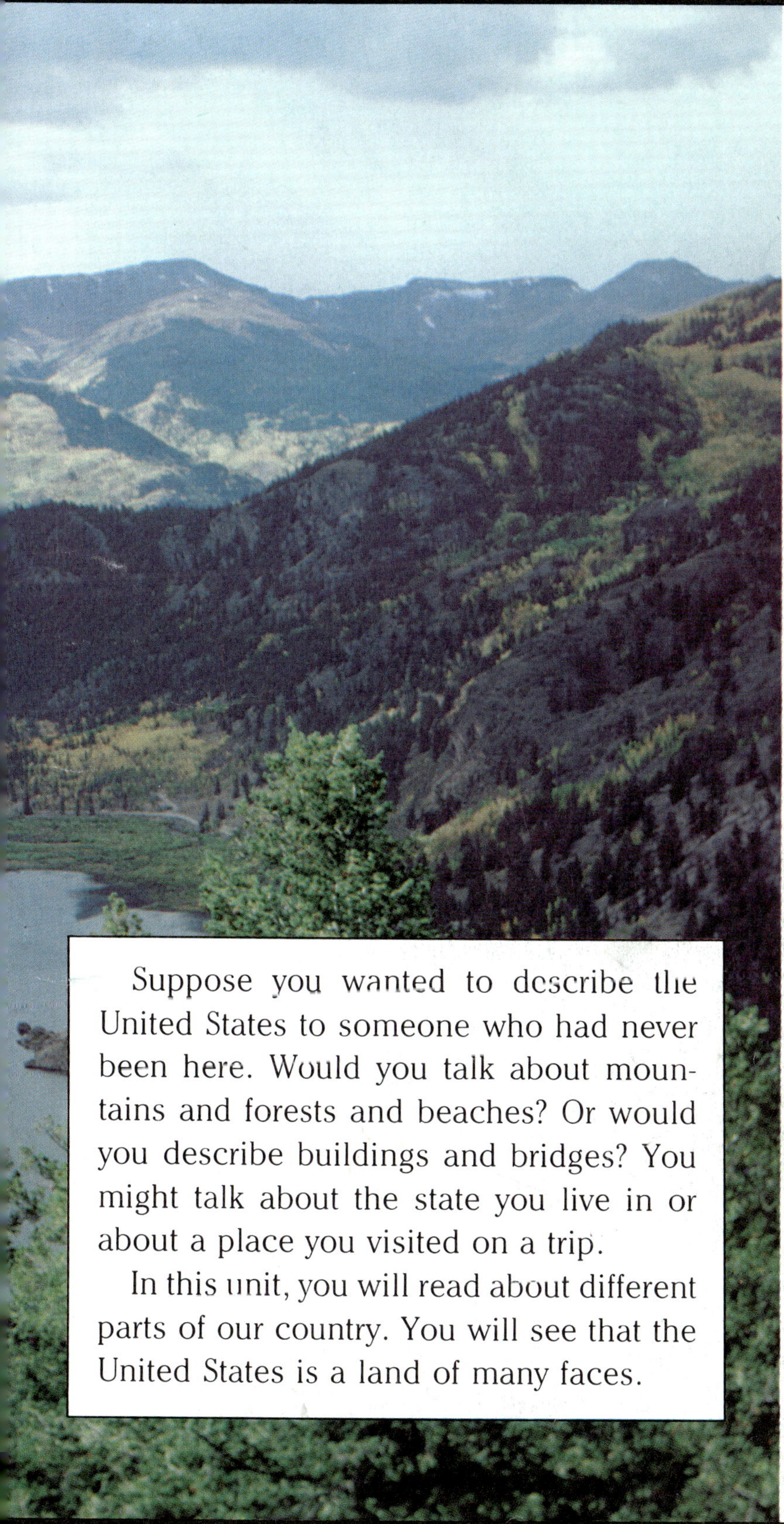

Suppose you wanted to describe the United States to someone who had never been here. Would you talk about mountains and forests and beaches? Or would you describe buildings and bridges? You might talk about the state you live in or about a place you visited on a trip.

In this unit, you will read about different parts of our country. You will see that the United States is a land of many faces.

CHAPTER 1

Our Country's Geography

If your family moved from Florida to Colorado, it would be a big change for you. Florida is very warm. It is much cooler in Colorado. In Florida, you saw the Atlantic Ocean. In Colorado, you would see huge mountains.

Our country is very big. In this chapter, you will read how some parts are different from others.

At the end of this chapter, you should be able to:

- ○ Name eight land regions of the United States.
- ○ Name some important waterways of our country.
- ○ Explain what climate is.
- ● Read a climate regions map.

1 A Varied Land

Suppose you were to travel all the way across our country. What you would see might surprise you. The United States is made up of many different areas of land, or **regions.**

region
an area of land

In some regions, you would climb hills and mountains. You would cross wide rivers. In other regions, the land would be flat. Sometimes, you might see only sand and rocks. Other times, you would walk through cool, green forests. Such natural differences affect the way people live in different parts of our country. They also affect the way the land is used and how people earn their living.

Our country can be divided into eight land regions. Look at the map on page 25 and see if you can find them.

The Coastal Plain

plain
a low, flat land area

The Coastal Plain region extends from the northeast to the southeast coast of the United States. A **plain** is a low, flat land area. Find this plain on the map on page 25. The Atlantic Ocean borders this plain on the east. What body of water is on the south?

The Appalachian Highlands

highland
an area of hills or mountains

West of the Atlantic Coastal Plain is an area of hills or mountains called a **highland** region. This is the Appalachian (ap-uh-**lay**-chun) Highlands. Find these highlands on the map on page 25. The Appalachian Highlands includes some mountains you may have heard of, such as the Blue Ridge Mountains of Virginia.

The Interior Plains

Look at the map on page 25 and find the Interior Plains. This huge, mostly flat region stretches across the center of the United States. The great Mississippi River flows through these plains.

The Interior Highlands

North of the Gulf Coastal Plain are the Interior Highlands. This area is known for its hills, rivers, and forests. Find the Interior Highlands on the map on page 25.

The Rocky Mountains

Look at the map on page 25 and find the Rocky Mountains. These high mountains extend north and south for more than 4,800 kilometers (3,000 miles). They reach all the way to Alaska. Look at the cutaway diagram on pages 26 and 27. Find the Rocky Mountains.

Land Regions of the United States
CANADA
Lake Superior
Lake Huron
Lake Michigan
Lake Ontario
Lake Erie
Hudson R.
Columbia River
Mississippi River
Missouri River
Ohio River
Tennessee River
Arkansas River
Red River
Colorado River
Rio Grande
ROCKY MTS.
APPALACHIAN MTS.
ATLANTIC COASTAL PLAIN
GULF COASTAL PLAIN
PACIFIC OCEAN
ATLANTIC OCEAN
GULF OF MEXICO
MEXICO
N
S
E
W
0 600 kilometers
0 400 miles
ARCTIC OCEAN
ALASKA
CANADA
PACIFIC OCEAN
0 200 kilometers
0 200 miles
PACIFIC OCEAN
HAWAII
0 150 kilometers
0 100 miles
Coastal Plain
Appalachian Highlands
Interior Plains
Interior Highlands
Rocky Mountains
Plateau Country
Pacific Highlands
Island Highlands

plateau
an area of flat land higher than the land around it

desert
a sandy area with no trees or water

canyon
a deep valley with steep sides

The Plateau Country

This is a region of high, flat places known as **plateaus** (plah-**toze**). In the Plateau Country, there are mountains and **deserts.** Deserts are sandy areas with no trees or water. There also are deep valleys with steep sides called **canyons** (**kan**-yunz). Find this region on the diagram below.

The Pacific Highlands

The Pacific coast is different from the low, flat land along the Atlantic coast. This coast is a region of mountains and valleys. Find the Pacific Highlands region on the map on page 25. What four states are part of the Pacific Highlands region?

Island Highlands

The islands of Hawaii make up the Island Highlands region. Here plains rim the islands along the shore. The land rises quickly to high mountain peaks inland from the Pacific Ocean.

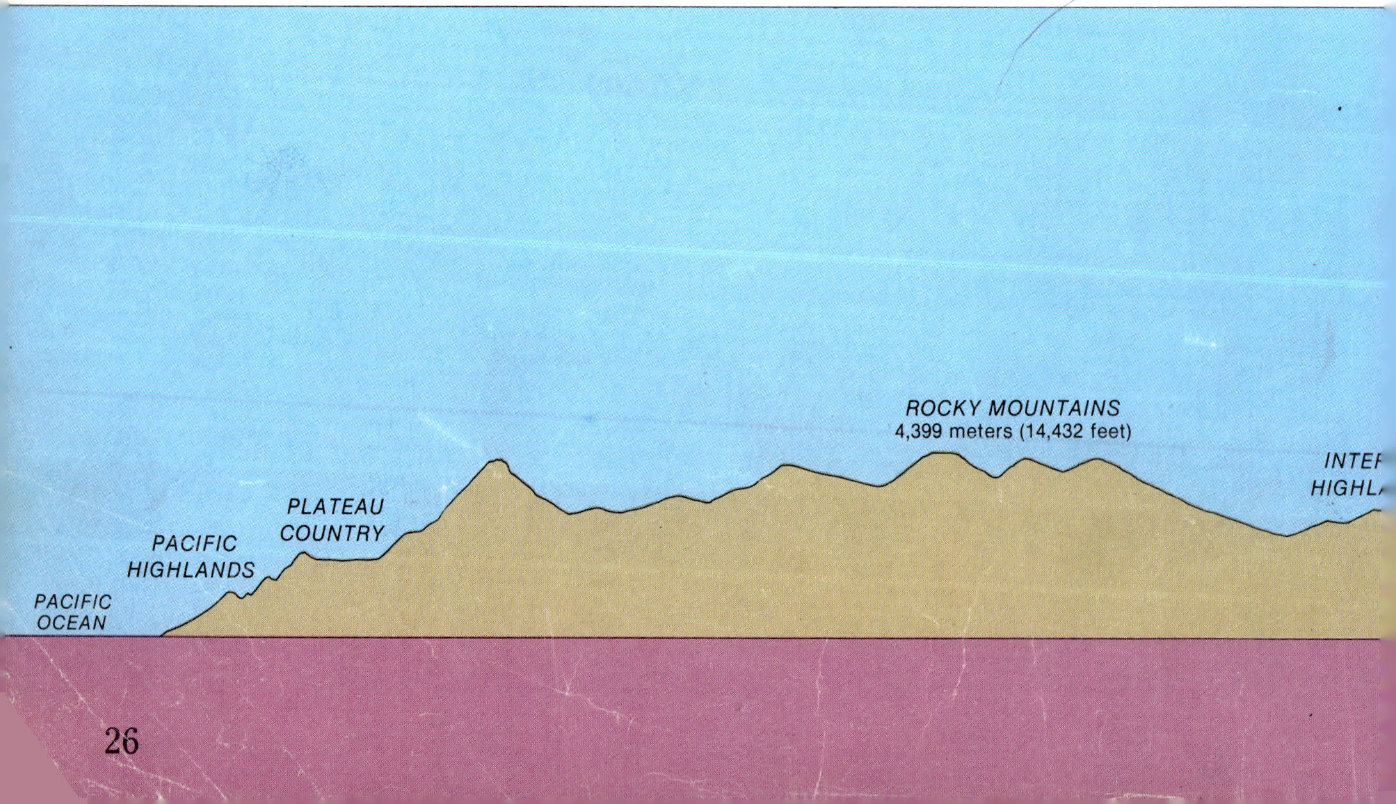

Land Affects Our Lives

The natural differences in the eight regions are important. They affect the way people live and work. For example, many parts of the Appalachian Highlands and the Rocky Mountains are rugged. That is why only a few cities and towns have been built there. But many people who live there earn their living by working in the forests of these two regions.

In the Interior Plains, the flat land and rich soil are good for farming. Here farmers grow corn and wheat. The short grasses of the Plains also help the farmers to raise cattle and sheep. Many people live and work in this region.

The Atlantic and Pacific coastal regions are near large bodies of water. Because of this, some people in the coastal regions make their living working in the fishing industry. Goods from other parts of the United States are shipped to cities in the Atlantic and Pacific coastal regions. From here, they go to cities all over the world.

Cutaway Diagram of the United States

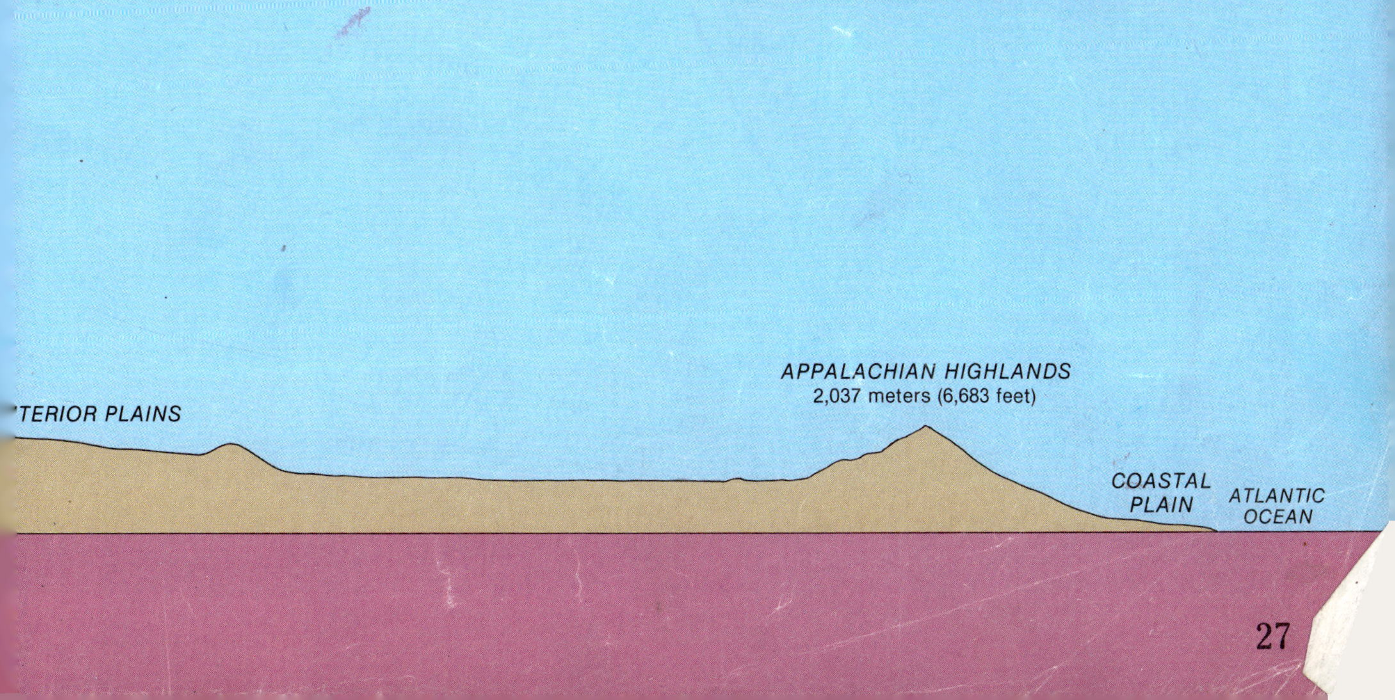

Important Waterways

As you have read, the United States is bordered by three important bodies of water. Look back at the map on page 25 and find the Atlantic Ocean, the Pacific Ocean, and the Gulf of Mexico. They give our country more than 19,000 kilometers (12,000 miles) of seacoast.

tributary
a river or stream that flows into a larger body of water

There are also many waterways inside our country. The largest of these is the Mississippi River. Hundreds of rivers and streams, called **tributaries** (**trib**-yuh-terr-eez), flow into the Mississippi River. Its chief tributary is the Missouri River.

The Mississippi River

Other major waterways in the United States are the Rio Grande (**ree**-oe **gran**-day) and the five Great Lakes. The Ohio River, the Arkansas River, and the Colorado River are also important waterways. Find these waterways on the map on page 25.

The rivers and lakes are important routes for ships to take goods from one part of our country to another. Ships can also carry goods from the United States to other countries across the oceans.

Dividing a Nation into Parts

In this section, you have read how our country can be divided into land regions. The United States can also be divided in other ways.

The map on this page shows how we divide our country into 50 states. Which state is the smallest? Which states border the Great Lakes? Which states border the Gulf of Mexico? Which states border the Pacific Ocean?

Sometimes we group the 50 states into six geographic regions. These regions are the Northeast, the Southeast, the Midwest, the Southwest, the Rocky Mountain region, and the Pacific Coast region.

A geographic region is usually known for certain things. These can include waterways, mountains, and kinds of land. The Midwest is mostly flat land. The Rocky Mountain region has many high mountains. In the Northeast, there are many waterways.

Look at the map on page 29. Find the six geographic regions. Name the states in each of the regions. Which regions are on the east coast? Which region is on the west coast? Which region has the most states? Which region has the least states? Which geographic region do you live in?

Section Review

Write your answers on a sheet of paper.

1. What is the difference between a plain and a plateau?
2. How is the Pacific Highlands region different from the Coastal Plain region?
3. Name the largest waterway in our country.
4. Describe three ways of dividing our country into parts.
5. Suppose you took a trip to the Interior Plains region of our country. What kind of land would you expect to see?

2 Climate

What is it like outside today? Is it warm and sunny? Is it cold and rainy? When you answer these questions, you are talking about the **weather.** Weather is what the air is like at a certain time or place. The kind of weather a region has over many years is its **climate.**

weather
the condition of the air at a certain time or place

climate
the kind of weather a region has over a long period of time

temperature
the measure of how hot or cold a place is

Describing Climate

We use several words to describe climate. One of these words is **temperature,** a measure of how hot or cold a place is. Places that have fairly high

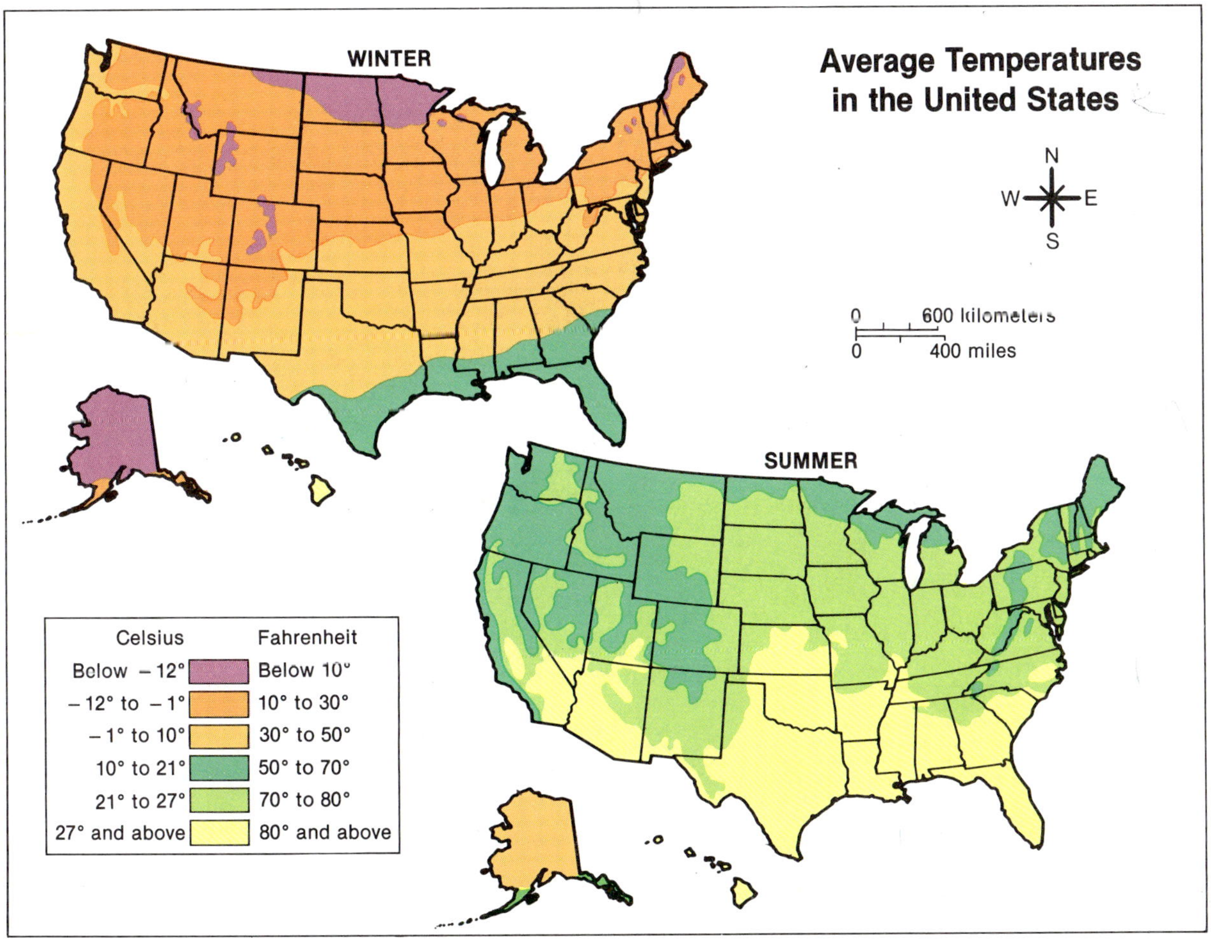

temperatures over a long period of time have warm climates. Places that have fairly low temperatures have cold climates. The map on page 31 shows differences in temperature in different parts of our country.

Heat comes from the sun. Because the sun shines during the day, temperatures are usually higher in the daytime than at night.

moisture
water or other liquids in the air or on the ground; wetness

humid
moist or damp

Climate can also be described as wetness and dryness. Some places receive a great deal of wetness, or **moisture.** Rain, snow, hail, and fog are forms of moisture we can see. There is also a form of moisture we cannot see. This moisture makes the air feel damp, or **humid.**

Places that receive a lot of moisture over a period of time have wet climates. Places that receive little moisture over a period of time have dry climates.

The United States has many different climates. The pictures on page 32 show the climate in winter in two parts of the country.

What does the picture at the left on the facing page tell us about the climate in Connecticut? Are winters hot or cold? Are they wet or dry? What does the picture at the right tell about Arizona's climate?

Differences in climate are important for many reasons. Climate affects the way people live. It affects the work they do. And it affects the way the land is used.

Climate Affects Our Lives

Imagine you live in a region with a cold, snowy climate. You would probably own a heavy, warm coat. At night, you would sleep under a thick blanket. Your favorite sport might be skiing. Now imagine you live in a warm, dry climate. You would need only a light jacket. At night, a sheet might be enough to keep you warm. You would probably do a lot of swimming.

The kind of climate also affects the kind of materials used to build houses. Look at the pictures on the facing page. How do the homes in these pictures differ? Why?

Climate is also very important to the kind of work people do. In the states of Florida and California, the warm, sunny climate is perfect for growing orange trees. Many people earn their living by growing oranges. In the western part of the states of Oregon and Washington, the cool, rainy climate helps forests grow. As a result, this region is a center for the lumber industry.

Climate Affects Land Use

The picture on this page shows how climate affects the way land is used. The picture shows a part of Wyoming that receives little moisture. The climate is quite dry. About the only thing that grows well here is short grass. So this land is used for grazing. Cattle, horses, and sheep feed on the grass.

The state of Iowa receives good rainfall. Corn is a crop that needs moisture to grow. So the farmers of Iowa plant corn on their land.

In parts of Arizona and New Mexico, there are desert areas. Little or no rain falls there. Few plants can grow in this dry climate.

The Everglades area of southern Florida shown on the next page has a very different climate. A great deal of rain falls each year in the Everglades.

The soil is too wet and soggy to be used for farming. Farm machinery would sink right into it. So, much of this land is left as it is. Few people live in the Everglades.

Section Review

Write your answers on a sheet of paper.

1. What is climate?
2. Give three examples of types of moisture.
3. Suppose you lived in an area that had a cool, dry climate. Describe the kind of homes people might build in your area.

SOCIAL STUDIES SKILLS

Reading a Climate Regions Map

What is the climate in your state? Is it hot in summer? Is it cold in winter? Is it warm and dry most of the year? Perhaps it is mostly humid and cool. You can find out something about the climate of a state by reading a climate regions map.

The map on the next page shows the eight climate regions of the United States. The map key describes what kind of climate each color stands for. What is the climate in the areas colored light green? in the area colored yellow? What section of the country has a cool, humid climate?

What can you learn about the climate of Hawaii from the climate map? What is the climate of the states along the Great Lakes? along the Gulf of Mexico? near the Rocky Mountains? What climate region do you live in?

Practice Your Skills

1. What area of the United States has the coldest climate? the hottest climate?
2. In what way is the polar climate region and the desert climate region alike?
3. Which is generally warmer all year long, a desert or a semiarid climate?
4. In which sections of the country is the climate rainy? In which is it dry?

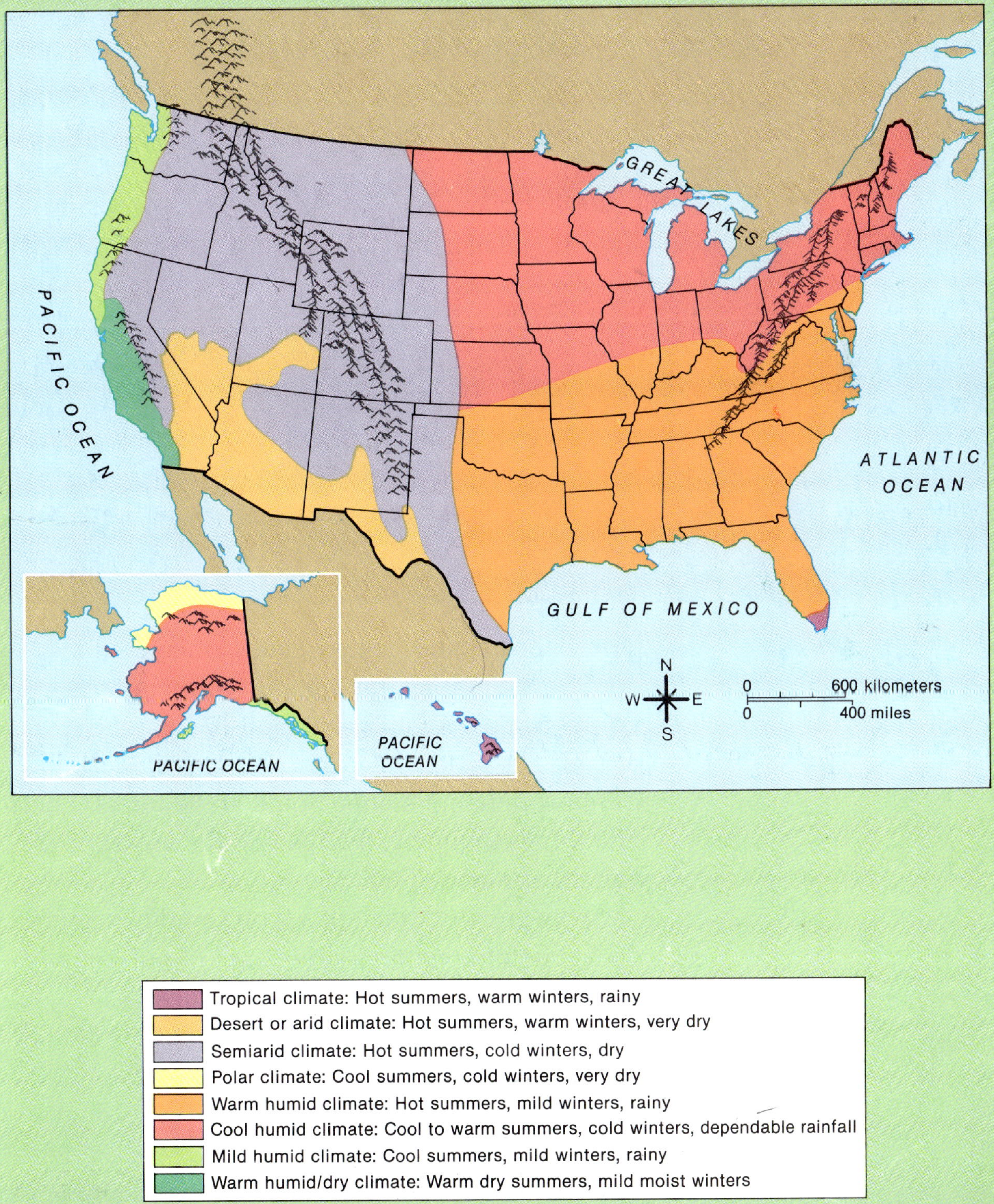
GREAT LAKES
PACIFIC OCEAN
ATLANTIC OCEAN
GULF OF MEXICO
PACIFIC OCEAN
PACIFIC OCEAN
N
W
E
S
0
600 kilometers
0
400 miles
Tropical climate: Hot summers, warm winters, rainy
Desert or arid climate: Hot summers, warm winters, very dry
Semiarid climate: Hot summers, cold winters, dry
Polar climate: Cool summers, cold winters, very dry
Warm humid climate: Hot summers, mild winters, rainy
Cool humid climate: Cool to warm summers, cold winters, dependable rainfall
Mild humid climate: Cool summers, mild winters, rainy
Warm humid/dry climate: Warm dry summers, mild moist winters

CHAPTER 2 Landmarks of Our Country

Houston Astrodome

A visitor to the United States once said that if you traveled long enough in our country, you could see just about every kind of sight there was to see. The visitor was right. Our country is a land of many different sights. Some are natural. Others are things built by people. Some are very old. Others are new.

At the end of this chapter, you should be able to:

○ Name three natural landmarks of our country.
● Use a road map to measure distances.
○ Name two human-made landmarks of our country.
○ Explain why we must preserve our country's landmarks.

1 Natural Landmarks

Look at the pictures on this page. Do you recognize them? One is a huge statue on an island in New York Harbor. It is the Statue of Liberty.

The Statue of Liberty is well known around the world. People think of the statue as an important part of New York and of our country. An important thing or place that stands out from everything around it is called a **landmark.**

landmark
an important thing or place that stands out from everything around it

North Stone Mountain in Georgia is known for its strange and beautiful shapes. But there is a big difference between the Statue of Liberty and North Stone Mountain. North Stone Mountain was formed by nature. It is a natural landmark. The Statue of Liberty was built by people. It is a human-made landmark.

Some landmarks are surprisingly beautiful or very unusual. Landmarks such as these are sometimes called **wonders.**

wonder
something that is surprisingly beautiful, or very unusual

(left) North Stone Mountain in Georgia with carving of historical figures important to the history of the South

(right) Statue of Liberty

The Grand Canyon

The Grand Canyon is one of the world's greatest natural wonders. Located in Arizona, this vast canyon is 443 kilometers (277 miles) long. In some places, it is almost 30 kilometers (18 miles) wide and 1.6 kilometers (1 mile) deep.

The great Colorado River formed this canyon. For millions of years, the river has flowed through Arizona. Slowly, it cut into the ground. As time passed, a deep, narrow passage, or **gorge** (**gorj**), was carved by the powerful water. This gorge is the Grand Canyon.

gorge
a deep, narrow passage between mountains

The canyon is so large it makes the Colorado River look like a stream. Layer upon layer of rock rises up to form the steep cliffs and canyon walls.

Weather in the canyon depends on how high up you are. In winter, it may be snowing and $-15°$ C (5° F) at the top, but 4° C (40° F) at the bottom. The farther down you go into the canyon, the warmer it is. In summer, the temperature at the bottom may reach 49° C (120° F).

The Giant Sequoias

In the Sierra Nevada (see-**err**-uh nuh-**vad**-uh) Mountains of California stand some of the oldest and largest living things in the world. They are the giant sequoia (sih-**kwoi**-uh) trees. Some are more than 3,000 years old and almost 100 meters (330 feet) high. That is as tall as a 30-story building. Some are 9 meters (30 feet) thick at the bottom and weigh more than 900,000 kilograms (1,000 tons). The bark of the sequoias is often 60 centimeters (2 feet) thick. It protects the trees against fire and insects.

Old Faithful

geyser
a hot spring that shoots water and steam into the air

One of our most famous natural landmarks is Old Faithful, in the state of Wyoming. Old Faithful is a hot spring that shoots water and steam into the air. This kind of spring is called a **geyser** (**gie**-zer). Old Faithful bursts forth almost every 70 minutes. For about four minutes, hot water and steam rise as high as 38 meters (125 feet). During this time, the geyser sprays more than 38,000 liters (10,000 gallons) of water into the air.

Section Review

Write your answers on a sheet of paper.

1. What is a landmark?
2. What is the difference between a natural landmark and a human-made landmark?
3. Name some landmarks that you have seen in our country.

FAMOUS AMERICANS

WOODY GUTHRIE

"This land is your land. This land is my land. This land was made for you and me." These are the words to a song written by Woody Guthrie. Woody Guthrie was a folksinger. He sang about the beauty of the United States. He sang about the hopes of the American people.

Woody Guthrie was born in Okemah (oe-**kee**-muh), Oklahoma. When he was a small boy, his mother sang old songs and ballads to him and the rest of the Guthrie children. His father taught the family American Indian songs and square dances. Woody Guthrie always loved to sing. And his uncle taught him how to play the guitar.

When he was 13, Guthrie began to travel and work all over the United States. He sang songs for people around the country. He wrote songs about what he saw and the people he met.

In the 1930's, Woody Guthrie sang songs to keep up the spirits of people who were out of work. Later he began to write songs about war. He also wrote a book called *Bound for Glory.* It tells the story of his life.

Woody Guthrie wrote more than 1,000 songs. His son, Arlo, is also a folksinger. He is continuing the work that his father began.

SOCIAL STUDIES SKILLS

Reading a Road Map

Suppose you are on a sightseeing tour of our country. You can use road maps to figure out how to get from one place to another. You also can use them to figure out the distance between places. One way of doing this is to use the map scale and measure the number of kilometers or miles from one place to another. For example, the distance between Fresno and Madera is about 38 kilometers, or 24 miles.

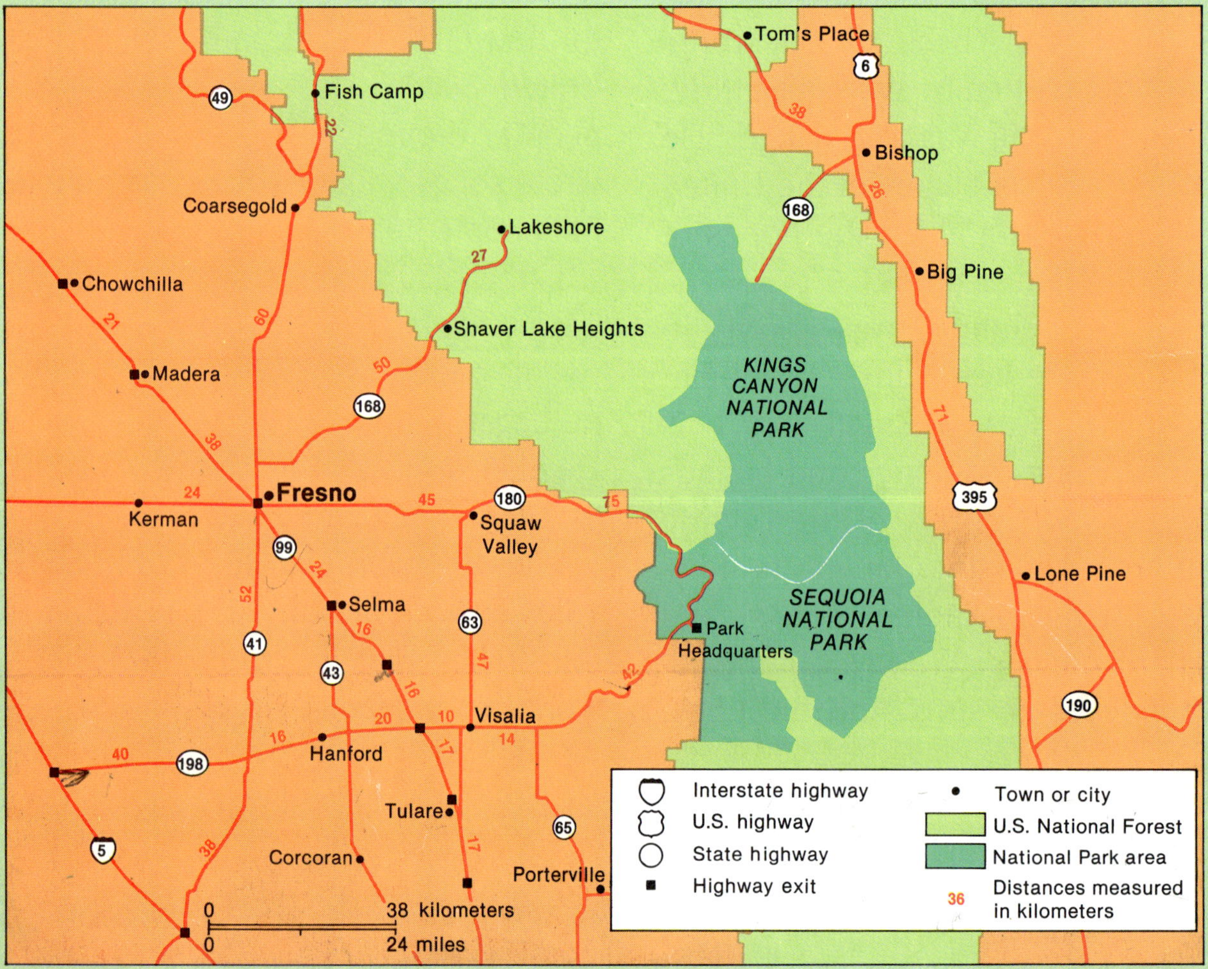

Another way of figuring distances on a road map is by adding up the numerals between places on a road or highway. The road map on page 44 shows a part of California near Sequoia National Park. Look closely at a main highway. The little squares show you where the highway exits are. Notice the little numerals between the exits. These numbers tell how far it is from each exit to the next. Find Highway 99. How far is it from the Madera exit to the Fresno exit? from the Fresno exit to the Selma exit? Along the smaller roads you can see other tiny numerals. These tell how far it is from one town or landmark to another. Find Highway 395. How far is it from Tom's Place to Bishop? from Bishop to Big Pine?

As you can see, the scale of this map is 38 kilometers (24 miles) to 2.5 centimeters (1 inch). Use the scale to find the distance from Fresno to Tulare. Now add up all the numbers along the route. You should get about the same answer.

Practice Your Skills

1. Suppose you wanted to travel to Sequoia National Park along Route 198. How far is it from Highway 99 to park headquarters?
2. Traveling along Highway 41, how far is it from Fresno to Fish Camp?
3. Traveling on Highway 395, how far is it from Lone Pine to Bishop?

2 Human-Made Landmarks

(left) Sears Tower in Chicago
(right) Hoover Dam

There are human-made landmarks all around our country. Some human-made landmarks are special because of their size. Others are special because they remind us of the past. Some seem almost like something from the future.

Human-made landmarks include buildings, bridges, tunnels, and statues. You can see two human-made landmarks in these pictures.

The Great Serpent Mound

Not all human-made landmarks were built in modern times. In southern Ohio, a long pile, or heap, of earth called a **mound** was built more than a thousand years ago. This mound is called the Great Serpent Mound. It was built by American Indians who lived in the area.

mound
a pile, or heap, of earth

There is a reason why it is known as the Great Serpent Mound. It is almost 400 meters (1,330 feet) long. And it winds through the countryside like a large snake, or serpent. In some places, the mound is about 6 meters (20 feet) wide and 1.5 meters (5 feet) high.

No one knows exactly why the mound was built or how it was used. It probably was built for religious reasons. The mound must have been very important to the Indians because building it must have taken back-breaking labor. All the soil used to build the mound probably had to be carried to it. The people who carried the soil probably used handmade containers.

The Verrazano-Narrows Bridge

Can you imagine 1,278 meters (4,200 feet) of concrete highway hanging more than 60 meters (200 feet) in the air? If you can, then you have begun to picture in your mind the Verrazano- (ver-uh-**zahn**-oe) Narrows Bridge.

suspension bridge a bridge suspended from cables hung between towers

The Verrazano-Narrows Bridge is in New York Harbor. It is suspended from cables hung between two tall towers. This kind of bridge is called a **suspension bridge.** The part of the Verrazano-Narrows Bridge that stretches between the two towers is one of the longest bridges in the world.

It took 10 years to build this bridge, and it cost $320 million. The result is a true human-made wonder. There are 97,263,000 kilograms (107,000 tons) of steel and concrete suspended from four cables. Each of these cables is made up of 26,108 wires tightly pressed together. The two towers that hold the cables are as tall as skyscrapers.

It is important for us to protect our country's landmarks. City and state governments try to take good care of their landmarks. Taking care to make sure landmarks are kept safe from damage is called **preservation.** People hope that their country's landmarks will not be harmed. They want them to be seen and used for many years to come.

preservation
taking care to make sure landmarks are kept safe from damage

Section Review

Write your answers on a sheet of paper.

1. What is the Great Serpent Mound?

2. Who built this mound?

3. What is a suspension bridge?

4. What makes the Verrazano-Narrows Bridge special?

5. Do you think 100 years from now the landmarks you have learned about will still be here? Explain your answer.

Close-up on

Fourth of July Celebrations

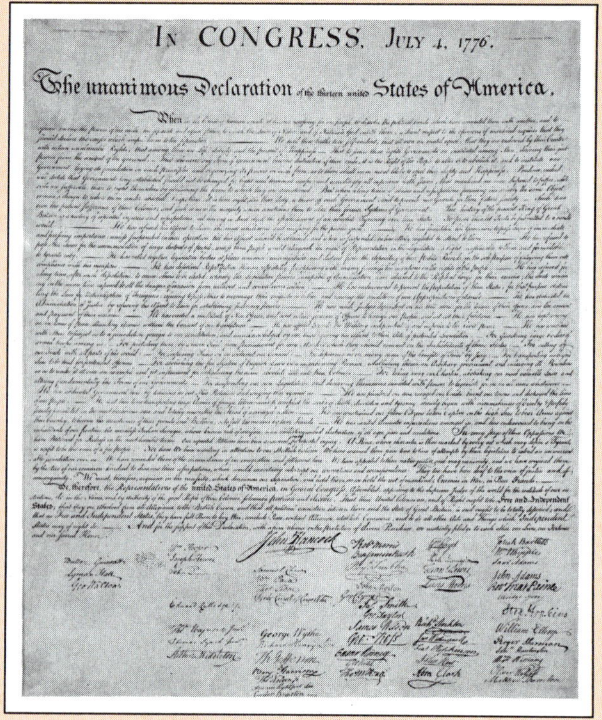
IN CONGRESS, JULY 4, 1776.

The unanimous Declaration of the thirteen united States of America,

The people of our country have been celebrating the Fourth of July since July 4, 1776. On that day, the Declaration of Independence was signed. This was a document written and signed by the early leaders of our country. Its purpose was to make our country separate, or independent, from Great Britain. We remember July 4, 1776, as the day on which our nation was born.

In 1876, 100 years after the signing of the Declaration of Independence, Philadelphia had a huge Fourth of July celebration. The city held a world's fair! About 10 million people came to the fair. They saw new inventions such as the typewriter and the telephone. A parade marched through town to Independence Hall.

On July 4, 1976, our country had another huge celebration. People called it the Bicentennial Celebration because it celebrated our country's two-hundredth birthday.

More than 200 sailing ships from 30 nations helped the United States celebrate its two-hundredth birthday. The ships sailed into New York Harbor. Then they sailed a short distance up the Hudson River. People all along the banks of the river could see these ships.

Many communities in different regions of the country buried time

1876 Centennial in Philadelphia

capsules. These will be dug up on July 4, 2076, the next huge birthday celebration.

Not every Fourth of July celebration is as special as the Bicentennial. But people celebrate the Fourth of July every year. Almost every town in the United States has a parade. You can always see a display of fireworks. Some cities have special feasts. In other places, people dress in clothes from the early days of our country. These are all the different ways of remembering our country's independence.

1976 Bicentennial in New York City

UNIT REVIEW

Word Work

Write the sentences below on a sheet of paper. Fill in the blanks with the correct words from the list.

canyon gorge landmark plain

1. An area of low, flat land is called a ____.
2. A ____ is a deep valley with steep sides.
3. A deep passage through mountains is called a ____.
4. A ____ is an important thing or place that stands out from things around it.

Knowing the Facts

Write your answers on a sheet of paper.

1. What are the eight land regions of the United States?
2. What three important bodies of water border the United States?
3. How does climate differ from weather?

Using What You Know

Choose one of the following activities to do. Follow the instructions given here.

1. Write a letter to a friend describing one region in our country that you have studied.
2. Describe how climate affects your life.

Skills Practice

Use the following road map to answer these questions. Write your answers on a sheet of paper.

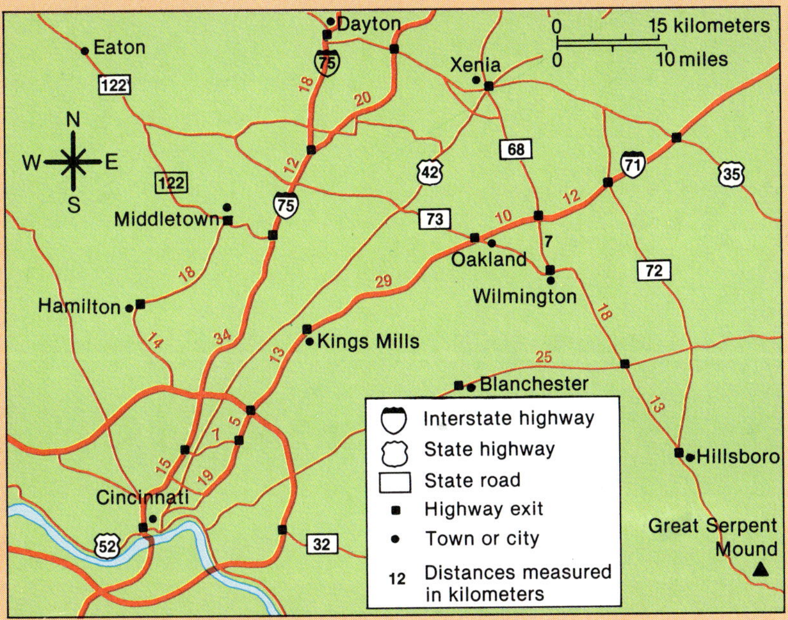

1. You are driving from Hillsboro along Route 73. How far is it to Wilmington?
2. Traveling along Interstate Highway 75, how far is it from Cincinnati to Dayton?
3. How far is it from the Kings Mills exit on Highway 71 to the exit for Route 73?

Your State

Every state has its own landmarks. What are the best-known landmarks in your state? Are they human-made landmarks? If so, when were they built or made? If they are natural landmarks, how were they formed? How are the landmarks used?

UNIT 2 The Northeast Region

Look at the scenes on these pages. How very different they are! Yet they all have one thing in common. They all show places that are part of the Northeast region.

This region is the smallest in land area of all the regions of the United States. But it has more than 54 million people. One out of every four persons in our country lives in the Northeast. In this unit, you will learn why the Northeast is one of the busiest regions in the country.

CHAPTER 3

The Northeast

The path you see in the picture above is part of the Appalachian Trail. This trail winds through the Northeast. Every year, thousands of hikers travel this trail. They want to see the mountains, rivers, and rich farmlands of the Northeast.

At the end of this chapter, you should be able to:

- ○ Name the states that make up the Northeast.
- ○ Describe the major landforms of the Northeast.
- ● Explain how the earth's movement affects the seasons.
- ○ Describe five major industries of the Northeast.
- ● Read an economic activity map.

1 The Land

Look at this map. What does it tell you about the Northeast? It shows the states that make up the region. There are 11 states in all. The District of Columbia is in the Northeast region too. This is the place where Washington, D.C., the capital of the United States, is found.

What else can you learn from the map? What are the names of the 11 states? What body of water lies east of the region? What bodies of water lie along the western part of the region? What country lies to the north?

Find the symbol for state capitals on the map below. What is the capital of Maine? What is the capital of Pennsylvania?

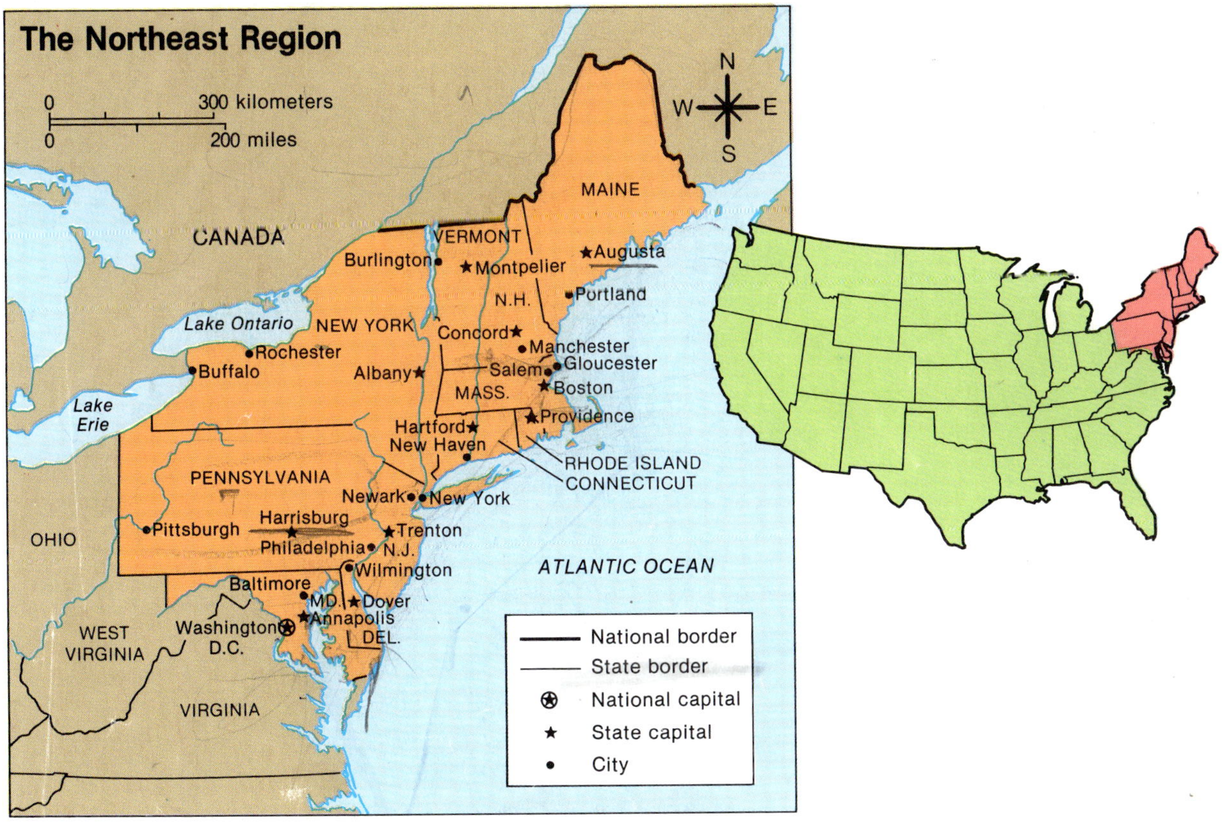

Highlands

lowland
a low, flat area of land

mountain range
a group or series of mountains

landform
a shape of land, such as a mountain, valley, or plateau

Look at the map below and find the map key. The key shows you that the Northeast has highlands. It also has low, flat places called **lowlands.**

As you can see, most of the Northeast is covered by the Appalachian Highlands. Part of these highlands contains groups of mountains called **mountain ranges.** These ranges are covered with forests.

Some parts of the highlands have valleys that dip down between mountains. Other parts of the highlands are plateaus.

Mountains, valleys, and plateaus are all shapes of land on the earth's surface. Such shapes are called **landforms.**

Lowlands

Now find the lowlands, or plains, on the map on the facing page. Most of the people of the Northeast live in these lowlands.

Find the Atlantic Coastal Plain. All along this area, the land is flat and the soil is rich. This is good for farming. Above the coastal plain, the lowlands are hilly and the soil is stony. This is not good for raising crops.

The lowlands area stretching to the west is a broad plain covered with good soil. Trace this plain on the map. What bodies of water do you see at its western edge?

Now follow the Atlantic coastline down its length. Find several bodies of water that seem to carve their way into the coastal plain. Note that each of them has land on at least two sides. Each of these bodies of water is a **bay.** What are the names of the bays?

bay
a body of water having land on at least two sides

In bays, the water is usually calm. Ships can draw up close to the land and load and unload their goods. A place where ships can do this is called a harbor or **port.**

port
a place where ships can load and unload goods

Section Review

Write your answers on a sheet of paper.

1. Name three landforms found in the highlands.
2. Where are the lowlands located?
3. Make a list of the cities of the Northeast you think are ports.

2 The Climate

Temperatures differ from place to place in the Northeast. In January, it is very cold in the northern part of the region, in such states as Maine and New Hampshire. There you would have to bundle up in a heavy coat and boots to go out. Yet in the southern part—in Delaware or Maryland—it is not very cold. There you could wear just a light coat. Why is this so?

Distance from the Equator

The answer is that distance from the equator affects climate. The sun shines more strongly on the equator than on any other part of the earth. So the closer an area is to the equator, the warmer its climate is. Such states as Maine and New Hampshire are farther from the equator than Maryland and Delaware.

New York City in April

Washington, D.C., in April

The northernmost states of the Northeast have long, cold, and snowy winters. Summers there are short and cool. In the southern part of the region, winters are short and mild. Summers are long, hot, and humid.

Growing Seasons

The period of time that crops can be grown is called a **growing season.** Differences in climate affect the growing seasons in the Northeast.

growing season the period of time in which the weather is warm enough for crops to grow

Warmer weather comes early to the lowlands and the southern part of the region. In April, cherry blossoms are blooming in Washington, D.C. Farmers in Maryland and southern New Jersey can start planting their crops. The growing season will last until the frost comes, in October.

However, in the highlands and the northern part of the Northeast, warmer weather comes later and frost comes earlier. Farmers in northern Maine cannot plant their crops until May, and there will be a short growing season. The frost comes four months later, in September.

Section Review

Write your answers on a sheet of paper.

1. Describe winters and summers in the Northeast.
2. Why are winters longer and colder in Maine than in New Jersey?
3. Why would people in Maryland go to Vermont to ski in January?

SOCIAL STUDIES SKILLS

Understanding the Effects of the Earth's Movements

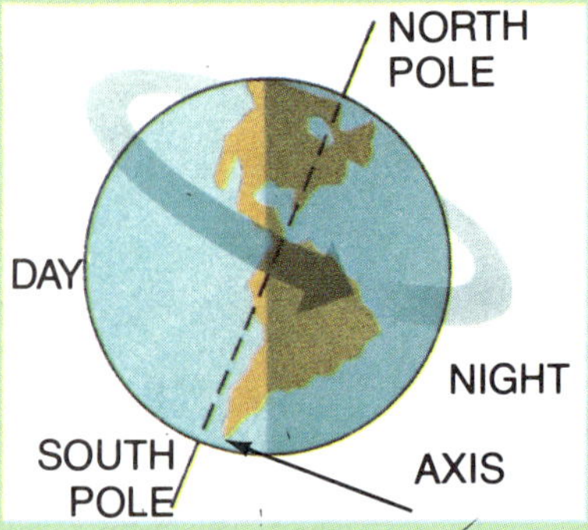

The sun gives the earth daylight. If it were not for the sun, the earth would always be dark. The sun also gives heat. If it were not for the sun, the earth would always be cold. But why is it sometimes dark and sometimes cold? The answer has to do with the way the earth moves in space.

The earth is like a round ball that is always turning. It turns, or rotates, from west to east on an imaginary line called an axis. The axis runs through the center of the earth from pole to pole. The earth rotates around its axis once every 24 hours, causing day and night.

revolution
the movement of the earth in a circle around the sun

As the earth turns, it is also traveling in a large path around the sun. It takes one year for the earth to make one full circle, or **revolution,** around the sun. The diagram on page 63 shows the path the earth takes. Notice that the earth tilts, or slants, on its axis as it travels around the sun.

At one end of the earth's journey around the sun, its Southern Hemisphere is tilted toward the sun. At the other end of its journey, its Northern Hemisphere is tilted toward the sun. The hemisphere tilted toward the sun receives more hours of sunlight during a day. Also, the rays of the sun are straight, not slanted, as they hit the hemisphere. These direct rays give much more warmth than slanted ones. When a hemisphere receives long days of direct sunlight, it is summer in that hemisphere. What season is it in the opposite hemisphere? Why?

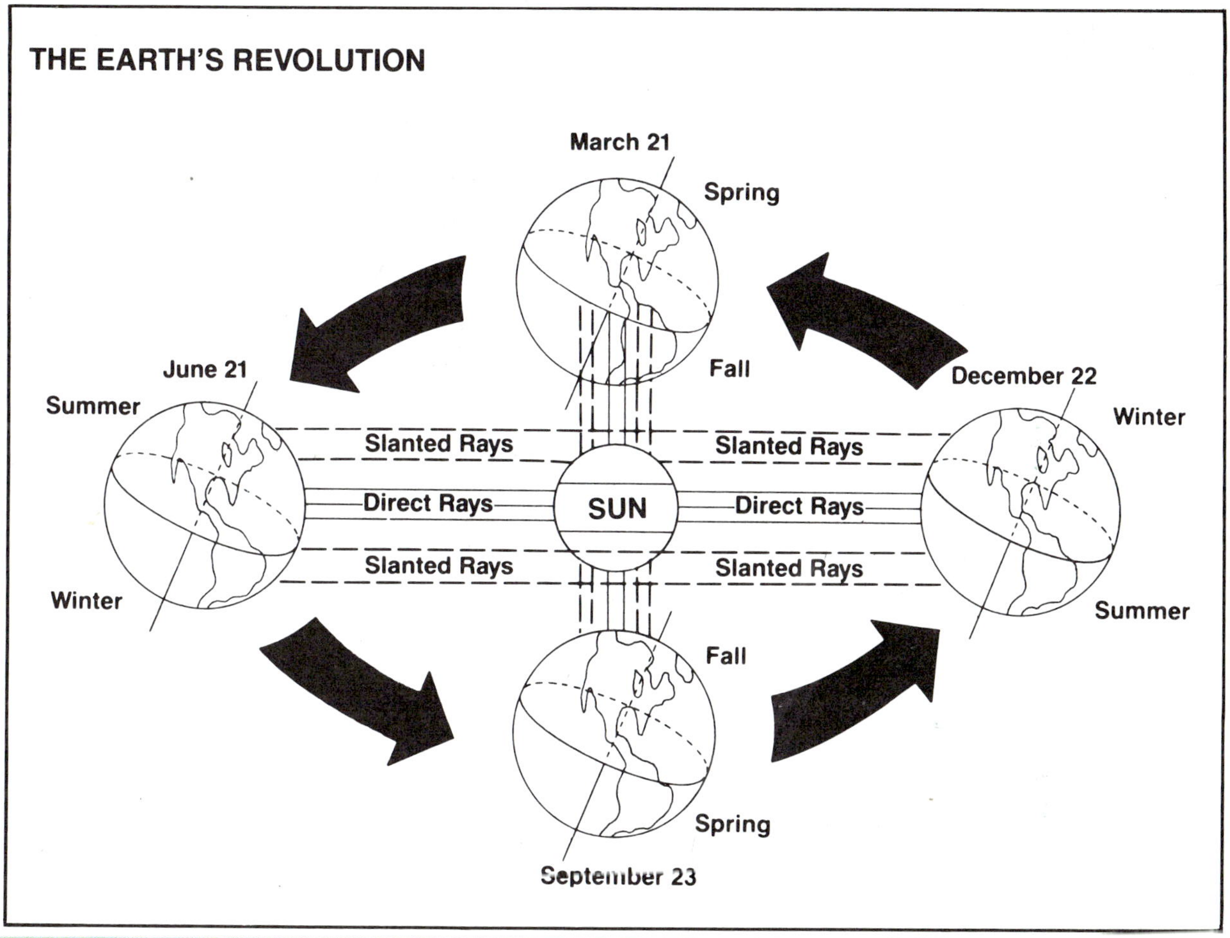

Practice Your Skills

1. When is it winter in the Northern Hemisphere? Is this hemisphere receiving direct or slanted rays?
2. When is it summer in the Northern Hemisphere?
3. What part of the earth is tilted away from the sun on June 21? What is the season?

3 Resources and Industry

natural resource something from nature that people need or want, such as water, coal, soil, and forests

Nature has provided the Northeast with many valuable things that people need and want. These valuable things are called **natural resources.**

Water is an example of a natural resource. Lakes, rivers, and a nearby ocean give the Northeast plenty of water. The fish that fill the waters of the region are another natural resource. So are the forests that cover much of the land.

We use natural resources to get and produce the things we need to live. For example, in the Northeast, people make their living catching fish and selling it to be used for food. People work in the lumbering industry. They make their living cutting down trees. The Northeast has many industries because of its natural resources.

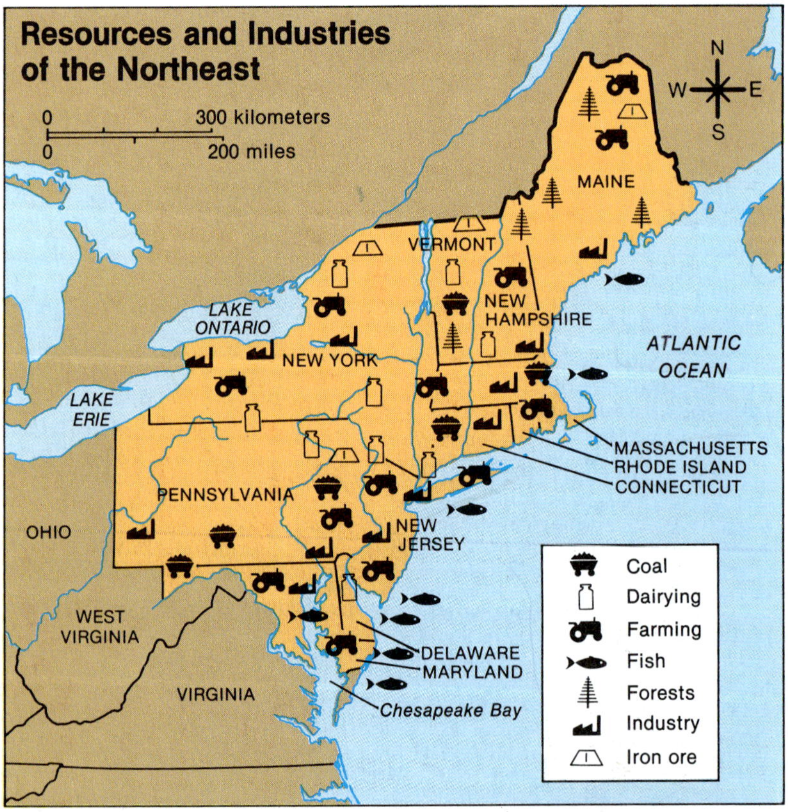

Farming

Good soil and a lot of water are natural resources needed to grow things. Southern New Jersey has plenty of both. Farmers there can produce many of the vegetables the people of the Northeast need. Southeastern Pennsylvania is another fine area for farming, or agriculture. Wheat and corn grow well there.

Farther south, in Maryland and Delaware, farmers produce fresh vegetables and fruits. Farther north and west, in the lowlands near Lakes Erie and Ontario, farmers grow apples and grapes.

Raising cows is a kind of farming done all over the Northeast. The milk these cows produce is the major farm product in the region. Chickens and eggs are the second major product in the Northeast. Delaware and Maryland lead the region in raising chickens.

A chicken farm in Maryland

Steelmaking

Have you ever passed a steel mill at night? If you have, you might have seen flames shooting up from tall smokestacks. These flames come from powerful blast furnaces. Inside these furnaces, intense heat helps turn iron into steel. Coal is the natural resource used to produce this heat.

Pennsylvania has great supplies of coal. This resource has helped to make the Northeast a leading steel producer. The city of Pittsburgh is the center of the steelmaking industry in the Northeast. Buffalo, New York, and Baltimore, Maryland, are also major steel producers.

raw material
a material in its natural state, used in making finished goods

manufacturing
making finished goods from raw materials

Manufacturing

As you read, iron is used in making steel. In its natural state, iron is called a **raw material.** Using a raw material, such as iron, to produce a finished product, such as steel, is called **manufacturing.**

Manufacturing is the Northeast's most important industry. Most of the people in this region work in manufacturing.

What kinds of goods do they manufacture? They make many steel products—everything from nails to huge factory machines. They may have made the clothes you are wearing. The cloth of your coat could have been woven in Massachusetts. Perhaps it was designed and sewn together in New York.

There are good reasons why the Northeast is a leading manufacturing center. One reason is that the region is rich in raw materials that can be made into finished goods.

Another reason is that the people of the Northeast make good use of their many waterways. They use some waterways to provide energy to run machines. The rushing waters of Niagara Falls produce electricity. This electricity helps run machines in factories. The waterways are also used to ship raw materials and finished products to and from factories. Also, there are plenty of people in the region to do the work. And there are plenty of people to buy the goods that are made.

Section Review

Write your answers on a sheet of paper.

1. Name five natural resources of the Northeast.
2. Name four of the region's farming products.
3. Give two reasons why the Northeast is a leading manufacturing center.
4. List the states of the Northeast that you think have a fishing industry.

SOCIAL STUDIES SKILLS

Reading an Economic Activity Map

economic activity
a way that people use their resources to live

Pennsylvania is a leading producer of coal. It is also a major manufacturing and farming state. You can learn more about Pennsylvania's many **economic activities** from a map such as this.

Economics has to do with how people use resources to live. Study the map and map key. Then name some of the activities that help make Pennsylvania a rich state. Describe the parts of the state in which each activity takes place. Are the activities near mountains? rivers? cities?

Practice Your Skills

1. In what area are most of Pennsylvania's crop farms found? What is this area called?
2. Where are Pennsylvania's two leading ports? Where are its main manufacturing centers?
3. In what parts of the state is tourism an important economic activity?

FAMOUS AMERICANS

BEVERLY SILLS

In 1932, when she was three years old, Belle Miriam Silverman sang her first song in public. By the time she was seven, she was singing every week on the radio. But now she called herself Beverly Sills.

One year later, Beverly Sills saw her first opera. She was thrilled as she watched people sing and act on the stage. From then on, she knew that she too wanted to appear in opera—and to be an opera star.

Beverly Sills began to read every book she could find on opera. She played opera records over and over again. She studied singing with a good teacher. She sang for the public whenever she had the chance.

After many years of hard work, Beverly Sills reached her goal. She became a major star of the New York City Opera. There, she has said, she played and sang the parts of "queens, madwomen, and country girls."

Life for Beverly Sills is very busy. As the mother of disabled children herself, she speaks out for the good of all disabled children. Beverly Sills also helps young people who want to become opera singers themselves.

Beverly Sills has retired from singing but not from opera. She is now the head of the New York City Opera.

CHAPTER 4

People and Places

New England today

The year is 1607. The place is the coast of Maine. Two sailing ships are heading for a bay. The ships land, and the people come ashore. They have sailed all the way from England.

At the end of this chapter, you should be able to:

- ○ Give three reasons why people settled in the Northeast.
- ● Read a pie graph.
- ○ Describe the parts of our government.
- ○ Name three reasons why a city can be a communications center.
- ○ Describe how fish products are made.

1 The Early Settlers

The people who landed in Maine on that long-ago day were settlers. They had come from England to make new lives in a land that was strange to them. They had been sent by a group of English business people, or **merchants.**

These merchants wanted the people to start a settlement, or **colony.** A colony is a place that is settled by people from another country and ruled by that country. The merchants wanted the settlers to set up new industries in the colony. These industries would give the settlers goods to trade with the merchants.

merchant
a business person who buys and sells goods

colony
a place settled by people from another country and still ruled by that country

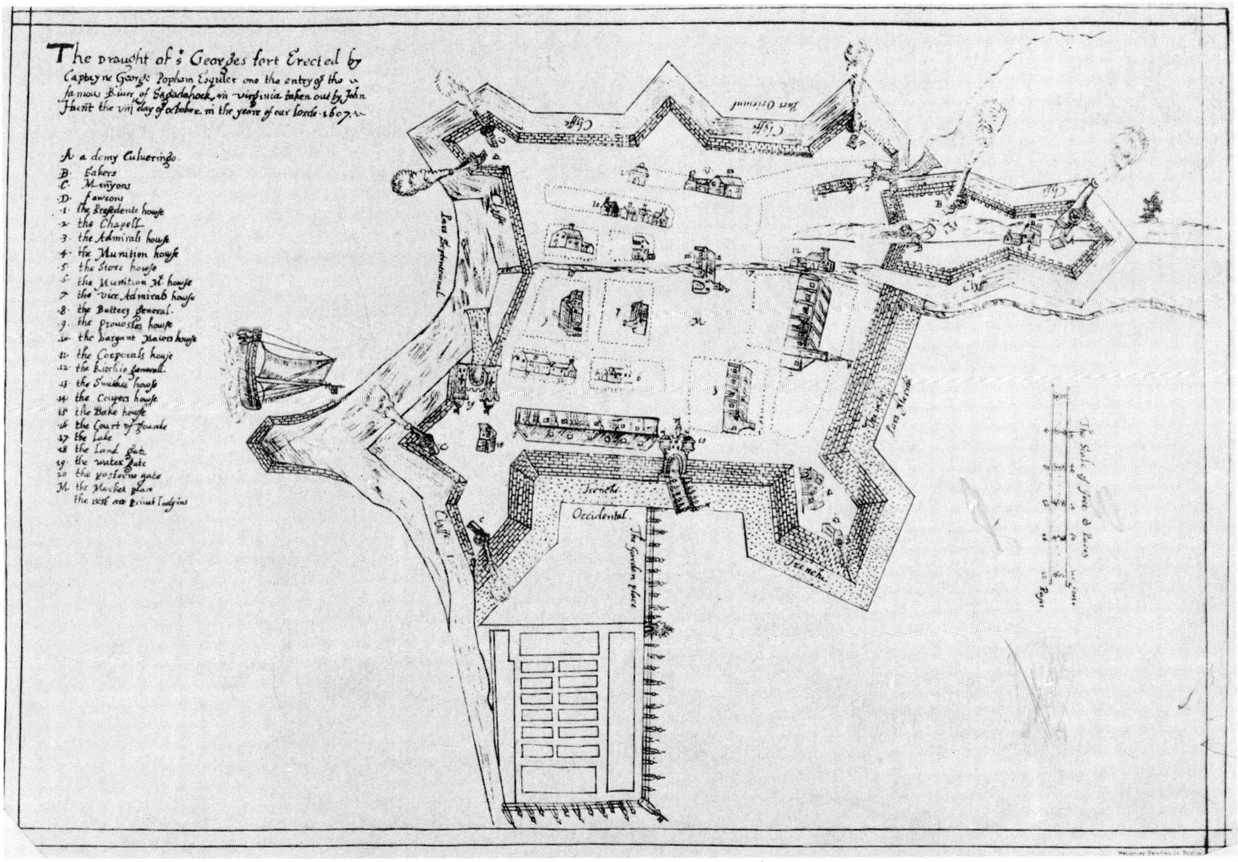

Map of the Popham settlement in Maine

The settlers started their community with high hopes. They named it Popham, after their leader, George Popham. But soon a hard and cold winter set in. The settlers did not have enough food. Many grew sick and died. In the spring, the few still alive returned to England.

In 1620, another ship filled with English settlers came to the Northeast coast. These settlers had left England because they wanted to practice their own religion. The English government did not want to let them do this.

The people landed their small ship, the *Mayflower,* on the coast of Massachusetts. There they founded a settlement called Plymouth. It was on the site of an old Indian village. These settlers were called Pilgrims.

Winter came, and life was just as hard in Plymouth as it had been in Popham. Hunger and sickness were everywhere. In the spring, though, there was new hope. The Wampanoag (wahm-puh-**noe**-ag) Indians had lived in the area for a long time. They came to help the Pilgrims.

The first Thanksgiving

Religion was an important part of Puritan life.

The Wampanoags taught the Pilgrims how to grow corn and other crops. They taught them how to fish the waters.

By the fall, there was food to harvest. Plymouth Colony and the Pilgrims were saved because of the Wampanoags' help.

More Colonies

The success of the Pilgrims was a hopeful sign to other groups of people in England. These groups also wanted freedom to practice their own religions.

One group was called the Puritans. They began arriving in Massachusetts in 1626. The colony they founded was called the Massachusetts Bay colony. During the next 10 years, 16,000 Puritans settled such towns as Salem, Boston, and Gloucester (**gloss**-tur).

The Puritans worked hard, and their colony grew strong. They made religion an important part of life in their colony. In fact, they made it a rule that everyone there must follow Puritan beliefs.

Everyone had to obey Puritan rules and pay taxes to the Puritan Church.

Some people who lived in the Massachusetts Bay colony did not share all the Puritan beliefs. These people wanted to be free to follow their own beliefs. The Puritan leaders refused. They ordered all the people who disagreed with them to leave the Massachusetts Bay colony. So these people went off to start their own colonies, in Rhode Island and Connecticut.

Like the Pilgrims and Puritans, Catholics did not have religious freedom in England. Lord Baltimore was a wealthy English Catholic. He decided to set up a colony in the Northeast where Catholics would have religious freedom.

Lord Baltimore called his colony Maryland, after Queen Mary of England. In 1634, about 200 settlers

William Penn bought land from the Delaware Indians.

moved to Maryland. The colony grew rapidly.

William Penn was another Englishman who wanted religious freedom for his people, the Quakers. In the 1680's, he bought land from the Delaware Indians for his colony, Pennsylvania.

Penn wanted Pennsylvania to offer more than religious freedom for just the Quakers. He wanted it to be a place where all people who believed in God would be free to live and worship. He worked to make his colony a place where everyone—whites, blacks, and American Indians—would be treated fairly and would live in peace with one another.

Soon more and more people came to these colonies and others that had been started. The colonies of New Hampshire, New York, New Jersey, and Delaware were all being settled.

Goods made in the colonies were shipped from the port of Boston.

Life in the Northeast Colonies

In the colonies to the north, hilly land, stony soil, and short growing seasons made farming hard. So, many of the colonists there made their living from the water and forests. They founded fishing villages along the coast. They cut down trees for wood and built ships.

In the colonies to the south, the land and climate were much better for farming. So farming became the main work of these colonies. Farmers produced wheat, vegetables, and tobacco.

Most of the people in the colonies lived in towns or villages, or on farms. But some lived in the growing cities. Boston became an important port. Ships from Boston carried fish all over the world. New York, Philadelphia, and Baltimore also became busy ports. These cities handled the shipping of the farm products.

Government

When large numbers of people live together, they need some people to make their laws and to lead them. These lawmakers and leaders make up the **government.**

government
a group of people who are elected to make laws and lead a community, state, or country

As you have learned, some settlers came to the Northeast to be free to practice their own religion. They also wanted to have some freedom in their governments. They wanted to choose the people who would govern them. They wanted to elect people who would act for them, or represent them, in making laws. A person who acts for other people is called a representative. Government in which a few people act for many people is called **representative government.**

representative government
a government in which lawmakers are elected by the people

The people of the colonies guarded their right to take part in their government. They worked to keep this right so that their government would represent them as they wanted.

Colonial town meeting

The Northeast Today

Suppose that a colonial family could come back to the Northeast today. What changes might they see? Perhaps they would want to take a walk down a quiet country lane to their farm. They might find that the lane is now a roaring superhighway. What would their farm look like? It is probably covered with hundreds of homes.

In 1700, about 227,000 people lived in the Northeast. The number of people who live in a place is called that place's **population.** Most of the population of the Northeast had come from England, Scotland, Ireland, or Germany. Or they were the children or grandchildren of these people.

population
all of the people who live in a particular place

Today, more than 54 million people live in the Northeast. They, or their parents, grandparents, or relatives, have come from nearly every country in the world.

The people of the Northeast have made many contributions to our country. You will meet a few of these people on the next two pages.

A town meeting today

Marian Anderson

Some Important People

Have you ever heard of Marian Anderson, Herman Badillo (buh-**dee**-yoe), or Albert Einstein? All of these people have lived in the Northeast. And all of them have done good things for our country.

From early childhood in Philadelphia, Marian Anderson dreamed of becoming a great singer. At age six, she began singing in the church choir. Then, for many years, she studied and practiced singing. Finally, her dream came true. A famous musician told her, "A voice like yours is heard only once in a hundred years." From then on, she was asked to sing all over the world. She became the first black American ever to sing at the Metropolitan Opera House in New York City.

Herman Badillo has been a leader in New York City for many years. He came to the city from Puerto Rico when he was 11 years old. As a young man, he worked at many jobs to pay for his schooling. The people of New York elected him to be a representative in Congress. As their representative, he went to their neighborhoods to listen to them. He helped them get better housing and streets. He worked to help them get the things they needed for their communities.

Albert Einstein was one of the most brilliant scientists who ever lived. As a boy in Germany, where he was born, he showed great ability to learn about science and to think about it. Within only a few years, his knowledge was helping him solve some of the puzzles of science, including the mystery of atomic energy. Albert Einstein brought his great knowledge to Princeton University in New Jersey. He was a teacher there for nearly 20 years. Students and other scientists came to learn all they could from him.

Herman Badillo

Albert Einstein

Section Review

Write your answers on a sheet of paper.

1. For what reasons did settlers come to the Northeast?

2. Who lived in the Northeast before the settlers came?

3. What is representative government?

4. Name two ways in which your community is like the early colonies of the Northeast. How is it different?

SOCIAL STUDIES SKILLS

Reading Pie Graphs

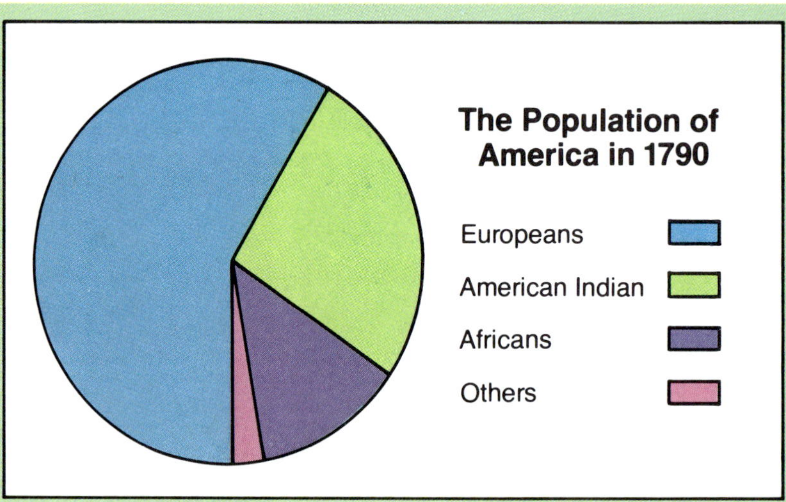

pie graph
a drawing of a whole circle divided into parts

The graph on this page is called a **pie graph.** It is divided into slices like the pieces of a pie. A pie graph shows a whole thing divided into parts. The circle stands for the whole. The slices stand for parts of the whole. What does the whole of the pie graph on this page stand for? What does each part, or slice, represent?

Practice Your Skills

1. For what year does this graph give population information?
2. Into how many parts is this graph divided? Name the group of people each slice represents.
3. Which group makes up the largest part of the population?
4. Were there more American Indians or Africans in 1790?

2 Washington, D.C.

Washington, D.C., is one of the most important cities in our country. The pictures on these pages show you some reasons why.

The picture below was taken inside the Capitol Building in Washington, D.C. The **Congress** of the United States works in the Capitol Building. The Congress is part of our national government. The men and women of Congress make many of our country's laws. All of us who live in the United States must obey these laws.

Like the early colonies, the United States today has a representative form of government. In fact, one branch, or part, of Congress is called the **House of Representatives.** These representatives are elected by the people of each state.

Congress
the part of the United States government that makes many of our country's laws

House of Representatives
the branch of Congress with members elected according to the state's population

States with small populations send only a few. States with large populations send more representatives to Congress.

Senate
the branch of Congress in which each state elects two members called senators

Congress has another branch, called the **Senate.** The people of each state also elect men and women as their senators. But each state, no matter what its population is, can have only two senators.

President
the leader of the United States government

The picture on this page shows the White House in Washington, D.C. This is where the leader of our government, the **President** of the United States, lives and works. The people of the United States help to elect the President.

Running the Government

Running the government of our country is a big job. It takes the work of many more people than just the President and the representatives and senators. In fact, more than 375,000 people work for the government in Washington, D.C., alone. That is half the number of people who live in this city.

People from all over the country come to Washington, D.C., to help run the government. There are many things that need to be done. Members of Congress must have a lot of information before they make new laws. Many people have jobs finding such information. It is the job of our government to print the paper money and postage stamps we use. Many people earn their living producing these items.

Visiting Washington

Every year, 10 million people visit Washington. They want to see the sights in this beautiful city built to house our government. Most of the places they visit are around the Mall (**mawl**). The Mall is a strip of land stretching more than 2 kilometers (1.6 miles) through the center of the city.

At one end of the Mall is the Capitol Building. At the other end is the Lincoln Memorial. This building stands in honor of Abraham Lincoln, who was President more than 100 years ago.

In the middle of the Mall is the Washington Monument. It was built to honor George Washington, our first President. It is a tall, slender building that is 169 meters (555 feet) from the Mall. From the top, you can see all over Washington. An elevator can take you to the top.

The Mall in Washington, D.C.

Section Review

Write your answers on a sheet of paper.

1. Describe the two branches of the Congress of the United States.

2. Where does the President live and work?

3. Does each state send the same number of representatives? Explain.

4. How many senators does the Northeast region send to Washington, D.C.?

3 New York, New York

New York City likes to think of itself as the biggest, tallest, busiest city in the country. Is it the biggest? Yes, its nearly 8 million people make it the American city with the largest population.

Is it the tallest? The answer is "yes" here too. Although New York City does not have the tallest building in the United States, it has more tall buildings than any other city.

Is it the busiest? If you walked down one of New York City's major streets at noon, you might think so. Every day more than 3 million people crowd into just one small part of it to do their jobs.

New York City is proud of its bigness and busyness. It is also proud of how important it is to the country. New York City is a major center for museums and for the performing arts. Actors, dancers, and singers all come to this city to perform. New York City is also a production center for newspapers, books, magazines, television, and radio.

Enjoying the Arts

About 25 years ago, New York City decided to build a place where people could go to operas, concerts, dance programs, and plays all in one area. So Lincoln Center for the Performing Arts was built.

Lincoln Center is not just a place to go to see artists perform. Young people who hope to be artists can go there to study. Lincoln Center includes a school for them. In one classroom, you might see a group of students taking a dance class. In another, you might see students practicing their instruments.

Students study dance at Lincoln Center.

Many museums in New York City set up art classes for school children.

Have you ever gone to a museum? In New York City you could go to 200 of them! In these museums, you can see just about anything you can imagine. You might go to the American Museum of Natural History. There you would see models of dinosaurs that lived long ago. You might go to the Fire Department Museum to see old-time fire engines and firefighting tools.

If you like paintings, you would probably go to the Metropolitan Musem of Art. There you could see thousands of paintings and drawings. The works of artists from all over the world are in this museum.

Words, Words, Words

Look at the book you are now holding. How did it get to be a book? First, it had to be written. Then pictures had to be found to be put in it. All the words and pictures had to be printed on the pages. Then the pages had to be bound together and a cover had to be put on. Only then was the book ready for you to read.

The work of making books is one of the largest industries in New York City. The city has more publishers, or companies that make books, than any other city in the country.

New York City is also home to the publishers of many magazines. The city has many newspapers too. Each day its printing presses turn out millions of papers.

Newspapers are not the only way we learn what is happening. We also watch television to find out the news. Many of the news programs we watch come from New York.

From your own television watching, can you name the three major television companies? All have their main offices in New York City.

communication
the sending out of ideas and information

Books, magazines, newspapers, and television are all ways of sending out ideas and information. Telephones are another way to send out information. All of these ways of sending information are means of **communication.** New York City is an important communications center.

Section Review

Write your answers on a sheet of paper.

1. Tell why New York City can call itself the biggest American city.
2. Describe Lincoln Center.
3. Why can New York City be considered a center for communications?
4. Name three jobs that might be easy to find in New York City.

4 Gloucester, Massachusetts

Gloucester began as a tiny fishing village in the Massachusetts Bay colony. Today, it is a city of nearly 28,000 people. Fishing and making fish products are still its most important work. Gloucester is a major fishing center of the Northeast.

The waters that lie 160 kilometers (100 miles) and more from Gloucester have always been rich in fish. Cod, haddock, and whiting live well there. Over the years, thousands of fishermen have sailed out from Gloucester to find them.

At first, the fishermen went out in wooden ships, moved by the power of the wind against the ships' giant sails. Today, the ships are made of steel. They are driven by powerful engines.

This statue was built to honor Gloucester fishermen.

Most Gloucester fishing boats are trawlers (**traw**-lerz). They carry huge nets. When the trawler crews reach the fishing waters, they lower the nets. Then the boats drag the nets along the bottom of the ocean. Fish swim in through an opening at one end. When the nets are full, the crews raise them. Then the crews empty the fish into the boats. After that, the boats turn around and head back to Gloucester.

Most Gloucester fishing boats carry huge loads of ice on which to put the fish. The ice keeps the fish fresh until the boats reach shore. Some of the fish is then sold just as it is. It is flown to restaurants all over the United States. Much more of it is delivered to the fish factories of Gloucester.

In the fish factories, workers clean the fish and then freeze it. At some factories, the fish is cooked and then frozen. Have you ever eaten frozen fish sticks or fish cakes? If you have, you may have eaten a fish product from Gloucester.

Every day, empty refrigerated trucks pull up to the fish factories of Gloucester. They pull out again, full and ready to carry their frozen contents to fish lovers all over the Northeast and beyond.

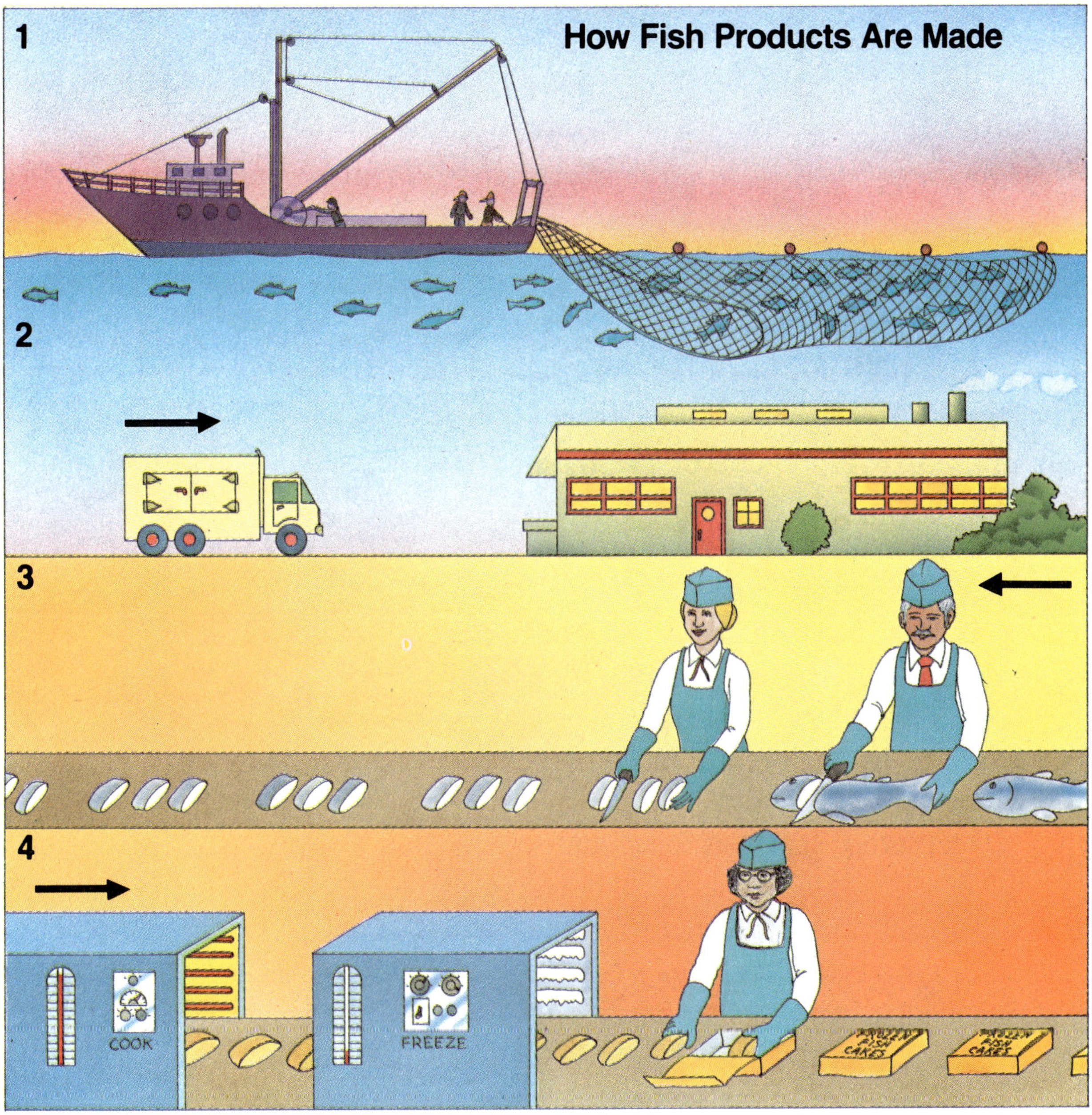

Section Review

Write your answers on a sheet of paper.

1. Why is fishing the most important work in Gloucester?
2. Describe how fish are caught in the waters off Gloucester.
3. How might water pollution affect life in Gloucester?

Close-up on

Peacham, Vermont, Piano Festival There is a quiet little town in the state of Vermont called Peacham. Only 38 homes are in this small village. Most of them are houses that were built more than 150 years ago. Peacham has one library. There is a church that was built in 1806, and one country store. Only one street in all of Peacham is paved!

Once every summer, Peacham is filled with music. Piano students and music lovers go there to take part in the Peacham Piano Festival. The people who go to the festival

are interested in listening to the piano. Many also want to improve the way they play the piano. At the Peacham Piano Festival, they can take piano classes with the woman who runs the festival. She has played the piano in concerts all over the world. She is an expert musician. First, she listens to the students play the piano. Then she gives them instruction.

The piano festival lasts for one week. Residents of Peacham open their homes to the musical visitors. They even serve their guests breakfast every day.

Peacham's church is the center of activity during the festival. Concerts as well as lessons and piano practice are held there.

By the end of the week, everyone is well fed, rested, and happy. The visitors like to become part of the life of Peacham for a week. The people of Peacham like to have the visitors come. They enjoy meeting them and listening to their music.

UNIT REVIEW

Word Work

Write the sentences below on a sheet of paper. Fill in the blanks with the correct words from the list.

growing season natural resource
population government

1. A valuable thing provided by nature is a ____.
2. The people who live in a place are its ____.
3. The time during which crops can be raised is a ____.
4. A group of people who are elected to make laws and lead a country are called the ____.

Knowing the Facts

Write your answers on a sheet of paper.

1. What are some landforms in the Northeast?
2. How does the revolution of the earth affect the growing seasons in the Northeast?
3. Why is the Northeast a major manufacturing center?

Using What You Know

Choose one of the following activities to do. Follow the instructions given here.

1. Write a report about the settlement of your state.
2. Using an atlas, make up a map showing the economic resources of your state.

Skills Practice

Use the following pie graph to answer the questions below. Write your answers on a sheet of paper.

1. What does each piece of the pie graph stand for? What does the whole pie graph stand for?
2. Which job type employs the greatest number of people?
3. In which job areas are there fewer people working than in government?

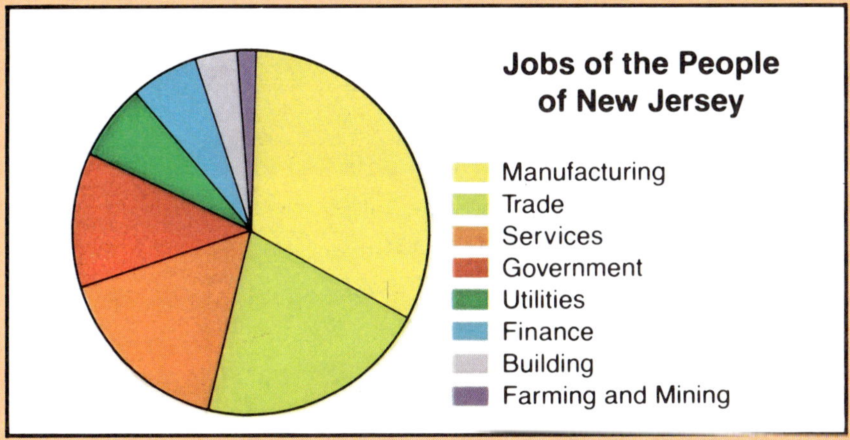

Your State

Think about some things in your state that you feel could be made better. Perhaps a waterway is no longer safe and clean. Maybe there is a landmark you think should be preserved. Write a letter to one of your senators in Washington, D.C., telling him or her your ideas.

UNIT 3

The Southeast Region

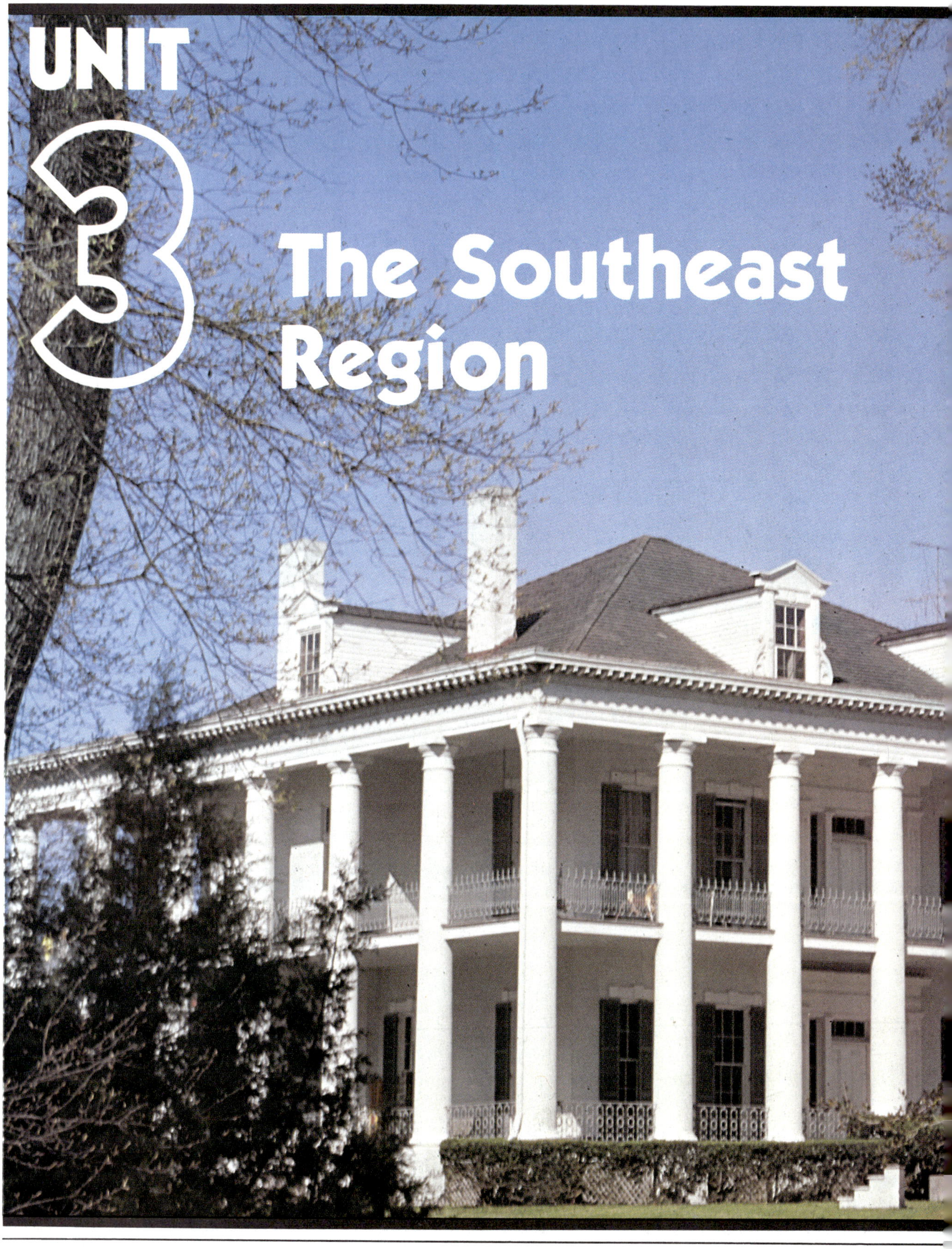

The scenes on these pages all tell something about the Southeast. A tall office building stands for the modern business communities in this region. A handsome old mansion represents the region's past. Fields of sugarcane show the importance of the Southeast as an agricultural region. In this unit, you will see that all of these scenes are part of the Southeast.

CHAPTER 5

The Southeast

Peanut fields in Georgia

A low plain extends inland from sandy beaches. Tall trees grow on rolling hills. Great rivers wind through green valleys. Mountain ranges stretch for great distances. This is the Southeast. In this chapter, you will read about the land and resources of this region.

At the end of this chapter, you should be able to:

- ○ Name the states that make up the Southeast.
- ○ Describe the Southeast's land and climate.
- ● Read a line graph.
- ○ Name the chief resources and industries of the Southeast.

1 The Land

Twelve states make up the Southeast region of our country. Look at the map below. Name the 12 states. What body of water forms the southern border of the Southeast? What body of water forms the eastern border of this region?

One state is surrounded by water on three sides. A body of land almost completely surrounded by water is called a **peninsula** (puh-**nin**-suh-luh). Which state is a peninsula?

peninsula
a body of land almost completely surrounded by water

Plains and Highlands

Find the broad coastal plain on the map on page 100. Here the land is flat. The rich, dark soil and mild climate are good for growing many kinds of crops. Parts of this plain are always covered

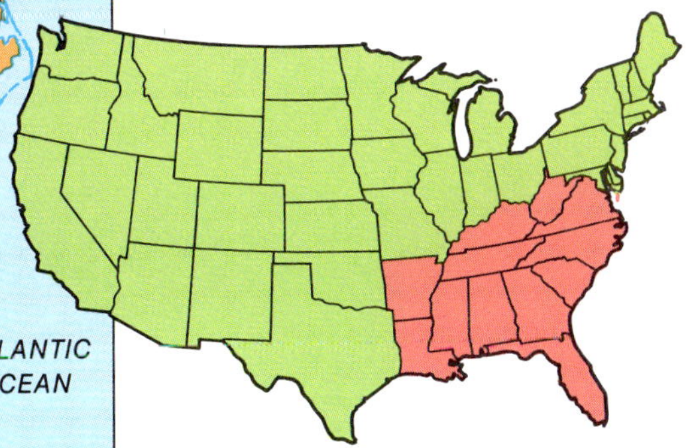

swamp
a lowland area covered with shallow water

with shallow water. An area like this is called a **swamp.** One huge swamp in Georgia and Florida is the Okefenokee (oe-kee-fuh-**noe**-kee) Swamp. Although the Okefenokee does not have good land for growing crops, it is the home of many wild animals. Bears, otters, alligators, deer, and bobcats all live there. Much of the swamp is owned by the national government. It has been set aside as a refuge, or safe place, for these animals.

Above the sandy coastal plain are the rolling hills and valleys of the Piedmont (**peed**-mont) Plateau. What states are part of the Piedmont Plateau?

West of the Piedmont Plateau, there are mountain ranges. The Blue Ridge Mountains and the Great Smoky Mountains are in this area. They are covered with thick forests of pine and oak. Beyond the mountains are highlands and plateaus. In western Tennessee and Kentucky, the land along the Mississippi River is flat.

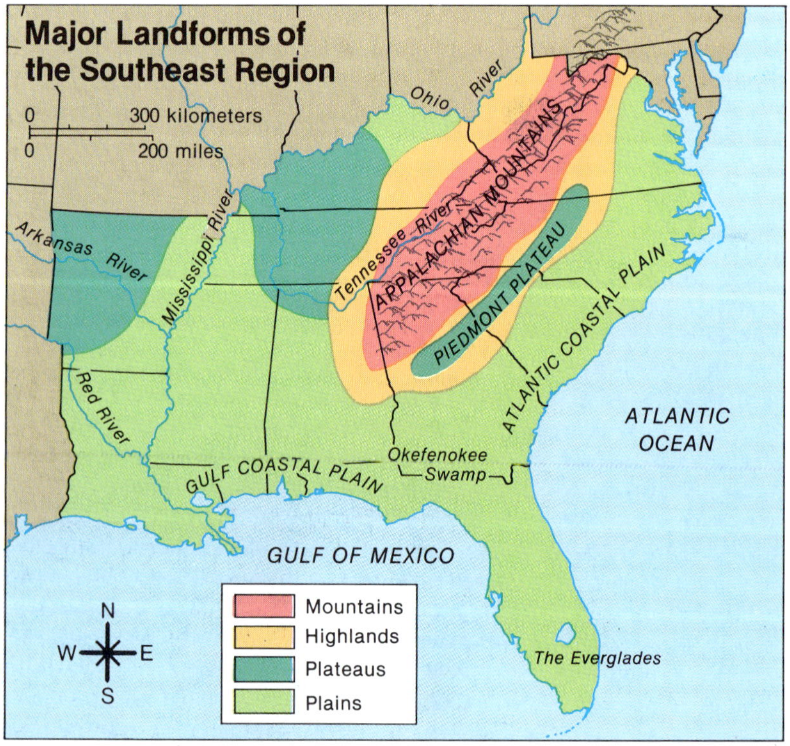

Look again at the map on page 100. What are some of the waterways of the Southeast? The Mississippi River is one. This mighty river is one of the longest in the United States. The soil along the Mississippi River is very rich and just right for growing cotton.

The Mississippi begins in northern Minnesota and flows for 3,780 kilometers (2,349 miles) to the Gulf of Mexico. It is one of the busiest rivers in our country. Day and night, boats carry grain, coal, and cotton up and down the Mississippi.

The Blue Ridge Mountains

hydroelectric power
energy produced by waterpower

dam
a wall-like structure built across a river to help control the flowing water

The rivers of the Southeast also help produce electricity. The power, or energy, that produces this electricity is called **hydroelectric** (hie-droe-ih-**lek**-trik) **power.**

Find the Tennessee River on the map on page 100. Along this river, wall-like structures called **dams** have been built to control the flowing water. These dams help prevent floods. They also make it possible to use the water for hydroelectric power. The diagram on this page shows how one dam holds back the water of the Tennessee River.

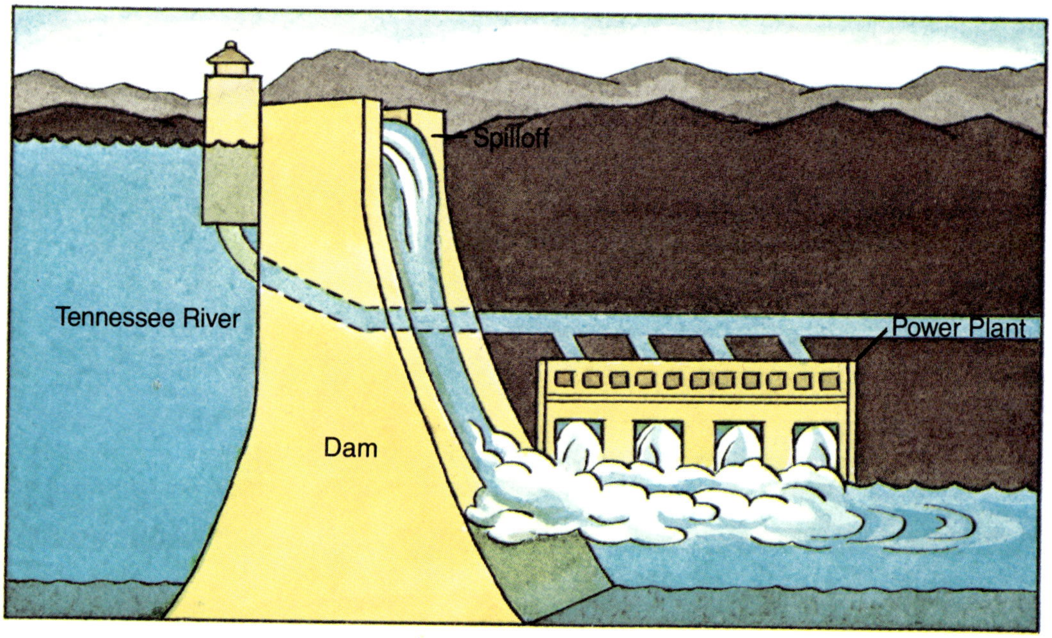

Section Review

Write your answers on a sheet of paper.

1. What is a peninsula?
2. What area of the Southeast is especially good for crops?
3. Why are dams so important?
4. Do you think many crops are grown in the mountain ranges of the Southeast? Explain.

2 The Climate

Most of the Southeast is warm and humid. Summers are long and hot. Winters are mild. But temperatures are not the same all over. In the Piedmont area and in the mountains, it is sometimes cool during the year. Along the coast, the climate is milder than it is in inland areas. This is because warm winds blow in from the Atlantic Ocean and the Gulf of Mexico.

In the southern states of the region, temperatures are warmer than in the northern states. The southern states of the region are closer to the equator.

The Southeast gets plenty of rain. Many areas receive 152 centimeters (60 inches) of rain a year. Along the southernmost coast, heavy rains come from moisture carried by winds from the Gulf of Mexico.

In summer and early fall, **hurricanes** sometimes strike the coastline of the Southeast. Hurricanes are fierce storms of wind and rain.

hurricane
a fierce storm of wind and rain

Tourists visiting Helen, Georgia

When a hurricane is on its way, weather stations send out warnings to communities in the storm's path. Sometimes people can board up their doors and windows and stay in their homes. Other times the hurricane is so strong that people must leave their homes and go farther inland.

The climate of the Southeast is sometimes called its greatest resource. Plenty of rain, mild temperatures, and a long growing season are typical of this climate. Because of this, farmers can raise many different crops. The long, sandy beaches in Virginia, North Carolina, and Florida are popular with tourists from all over the United States. The Shenandoah National Park in the Blue Ridge Mountains is also a favorite spot. Many people visit the Southeast each year.

Section Review

Write your answers on a sheet of paper.

1. In what way does the Southeast's location affect its climate?
2. Why is the climate of the Southeast called its greatest resource?
3. What problem does the Southeast have with its weather? How do the people of the region deal with this problem?
4. List three states in the Southeast you think would have cool winters. List three states you think would have warm winters. Explain why you chose the states you did.

Reading a Line Graph

December and January are often the coldest months in most of the United States. July is often the hottest. What kind of graph would you use to show this information? A **line graph** is a good way to show how things change over a period of time.

line graph
a graph that uses lines to show information and how that information changes

This line graph shows how the average temperature in Lexington, Kentucky, rose and fell for one year. The numbers running up the sides of the graph represent degrees in Celsius and Fahrenheit. The 12 months of the year are spaced across the bottom of the graph.

On the line above each month, there is a dot next to the temperature for that month. If you connect these 12 dots with a line, you can see clearly how Lexington's temperature changed from one month to another.

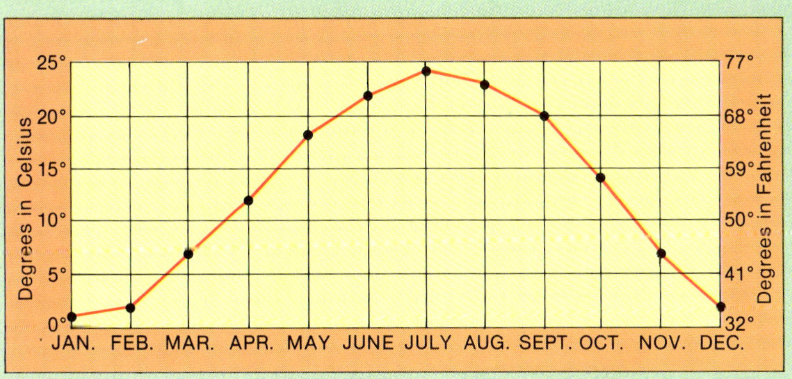

Practice Your Skills

1. What was the average temperature in Lexington in March?
2. What was the warmest month in Lexington?
3. Which month was the coldest?
4. Was it warmer in May or September?

3 Resources and Industry

You have learned that the waterways of the Southeast are a key resource. This region also has many other important natural resources. Coal, iron, and oil are only three. Materials, such as coal and iron, that are dug from the earth are called **minerals.**

mineral
a material dug from the earth

Getting coal out of the ground is a major industry in the highland areas of the Southeast. Look at the map on page 100. Find the highland area. What states are in this arca? Iron ore is dug from the ground in Georgia and Alabama. In Louisiana and Mississippi, giant machines take oil from under the ground and sometimes from under the water.

The Southeast's pine and oak forests provide wood for building homes and manufacturing furniture. In the waters of the Atlantic Ocean and the Gulf of Mexico, many kinds of fish can be found. Some important catches are grouper, red snapper, and shrimp.

Farming

When soil is good for growing plants, it is called **fertile.** The Southeast's coastal plain has fertile soil. So do the river valleys, especially along the Mississippi River. Find the Mississippi River on the map on page 107. Note the many kinds of crops that are grown along the river.

fertile
good for growing plants and crops

The Mississippi River flows into the Gulf of Mexico in Louisiana. The place where a river empties into a larger body of water is called the **mouth** of the river.

mouth
the place where a river empties into a larger body of water

As the Mississippi flows south, it often floods. Then the river carries along huge amounts of soil from its banks. The river leaves this soil at its mouth. This area of land at the mouth of the river is called a **delta.** The delta of the Mississippi River has built up large amounts of rich soil over many years.

delta
an area of land at the mouth of a river

This fertile soil is good for growing sugarcane and other crops. Look at the map on this page. What crops are grown around the Mississippi delta? Name the states that grow soybeans. Which states grow tobacco? What are the chief peanut-growing states?

The crops in the Southeast have led to another important industry. This is called **food processing.** In the food-processing industry, crops such as soybeans are turned into products such as margarine or cooking oil.

food processing
turning crops into food products

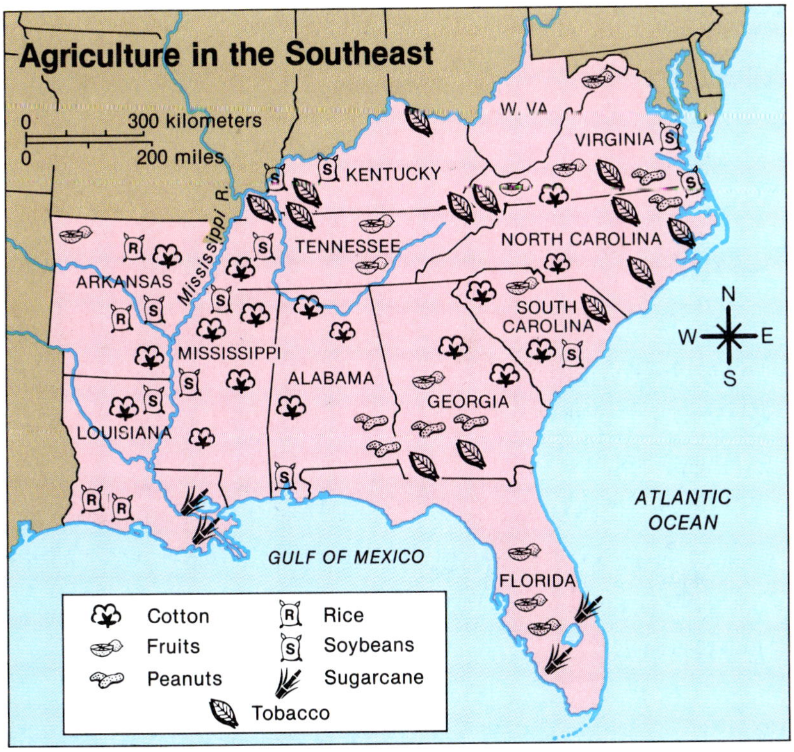

A textile worker

Manufacturing

The good climate and resources of the Southeast have brought many people to the region in the past 10 years. Factories have been built. Workers have moved to the area to fill the jobs. Today, the Southeast is a major manufacturing center.

Iron from the southeastern states is used in steelmaking. Oil is an important resource of the Southeast that is used to make many things. Fertilizer is one. It is used to help plants grow. Plastic is another product made from oil. It is used to make records, toys, bottles, dishes, clothes, and telephones.

Other factories in the region make cloth. Clothmaking is called **textile** manufacturing. Textiles can be made from cotton, linen, and silk. Some textiles, such as nylon, are made from oil.

textile
cloth made from cotton, linen, or other materials

Perhaps the paper in the book you are reading was made in the Southeast. The region's forests are a source of wood for a large papermaking industry there.

Section Review

Write your answers on a sheet of paper.

1. Name five of the Southeast's resources.
2. Why is the delta good for growing crops?
3. List five crops grown in the region.
4. List the resources of the Southeast. Next to each, list the products that are manufactured from this resource.

FAMOUS AMERICANS

DR. MARTIN LUTHER KING, JR.

When Martin Luther King, Jr., was growing up, many laws kept black people from going to the same places that white people went. Some restaurants had signs saying "For whites only." Some schools would not let black students in.

Martin Luther King, Jr., did not agree with such laws. He believed that color of skin should not keep people apart. He believed that people of all colors are equal.

King believed that the laws separating blacks and whites were unjust. In 1955, he began to organize many people to protest these laws. These protests were to be peaceful. "Meet hate with love," said King.

Many people heard King's powerful words and joined his protests. At last, the United States Supreme Court agreed with King too. The Court began to change the laws separating blacks and whites. For his work, King was given a special award called the Nobel Peace Prize.

Martin Luther King, Jr., lived for only 39 years, from 1929 to 1968. During his lifetime, he was greatly admired for the difficult work that he did. Today people still honor King for his peaceful fight for justice in the United States. The third Monday in January is a national holiday to celebrate his birthday.

CHAPTER 6

People and Places

French Quarter, New Orleans, Louisiana

The American Indians who first lived in the Southeast came from many different places. So did the European settlers who came later. The settlements they founded became the large cities and modern farming communities of today.

At the end of this chapter, you should be able to:

○ Describe the early settlements of the Southeast.

● Read a time line.

○ Describe two major cities of the region and give reasons for their growth.

○ Explain how oranges are made into orange juice.

1 The Early Settlers

Long before settlers arrived in the Southeast, many American Indians lived in the region. About 2 million Indians may have lived in the Southeast. One group, the Cherokees (**cher**-uh-keez), lived in Georgia, Alabama, Tennessee, and the Carolinas. They grew crops such as corn and beans. They also hunted and fished in the rich lowland areas.

Other Indians, the Seminoles (**sem**-uh-nolez), lived in the swamp areas of Florida. They built their homes on poles above the water. They also made low, flat boats that could move easily through the shallow water. From these boats, the Seminoles could fish in the swamp.

Look at the map below. What other Indians lived in the Southeast?

American Indians of the Southeast

Spanish Settlements

In 1513, a Spaniard named Ponce de León (**pons** duh lee-**on**) landed his ship on the coast of what is now the state of Florida. He named the area Florida. The word "Florida" comes from the Spanish word for *flower.*

Ponce de León was looking for a magic fountain of youth. He had heard that if you drank the water of this fountain, you would never grow old. De León did not find this fountain, but he did lead the way for Spanish settlers.

By 1565, the Spanish had founded a colony in Florida. They called the settlement St. Augustine. At first, St. Augustine had just a fort and some huts. By the 1600's, people had built bigger houses around a main square, called a plaza. Today St. Augustine is the oldest city in the United States. The buildings in the picture below are hundreds of years old.

St. Augustine, Florida

English Settlements

England was also eager to begin colonies in the Southeast. One of the first settlements began in 1587 on Roanoke (**roe**-uh-noke) Island, off the coast of North Carolina. The colony was not a success. Settlers lived there for a short time. Then they disappeared and no more was ever heard of them.

When other settlers from England landed on Roanoke Island, all they found was a huge tree with the letters "CROATOAN" carved on it. This was the name of a neighboring island. Did the people of Roanoke flee to this island? The mystery remains to this day.

What is the word carved on the tree?

Jamestown

The first permanent English settlement in America was Jamestown. It was begun in 1607.

The settlers who founded the colony were looking for gold. Instead, they ran into many problems. The settlement was near a river. Much of the land was low and swampy. The settlers did not know how to farm or fish. So food soon ran out. Many people starved or became ill and died.

But Jamestown had a strong leader named John Smith. He took charge of the colony and made the settlers work together. John Smith tried to be friendly with the American Indians too. The Indians helped the colonists to grow crops such as corn. Several years later, the colony began to prosper.

In 1619, a ship brought a group of blacks from Africa to Jamestown. Some colonists agreed to pay for the passage of these blacks. In turn, the blacks would work on the colonists' farms. At first, the colonists set the blacks free after they had paid back the cost of the passage. But by 1640, few blacks were set free any more. Instead they were owned by the white settlers. People who are owned by other people are called **slaves.** For the next 170 years, more and more blacks were brought from Africa to work in the colonies.

slave
a person who is owned by another person

Other English Settlements

As Jamestown grew, many new English settlers came to the Southeast to form colonies. The king of England gave a large area of land to a group of his friends. These people founded colonies that became North and South Carolina. The colonists who settled Georgia were led by a man named James Oglethorpe (**oe**-gul-thorp). Georgia was the last English colony to be settled in the Southeast.

Charleston, South Carolina, in the 1730's

French Settlements

The first French explorers came down the Mississippi River from Canada in 1673. Two early settlements were at Biloxi (buh-**luck**-see), Mississippi, and Mobile (moe-**beel**), Alabama. But the most important town was New Orleans (**noo or**-leenz) in Louisiana. New Orleans is near the mouth of the Mississippi River. Boats carrying furs from the North could sail down the Mississippi. In New Orleans, the furs were traded for goods from Europe. New Orleans' location and trade helped the town to grow.

In the mid 1700's, France fought a long war with Britain. France lost the war and most of its land in America. Britain now controlled Canada. After the war, Britain forced a group of French settlers in Canada to settle in the Southeast. These people were the Acadians (uh-**kay**-dee-unz) from Nova Scotia. It was a long, hard journey. Most of the Acadians finally settled in the area near what is now Lafayette, Louisiana. Today people descended from the Acadians are known as Cajuns.

The Southeast Today

The Southeast has changed a great deal since Spain, England, and France first began their settlements. Early settlements became towns and then large centers of industry. The early trails and rugged roads are now superhighways. The rivers are busy waterways for trade.

The population of the Southeast has grown to more than 52 million people. The Southeast has about one fourth of the total population of the United States.

Many of the people are descendants of English, Irish, or Scottish settlers. Others are descendants of the French and Spanish settlers. About 25 percent of the people of the Southeast today are blacks. Most blacks are descended from people who came to the United States from Africa. Although many American Indians once lived in the Southeast, not many of their descendants remain. Most Indian tribes were forced to move to the west by 1839.

Some Important People

Many people of the Southeast have made important contributions to our country.

Louis Armstrong, born in New Orleans, was famous all over the world as a trumpet player. He played a lively kind of music called jazz. His many hit records are considered to be among the best jazz records ever made.

Writer Margaret Mitchell was born in Atlanta, Georgia. She wrote a famous book called *Gone with the Wind.* Most of the story takes place in Atlanta. Readers of the book learn about life in the region during the 1860's.

Louis Armstrong

Helen Keller was born in Tuscumbia (tuss-**kum**-bee-uh), Alabama. She lost her sight and hearing when she was a small child. But with the help of her teacher, Anne Sullivan, she learned to read and write. Keller helped others who were blind. She also gave talks all over the country. Her courage and hard work still inspire people today.

Margaret Mitchell

Helen Keller

Section Review

Write your answers on a sheet of paper.

1. What is the oldest city in the United States? Who founded it?
2. What made Jamestown a successful colony?
3. Name five groups of people who settled in the Southeast. Why did each group settle there?
4. Why do you think there are so many people of French heritage in Louisiana today?

SOCIAL STUDIES SKILLS

Reading a Time Line

time line
a way of listing important dates or events in the order in which they happened

A **time line** is a way of listing the dates of important events in the order in which they happened.

The time line below covers more than 200 years of history. The earliest date, the one that happened longest ago, appears at the left. The most recent date appears at the right. To read the time line, you move from left to right.

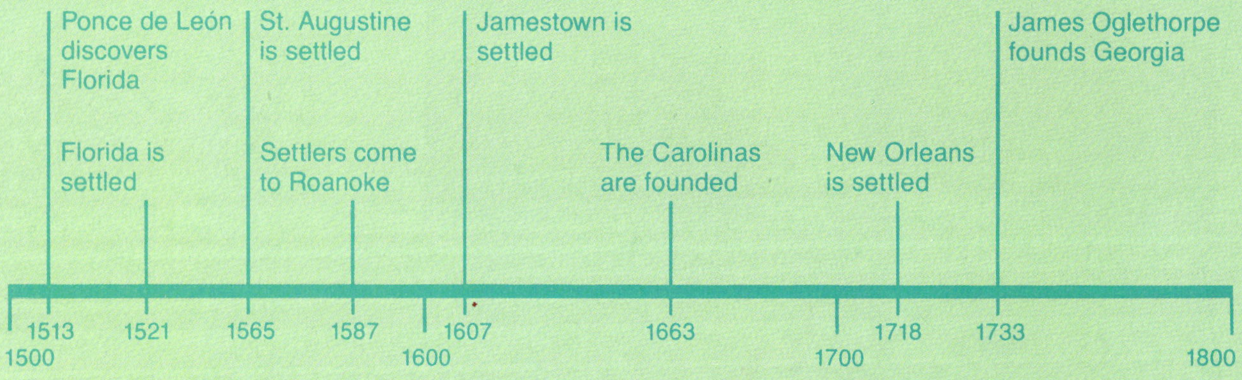

Practice Your Skills

1. What happened in 1513?
2. In what year was Jamestown founded?
3. What is the most recent event on the time line?
4. How many years are there between the settlement of Jamestown and the settlement of New Orleans?

2 Atlanta, Georgia

Atlanta — Georgia's capital — is a big, busy, and beautiful city. It is almost exactly in the center of the Southeast. This location has made it the center for trade and business in the region. In downtown Atlanta, you can see many gleaming skyscrapers. One is the 73-story Peachtree Plaza. It is the tallest hotel in the world!

Atlanta is a busy city today. But not very long ago it was a city in trouble. Many of its businesses had closed down. Its people needed jobs. Some newspapers called Atlanta a dying city. The story of how Atlanta changed and grew is an exciting one.

When Atlanta was rebuilt, many of these buildings were torn down. Peachtree Center was built in place of them.

A City in Trouble

Atlanta's problems began around 1945. This was when World War II ended. During that war, many army bases and airplane and automobile factories opened in Atlanta. Some of these places closed after the war. Many people were out of work.

Even so, more people moved to Atlanta hoping to find work. Many were farmers from the Southeast. Their farmland had been bought up after the war. People wanted to build houses on this land. But the farmworkers did not have skills to work in city stores and factories. They could not find jobs.

Some sections of Atlanta became crowded and dirty. In 1952, the city's leaders obtained 260 square kilometers (100 square miles) of land to make Atlanta larger.

The City Rebuilds

In the 1960's, Atlanta's leaders worked hard to rebuild the city. They asked banks for money so they could put up new buildings, hotels, and apartments. The leaders said that people from other places would want to visit, live, and work in a city that was growing. They told business leaders in other parts of the country about Atlanta's warm climate and beautiful parks.

Slowly, the city grew. Between 1960 and 1970, more than 50 apartment buildings, hotels, and office towers were built. New factories opened. Atlanta's people got jobs making car parts, chemicals, textiles, and iron goods. The area in and around Atlanta grew from 487,000 people in 1960 to more than one million people in just 10 years.

Atlanta being rebuilt

Inside a hotel in Peachtree Center

Atlanta Today

Atlanta kept on growing. More office buildings and factories were built. The city also built places where people could relax. Today sports fans in Atlanta can enjoy two new stadiums, built in 1965 and 1975. They can watch hockey, basketball, football, and baseball games in these stadiums. The Atlanta Memorial Arts Center, opened in 1968, is a home for plays, operas, and ballet.

Atlanta even has a "mini-city" in its downtown area. It is the 18-hectare (45-acre) Peachtree Center, built in the 1970's. Peachtree Center includes office buildings, hotels, apartments, and museums. In the photo to the left, you can see part of this "mini-city."

Atlanta's leaders believe the city will keep growing. They are asking people from other countries to open businesses there. They want to put up even more buildings in Atlanta. The people of Atlanta believe that their city is a place the whole world can enjoy.

Section Review

Write your answers on a sheet of paper.

1. Why did people in Atlanta lose jobs after World War II?
2. How did Atlanta's leaders rebuild the city?
3. How do places like a sports stadium and an arts center help a city to grow?

3 Nashville, Tennessee

What kind of music do you like? Are you a fan of rock music? Do you listen to tunes from shows and movies? Do you like other kinds of music?

If you lived in Nashville (**nash**-vill), Tennessee, chances are you would be a fan of country music. Nashville is called the country music capital of the world. Nashville also has the nickname Music City, U.S.A.

The Music Center

Over the last 35 years, Nashville has grown a great deal. One reason is that there has been more interest in country music. The words of this music tell about everyday things and ordinary people. Country songs about home life, railroads, truck drivers, and caring for someone have become popular. Today country music has fans throughout the United States and in many foreign countries.

Outdoor concert in Nashville

Grand Ole Opry House in Nashville

How Country Music Began

Country music began in the Southeast. It started with the music of settlers nearly 200 years ago. People made up their own words to songs and played along on fiddles or guitars. In these songs, they told about their work, their problems, and their feelings. Many of these people had come from Great Britain, Scotland, and Ireland. Often the music was based on songs from these homelands.

Two inventions helped spread country music. They were the phonograph in 1877 and the radio in the 1920's. By 1925, country music could be heard on radio stations. In Nashville, one country music program was called "Barn Dance." Today that program is called "Grand Ole Opry." It has been broadcast for more years than any other radio program in the country. Many people say that the "Grand Ole Opry" started the country music boom.

The "Grand Ole Opry" was broadcast live every week from the Grand Ole Opry House. Today the program comes from a new theater built especially to broadcast the program. It has 4,400 seats and is the largest broadcast studio in the world. But the Grand Ole Opry House will always be part of the tradition of country music—and of Tennessee.

Country Music Today

Country music is more than just a radio program. It is a major industry. There are hundreds of companies that make and sell phonograph records in Nashville. There are also many song-publishing companies. These companies print the words and notes to music on paper. This is called sheet music. There are about 70 recording studios in Nashville. At these sound studios, singers and musicians record their songs for record albums.

These people are recording music in a sound studio.

A country music group

Today many kinds of musicians come to Nashville. They hope to record and sell hit record albums. Rock groups, blues singers, and other kinds of musicians all make recordings of country songs.

Now you know why Nashville, Tennessee, is called Music City, U.S.A. The city is as important to many musicians as Hollywood, California, is to many actors and actresses.

Section Review

Write your answers on a sheet of paper.

1. What is Nashville's nickname? How did it get this name?
2. What is the "Grand Ole Opry"?
3. Do you think television has helped spread country music? Explain.

4 Winter Haven, Florida

Do you like orange juice? Maybe you even drank some this morning. Did you know that the United States produces about one third of all the oranges in the world?

Nearly all the oranges grown in our country come from just two states: Florida and California. The warm climate and good rainfall in these states are perfect for growing this fruit. If you drive through the central part of Florida, you will see orange **groves.** Groves are large fields of trees.

grove
a large field of trees

In the heart of orange country is the city of Winter Haven. All around the city, the land is covered with orange and grapefruit groves. These groves make Winter Haven an orange-growing center.

An Important Discovery

Fifty years ago, nearly all oranges were sold as fresh fruit. Some people ate the oranges. Others squeezed them to make fresh orange juice. Then, in 1944, scientists made an important discovery. They found a way to make frozen orange juice that tasted almost as good as freshly squeezed juice.

People did not have to squeeze oranges any more. They could just open a can and add water. Soon almost everyone was buying frozen orange juice instead of fresh oranges. Today about 90 percent of Florida's oranges are used to make frozen juice and other products. Some of these products are cattle feed, perfume, and candy.

What Happens to Oranges

How do oranges get from Florida orange groves onto your breakfast table? Whether you drink frozen or freshly squeezed orange juice, the oranges come from the same place: trees.

Oranges are loaded onto a truck and taken to an orange-packing plant or a processing plant.

An orange-packing plant

Orange trees may grow 9 meters (30 feet) high. They need warm weather and plenty of water to grow well. Temperatures below 4° C (25° F) may harm both the orange tree and its fruit.

Orange pickers, often standing on ladders, pick ripe oranges from the trees. The fruit is then loaded onto trucks. Oranges that will be sold fresh are taken to a packing house. Oranges that will be made into frozen orange juice are taken to a processing plant.

At the Packing House

Oranges used for eating are unloaded. Then they are carried by belts into the packing house. There they are washed in hot, soapy water, rinsed, and dried. Next they are waxed to protect and keep them fresh. After waxing, the oranges are sorted by size and quality. Finally they are packed in cartons or bags for shipping to other regions of the country.

HOW ORANGE JUICE IS MADE

At the Processing Plant

To make frozen orange juice, oranges are taken to a processing plant, or cannery. There the oranges are washed and squeezed. How many oranges do you think you could squeeze in an hour? Some juicing machines can squeeze 700 in one minute!

Next the squeezed juice is processed to take out the water. The remaining juice is then moved to a large blender tank. Then a small amount of fresh juice is added. This is done to put back any flavor lost during the squeezing process. Finally the orange juice is cooled, put into cans, and frozen solid. Refrigerated trucks and railroad cars then take the juice to towns and cities all over the United States.

After the juice is squeezed out, the rest of the orange is not thrown away. It is used to make jam, flavoring oil for cooking, cattle feed, and many other products.

Winter Haven has packing houses and processing plants. In fact, most of the people in Winter Haven work at making oranges and their products available to people all over the country.

Section Review

Write your answers on a sheet of paper.

1. Which states do most oranges grown in the United States come from?
2. What is a grove?
3. Where are oranges taken if they are to be sold as fresh fruit?
4. How is frozen orange juice made?
5. What do you think would happen in Winter Haven if the weather became very cold for a while?

Close-up on

Quilting Since early times in America, quilting has been a popular craft. The art of making beautiful quilts has been handed down from mother to daughter over and over again.

All kinds of fabric scraps are saved to make a quilt. They are sorted and kept in scrap boxes. When enough scraps have been gathered, a quilter cuts them and forms them into a pattern. There are many quilt patterns to choose from. The patterns have wonderful names, such as Pickle Dish, Wild Goose Chase, Crazy Ann, and Double Wedding Ring. Or, if the scraps are bits and pieces of different patterns, they might be sewn together any-which-way to make a one-of-a-kind Crazy Quilt.

Once the top part of a quilt is made, it is stitched to a bottom layer

(left) A quilting cooperative today
(below) A portion of an 1840's quilt

America

A quilting party in early America

with a fluffy stuffing in between. Since quilts are so big, quilters help each other. In the old days, there were quilting parties, or bees. Today there are quilting cooperatives. They are not so different from the early quilting bees. A big frame is set up. Quilters sit all around the frame and sew and chat. At the end of the evening, a quilt may be finished. Then it is time for supper and a square dance.

The layers of a quilt make it a warm cover for a bed. But a quilt is much more than that. A child tucked under a quilt might recognize a patch from a favorite shirt, long outgrown. Or a family member might touch a soft square that came from a grandfather's vest.

Whether it's Wagon Wheel, Jacob's Ladder, or Dove-in-the-Window, a quilt is a blanket of memories. A quilt is a family album made of bits and pieces of cloth lovingly stitched together.

UNIT REVIEW

Word Work

Write the sentences below on a sheet of paper. Fill in the blanks with the correct words from the list.

grove peninsula delta textile

1. A group of fruit trees is called a ____.
2. Clothmaking is called ____ manufacturing.
3. The area of land at the mouth of a river is called the ____.
4. A ____ is a body of land almost completely surrounded by water.

Knowing the Facts

Write your answers on a sheet of paper.

1. Why is the Southeast good for farming?
2. Why do coastal areas of the Southeast have a milder climate than inland areas?
3. Explain why Jamestown grew.
4. How was the city of Atlanta rebuilt?

Using What You Know

Choose one of the following activities to do. Follow the instructions given here.

1. Write a report on how people protect themselves and their property from hurricanes.
2. Pretend you are a colonist at Jamestown. Write a letter to a friend in England.

Skills Practice

Use the following line graph to answer these questions. Write your answers on a sheet of paper.

1. Which month is the rainiest in Miami?
2. Which month is the driest in Miami?
3. How many more days of rain are there in October than there are in November?
4. Which four months make up the rainy season in Miami?

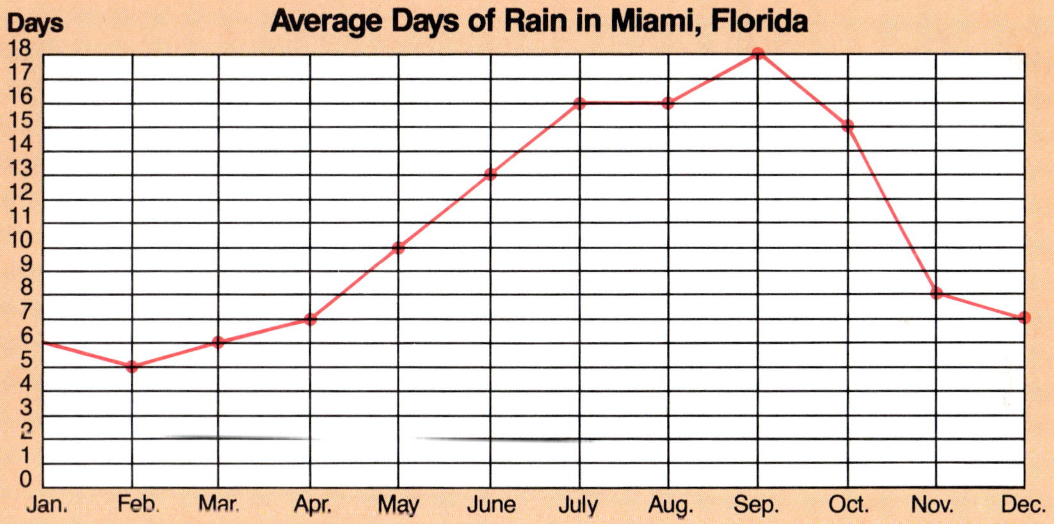

Your State

If a friend were visiting your state, which places would you tell him or her to see? What is your state most famous for? What important events happened in your state? Make a time line to show some events in the early history of your state.

UNIT 4 The Midwest Region

Look at the scenes on these pages. You can see a large farm and a busy waterway. You can also see a big city. These are all parts of the Midwest.

You might eat something today that was grown in the Midwest. It probably came to you through a midwestern city. The farms and waterways of the Midwest helped its cities grow. In this unit, you will read how the Midwest helped our country grow.

CHAPTER 7

The Midwest

Harvesting corn in Iowa

The Midwest lies in the center of our country. The region has mighty rivers and giant lakes that connect it with the rest of the country. Fertile soil and mild climate help to produce enough food to feed the country.

At the end of this chapter, you should be able to:

○ Name the states that make up the Midwest.

○ Describe the region's land and climate.

● Compare and contrast two kinds of maps.

○ Name some important resources and industries of the Midwest.

1 The Land

The Midwest is made up of 12 states. Look at the map below. What are the names of these 12 states? Now look along the northeastern part of the Midwest. The bodies of water you see are called the Great Lakes. In all, there are five Great Lakes in the northern United States. Four of them are part of the Midwest. What are the names of the four lakes shown here?

The Plains

If you were to fly over the Midwest toward the Rocky Mountains, you would see mostly flat land

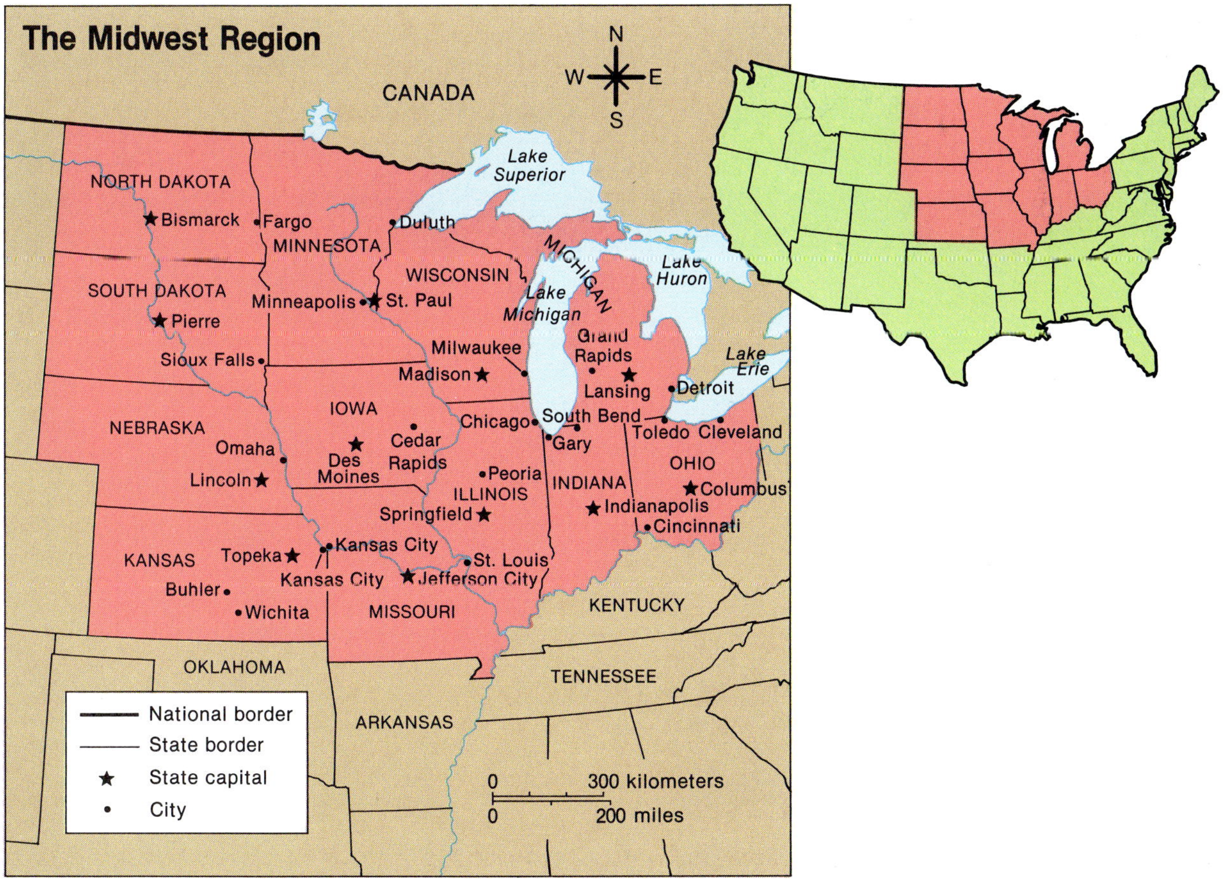

or low hills. This area is part of the Interior Plains. The Interior Plains has two major parts. They are the Central Plains and the Great Plains.

Look at the map on this page and find the Central Plains. The Mississippi, Ohio, and Missouri rivers flow through this area.

Crops grow well in the fertile soil of the Central Plains. The rich soil and the heavy rainfall each year make this area one of the best places in the world for farming.

prairie
large area of flat land covered with tall, thick grass

Nearly all the Central Plains were once a **prairie,** or flat land covered with tall, thick grass. Today much of this land is planted with corn. Corn grows well in a mild, humid climate. So much corn is grown on the Central Plains that the area is called the Corn Belt.

The four states farthest west are part of the area called the Great Plains. Look at the map on the

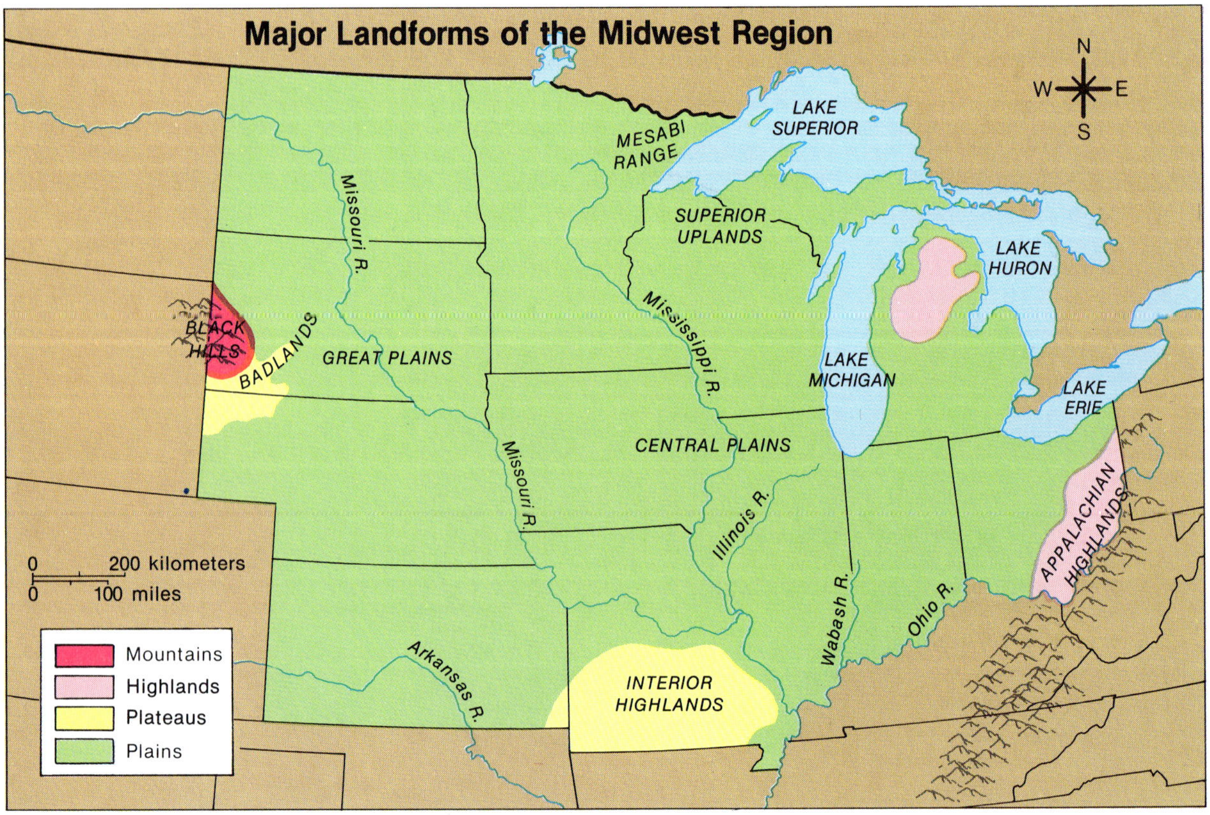

facing page and on page 139. Which midwestern states are in the Great Plains?

The Great Plains rise gently toward the Rocky Mountains. Parts of the Great Plains are covered with short grass. The short grass makes this part of the Midwest good for cattle grazing. Other parts are covered with wheat.

The Highlands

Look at the map on the facing page. Find the highland areas on it. You can see that the highlands cover only a small part of the Midwest. Find the Interior Highlands and the Appalachian Highlands. In these areas, the soil is too rocky for farming. But the land contains important resources for industry.

Badlands National Park, South Dakota

The Superior Upland area is in the northern parts of Minnesota, Wisconsin, and Michigan. The Mesabi (muh-**sah**-bee) Range is in the Superior Uplands. The Mesabi Range is a hilly area with large amounts of iron. Find the Mesabi Range on the map on page 140. Which of the Great Lakes is in this region?

The only mountains in the Midwest are the Black Hills in South Dakota. Some of these mountains are more than 2,134 meters (7,000 feet) high. They are named for their dark green pines. The pines make the mountains look black from a distance. There is valuable gold in the Black Hills.

ravine
a narrow valley with steep sides

Not far from the Black Hills lies a very dry plateau called the Badlands. Both the stony soil and the dry climate make this area useless for farming. But the scenery is very beautiful. Strange stone shapes rise up from the land. Narrow valleys with steep sides, called **ravines,** cut through the land.

Section Review

Write your answers on a sheet of paper.

1. Name five land regions of the Midwest.
2. What are the chief rivers of the Midwest? What lakes lie northeast of the Midwest?
3. Why is there a "Corn Belt" in the Central Plains?
4. Why do you think there are more cities in the Central Plains than in the Great Plains?

2 The Climate

The climate of the Midwest is a little like the climate of the Northeast. Winters can be quite cold. Summers can be quite warm. The reason for this likeness is that both regions lie about the same distance from the equator.

Yet there are differences between the climates of the two regions. For example, Chicago, Illinois, and New York, New York, are about the same distance from the equator. Yet Chicago has colder winters than New York. Why?

One reason for this difference in temperature is that New York is near the ocean and Chicago is not. During the winter, warm winds blow off the Atlantic Ocean. These winds make winter temperatures in New York warmer than in Chicago.

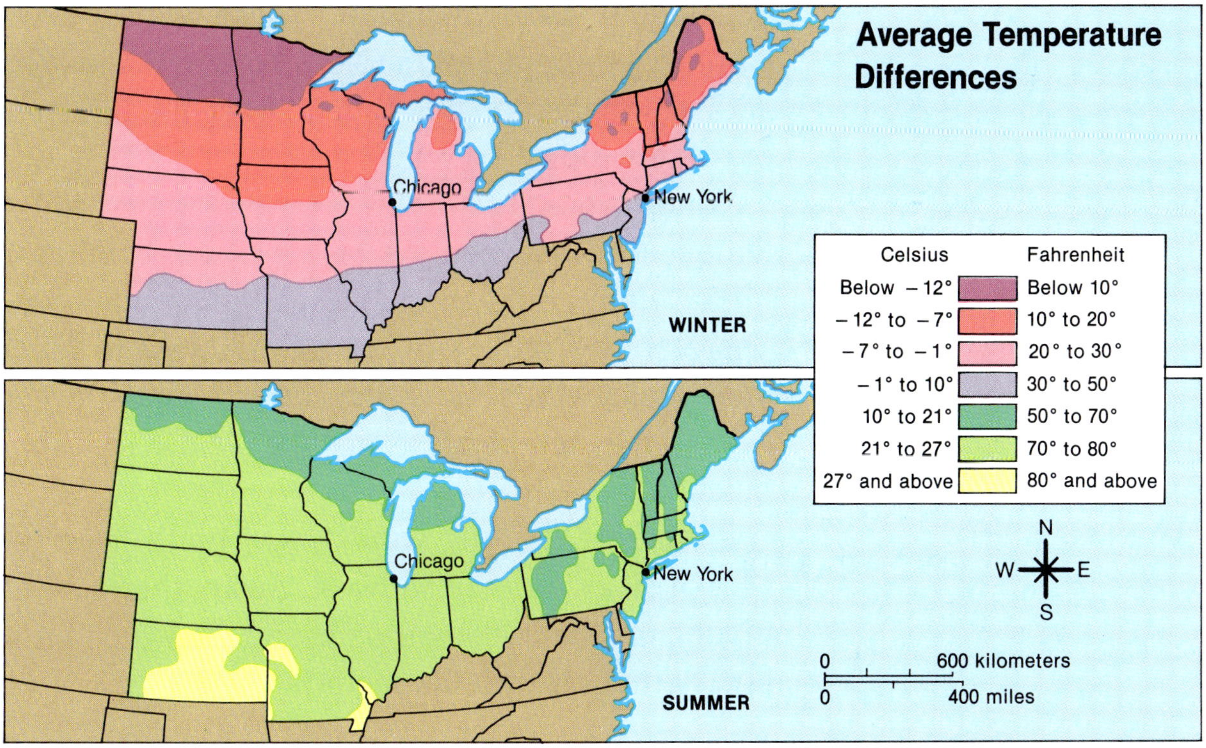

During the summer, cool winds blow from the ocean and Lake Michigan. These winds affect summer temperatures in New York and Chicago. Look at the map on this page to trace the direction of these winds.

Winds are another reason for differences in the temperature between the Midwest and Northeast. In the winter, cold winds blow from the icy north. There are no mountains in the Midwest to block these cold winds. So when the icy winds sweep down, the temperature in the Midwest drops quickly.

In summer, strong winds blow north from the Gulf of Mexico to the Midwest. Again, there are no mountains to block their paths. So the winds bring hot, humid air into the region.

The strong winds also bring rain and snow. From the south, the winds bring moisture from the Gulf of Mexico. When the wind brings cold air from the north, the cold air pushes the warm air upward. As the warm air rises, the moisture in it falls as rain or snow.

The rain is good for the Midwest. It makes possible the farming that is so important to the area. Yet some regions receive more rainfall than others. In the highlands and the Great Plains, the rainfall is less than 76 centimeters (30 inches) per year. The Central Plains are closer to the Gulf of Mexico. So this area receives as much as 127 centimeters (50 inches) of rain per year.

The difference in rainfall affects the kinds of crops that each part of the region grows. For example, wheat does not need a great deal of rain to grow. That is why it is grown in the Great Plains. Corn needs more rain than wheat. So corn is grown in the Central Plains.

Section Review

Write your answers on a sheet of paper.

1. Why are temperatures in the Midwest different from temperatures in the Northeast?
2. Why do the Central Plains receive more rainfall than the Great Plains?
3. What effect does the amount of rainfall have on the kinds of crops that are grown?
4. What do you think would happen to the supply of cornflakes if corn were grown in the Great Plains instead of the Central Plains?

SOCIAL STUDIES SKILLS

Comparing Maps

In this section, you read about which crops grow best in each part of the Midwest. With a little map detective work, you can discover this information for yourself. All you have to do is compare the following two maps.

First, study the temperature regions map and map key. You can see that most of the Midwest is in two temperature regions. In the upper region, colored yellow, summers are short and warm. The winters are long and very cold. In the zone colored red, the summers are longer and hotter. The winters are a little milder. In the zone colored green, summers are hot and winters are mild.

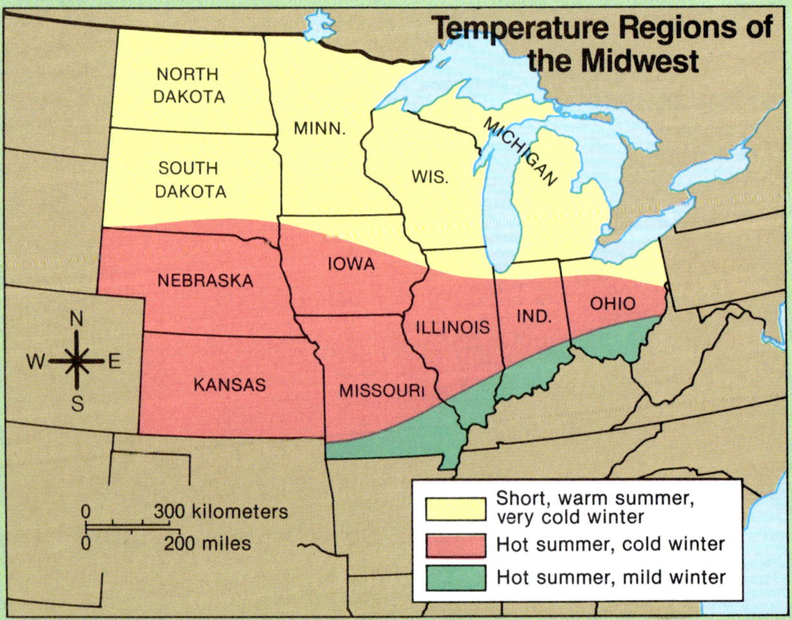

Now look at the agricultural regions map on the next page. The colors stand for the main crops and animals raised by the farmers of the area. Find the state of Iowa. There are about 10 million hectares (24 million acres) of farmland in Iowa. Most of this land is used for growing corn. Now find Iowa on the temperature regions map. What can you say about the climate needed for corn?

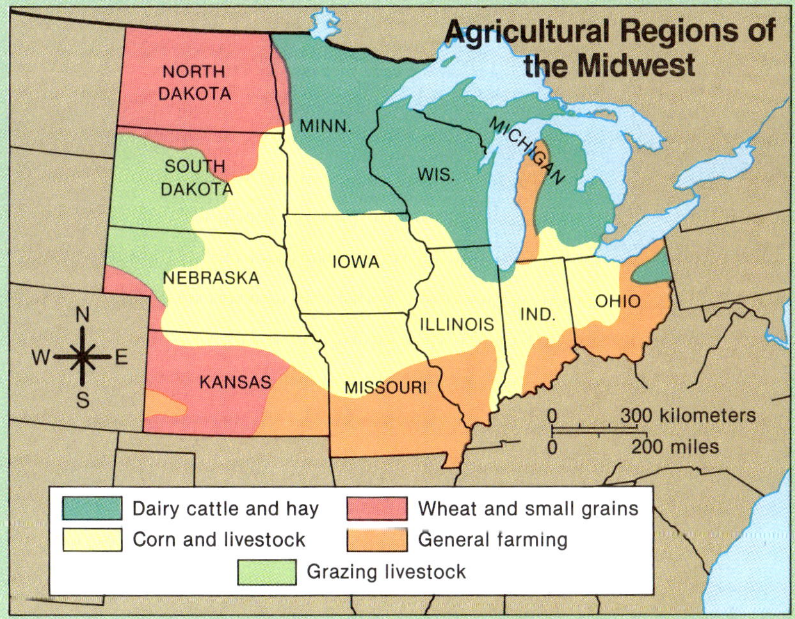

Practice Your Skills

1. Name the midwestern states in which dairy cattle and hay are raised. In which temperature region are these states located?
2. In which two temperature regions does general farming take place in the Midwest?
3. If you want to grow wheat, should you buy a farm in North Dakota? Why or why not?

3 Resources and Industry

The fertile soil of the Midwest produces food that is eaten throughout the world. The region is rich in minerals. Coal, iron ore, and other minerals can be found here. The many waterways of the region make it easy to carry goods all over the Midwest and beyond. The many roads and railways that cross the Midwest also carry goods.

The people of the Midwest have used their many resources and good transportation to make their region one of the richest in the world.

Manufacturing

Steelmaking is one of the Midwest's most important industries. Many steel mills line the southern shore of Lake Michigan. Each day boats arrive

Minerals are being loaded at the port of Chicago on Lake Michigan.

at these mills carrying a load, or **cargo,** of iron from the Mesabi Range. Look at the map on page 140. By what route might these boats take their cargoes?

cargo
a load of products carried from one place to another

As you know, coal is necessary in the steelmaking process. Illinois, Ohio, and Indiana are all leading coal-producing states. By what route might the coal reach the steelmaking plants? Another material that is needed to make steel is **limestone.** Limestone is a rock that is ground up and put in steel to make it stronger.

limestone
a kind of rock used in steelmaking and in building

Once the steel is made, it is manufactured into other products in the Midwest. In Michigan, it is made into cars, trucks, and buses. The Midwest is the country's leading producer of all these manufactured goods.

A farm tractor is being checked by workers at a Midwest factory.

Cheese is one dairy product made in the Midwest.

Farming

The many farms of the Midwest make this region the country's leading supplier of food. Much of the wheat grown here is shipped to Minneapolis, Minnesota. There it is made into flour to make bread or cakes. Or it is made into breakfast cereal.

The grassy lands of the Midwest provide food for cows. The milk of the cows is made into such products as cheese and butter. Wisconsin produces more cheese than any other state in the country. Minnesota, Michigan, and Iowa are other important dairy states.

Beef cattle also graze on the grassy lands. And much of the corn grown is used as feed for pigs. Because of the Midwest's good roads and railroads, it is easy to ship these animals to meat-packing plants. As a result, the Midwest is the country's leading meat-packing region. And Omaha, Nebraska, is the leading meat-packing center in the world!

Section Review

Write your answers on a sheet of paper.

1. Why is the Midwest one of the richest regions in the world?
2. What minerals are used in steelmaking?
3. Name three farm products of the Midwest.
4. Why do you think several of the Midwest's largest manufacturing cities are located on the Great Lakes?

FAMOUS AMERICANS

MARK TWAIN

Hannibal, Missouri, was the town where Samuel Clemens grew up in the 1840's. As a boy, he worked to help his family make a living. Sam worked for a printer. He went to school too. But when he could, he liked to go with his friends to the Mississippi River.

In those days, so much was happening on the river. There were catfish to catch and caves to explore. And there were the huge paddlewheel riverboats. Boat workers lowered long poles into the muddy river to see how deep it was. When the water came to a certain mark, they would call to the pilot, "Mark twain!" This was their way of saying that the water was a certain depth.

Perhaps Sam Clemens remembered this call years later. He used Mark Twain as his writing name, or "pen" name. He wrote stories about the exciting times he remembered when he grew up on the Mississippi River.

At this time, many American writers wrote about people in Europe. But Mark Twain was different. He told about life in America in the 1800's.

Mark Twain wrote *Tom Sawyer* and *Huckleberry Finn* more than 100 years ago. He made Tom and Huckleberry seem like real people. Their adventures are just as exciting to read about today as they were so many years ago.

CHAPTER 8

People and Places

The Mississippi River played an important role in the early settlement of the Midwest.

In the year 1673, American Indians who lived along the northern end of the Mississippi River saw a strange sight. A band of white men in canoes was slowly making its way down the river. The Indians had never seen such men before. Who were these men? Where did they come from? Where were they going?

At the end of this chapter, you should be able to:

○ Tell how the Midwest was settled.

○ Explain how transportation helps cities to grow.

● Compare a map and a photograph.

○ Describe how wheat is turned into bread.

1 The Early Settlers

The white men who came down the Mississippi in 1673 were French. They had come from settlements the French had built in Canada. Their leaders were a priest named Jacques Marquette (mahr-**kett**) and a mapmaker named Louis Joliet (zhol-**yay**). Their journey took them as far south as the Arkansas River.

Nine years later, another Frenchman, Robert La Salle (**luh sal**), made the same journey. With a group of American Indians and Frenchmen, La Salle traveled down the river to the mouth of the Mississippi. He claimed the land he passed through for France. In honor of King Louis of France, La Salle named the area Louisiana.

These trips showed the French that the Mississippi Valley was rich in fur-bearing animals. So the French started settlements along the Mississippi River. They used them as places where they could trade with the Indians for furs.

La Salle met the Taensa Indians on his journey down the Mississippi.

The Pioneers

In 1775, the American colonies along the Atlantic coast were at war with Great Britain. This war was called the American Revolution. The American colonies won the war. They became a free and independent country called the United States of America. The new country gained control of a huge area of land south of the Great Lakes. This land had once belonged to Great Britain.

Several of today's states were part of the area. Ohio, Indiana, Illinois, Michigan, Wisconsin, and parts of Minnesota were included in this land. The area was known as the Northwest Territory. Find this area on the map below.

Soon settlers from the east began moving into the Northwest Territory. They were searching for fertile soil and more space to farm. These new settlers thought of the Midwest as a great unsettled land, or **frontier.** They believed that its good land

frontier
land that is mostly unsettled

was open to them, even though American Indians had settled there many years earlier. These new settlers were **pioneers** (pie-uh-**nirz**). This is the name given to people who try something first and open the way for others to follow.

Life on the frontier was hard. The pioneers had to clear huge forests before they could grow crops. They had to build homes and find food. But the land gave the pioneers much of what they needed. By cutting down forests, they had logs to build cabins. By hunting wild animals, they had food as well as animal skins for clothing.

Good waterways—the Ohio and Mississippi rivers, for example—helped the pioneers move to the Northwest Territory. The rivers also helped them trade with other new settlements.

pioneer
a person who tries something first and opens the way for others to follow

As more and more settlers came to the area, the national government built a road called the National Road. It stretched from Cumberland, Maryland, to Vandalia, Illinois. The road was made of hard-packed dirt and logs. Find the National Road on the map on page 154.

You read earlier about the area called Louisiana. In 1803, the United States bought the land from France. This was called the Louisiana Purchase. The land the United States bought was west of the Mississippi River. Look at the map on page 150. What large land region of the Midwest did the Louisiana Purchase cover?

Settling the Great Plains

At first, most pioneers did not want to settle on the Great Plains. The land was flat and treeless. The soil was often dry and hard. It was covered with tall, tough grass. The Great Plains was also the home of the Plains Indians.

For hundreds of years, the Indians had lived and hunted on the Great Plains. Most of them depended on the huge herds of buffalo that fed on the tough grass. The Plains Indians used the meat of these animals for food. They used the buffalo skins for clothing and for their homes.

Then, in 1869, the first railroad to cross the entire country was finished. At the same time, the national government began to give the Plains Indians' land to settlers. The government wanted settlers to live on the land and farm it. People who settle on land provided by the government are called **homesteaders.**

homesteader
a person who settles on land provided by the government

Many homesteaders began to settle on the Great Plains. Some came in wagon trains or traveled on the rivers. Others rode on the new railroad.

Plains Indians chasing buffalo

The homesteaders moved onto the lands where the Indians hunted. The homesteaders' heavy steel plows cut through the hard soil and thick grass. They plowed up the grass that the buffalo fed on. As the grass disappeared, the buffalo died. Soon great fields of wheat replaced the grass. Herds of cattle took the place of the buffalo. As more and more homesteaders came, the Plains Indians were pushed farther and farther west.

The railroad made it easy for the homesteaders to ship their wheat and cattle to the towns that were being built. These towns grew up along the railroad line. As the farms grew, so did the towns. Some towns had mills to process the farm products. Other towns had factories to manufacture farm machinery.

Around 1900, new and better farm equipment made farming easier. Fewer people were needed to plow the ground and harvest the crops. Many people moved away from **rural,** or farming, areas. They went to the growing cities to find jobs.

rural
away from cities and close to farms

This family were homesteaders in Nebraska in the 1880's.

The Growth of Cities

Not all the settlers of the Midwest were Americans from the east. People also came from other countries to build homesteads. The earlier settlers had been French, English, Scottish, and Irish. Later, Germans found work in cities such as Milwaukee, St. Louis, and Cincinnati. Other people, from Sweden, Norway, and Denmark, settled in Wisconsin, Minnesota, and the Dakotas. They had been farmers and loggers in Europe. They found the same kind of work here.

Between 1890 and 1920, people came from eastern Europe, Italy, and Greece. Many of them settled in Chicago and other cities around the southern part of Lake Michigan. The growing industries there offered plenty of jobs.

In the 1900's, both black and white Americans left the rural areas of the Southeast and went north to midwestern cities. They were looking for better jobs. More recently, Spanish-American people have come to these cities as well.

St. Louis, Missouri, in the early 1900's

Some Important People

As a young woman in Mattoon (ma-**toon**), Illinois, Patricia Harris wanted to become a lawyer. After her studies, she decided to teach law to others. She also worked hard for equal rights for black people. In 1977, she became the first black woman to hold an important job in the national government. In this job, Harris was able to help the people in cities who needed better housing and jobs.

Patricia Harris

Amelia Earhart (ar-**hahrt**) came from Atchison, Kansas. In the 1920's, she wanted to learn to fly a plane. In those days, there were few women pilots. But Earhart worked hard and became a very good pilot. In 1932, she was the first woman to fly a plane across the Atlantic Ocean alone.

Amelia Earhart

Harry Houdini (hoo-**dee**-nee) was from Appleton, Wisconsin. As a boy, he joined a circus and learned to do magic tricks. But he wanted to entertain people with very exciting tricks. So he became an escape artist. One of his escapes was from a large box that had been nailed shut. Houdini was one of the greatest magicians of his time.

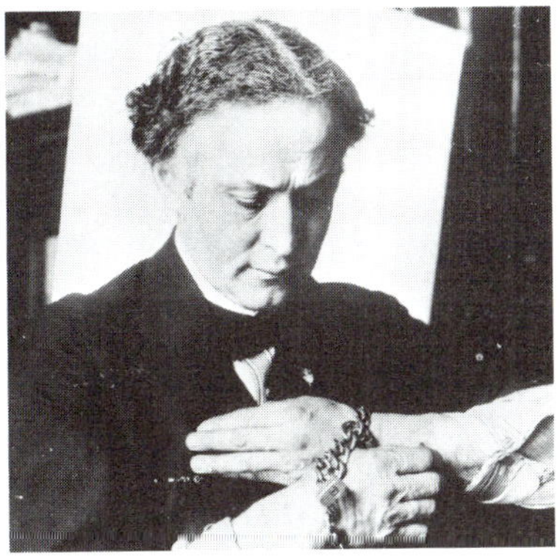

Harry Houdini

Section Review

Write your answers on a sheet of paper.

1. What contributions did the French make to the early settlement of the Midwest?
2. Why did settlers come to the Midwest?
3. Did the railroad help all people of the Midwest? Explain.

2 Chicago, Illinois

Chicago is the largest city in the Midwest. Its waterfront along Lake Michigan is about 40 kilometers (25 miles) long. South of the city are large factories, including many huge steel mills. North and west of the city are smaller towns that are part of Greater Chicago. Chicago is a center for industry, transportation, and shipping.

Early Chicago

Chicago became a city in 1837. It grew quickly, mostly because of its central location. It is right in the center of the area stretching from the Atlantic Ocean to the western edge of the Midwest.

Chicago in 1866

Riverboats brought farm products to Chicago from the rich Mississippi Valley. Railroads later connected the city with areas to the south, east, and west. And as a port on Lake Michigan, it was open to Great Lakes shipping. By 1870, Chicago had become a major center of transportation.

Look at the map on this page. Why do you think Chicago could easily receive goods from the west? Why could it ship them easily to the east?

Chicago Today

Chicago is still one of the most important centers of transportation in the country. Major highways and railroads lead in and out of the city. The Great Lakes have been connected to the Atlantic Ocean through the St. Lawrence Seaway. Ships in Chicago's port fly the flags of many nations. Chicago's O'Hare Airport is one of the busiest in the world.

One of Chicago's earliest industries was meat packing. Cattle and pigs brought in from Midwestern ranches and farms were made into meat products. The city is still a center of food processing. Its grain market is the country's largest. The iron and steel produced in Chicago and nearby are made into many kinds of machinery. Chicago's location has made it a great center of transportation. And its good transportation has helped it to grow into a large industrial center.

Chicago today

Section Review

Write your answers on a sheet of paper.

1. What kinds of transportation helped Chicago to grow into an important industrial center?
2. What are some of Chicago's industries?
3. Give two reasons why a city must have transportation in order to grow.

3 Detroit, Michigan

Detroit began as a French trading post. Like Chicago, its location helped to make it a leading trade and manufacturing center.

Downtown Detroit in 1910

The Coming of the Automobile

In 1896, Charles B. King drove through Detroit in what was called a horseless carriage. It was the first automobile ever seen in that city. Soon many automobile factories were being built in Detroit.

At first, automobiles took a great deal of time to make. Because it took so long to make them, they were very costly. Only the rich could afford them.

Then, in 1912, Henry Ford, an automobile maker, had an idea. He decided to speed up car making. First he divided the work of making a car into many small jobs. Then Ford designed a moving belt that slowly carried a car body past a row of workers. As the body passed, each worker did one job on it. At the end of the line, the car was complete.

By using this **assembly line,** Ford cut the time it took to make a car from 12.5 hours to about 1.5 hours. Since it took less time to make a car, more cars could be manufactured. And, each car could be sold at a lower price. The assembly line plan made the auto industry the major industry in Detroit.

assembly line
a way of manufacturing in which work is moved from one worker to another

The Motor City

Cars changed the way Americans lived and worked. Cars changed Detroit too. By 1950, it was the fifth-largest city in the country. It had a population of 1.5 million. Many of these people worked in Detroit's major industry—car making. Detroit had become known as the Motor City.

Then, in the 1970's, Detroit's car industry began to suffer. The price of gasoline was rising quickly. Car buyers wanted cars that used less gasoline than cars made in Detroit used. Small cars made in other countries became more popular than big cars made in Detroit.

What happens to a city when its major industry begins to lose money? Many of its people lose their jobs. Some of them leave the city, hoping to find jobs elsewhere. People are important to the industry of a city. When people leave a city, its factories and businesses can no longer run.

Looking to the Future

Detroit has not given up. The auto makers have designed new, smaller cars. They hope that these models will make people buy more American-made cars. Better sales for American-made cars will mean more jobs for Detroit's people.

Automobile assembly line

Renaissance Center in Detroit

But even when car sales increase, Detroit does not want to have to depend so much on one industry again. So the city is trying to get new industries to come to Detroit. If many industries grow, there will be more jobs. Then, even if people lose their jobs in one industry, there will still be jobs for them in other industries.

The leaders of Detroit have begun to rebuild parts of Detroit's downtown area. Today there are many new buildings in an area called the Renaissance (**ren**-uh-sahnss) Center. Near the center are a huge meeting hall and a sports arena. "Renaissance" means rebirth. When people change their city, it can be reborn.

Section Review

Write your answers on a sheet of paper.

1. Why is Detroit called the Motor City?

2. What new ideas did Henry Ford have about making cars?

3. Why might rebuilding run-down sections of a city draw new industries to it?

SOCIAL STUDIES SKILLS

Comparing a Map with a Photograph

After the invention of the airplane, the mapmaker's job became much easier. Before the airplane, a mapmaker had to stay on the ground to measure distance and direction. Then the measurements had to be transferred carefully to a map. After the airplane was invented, photographs could be taken from planes flying high above a place. Now a mapmaker could see everything in its correct position.

The photograph on this page shows an area around Chicago, Illinois. The photograph was taken from an airplane. Compare the photograph with the map of the Chicago area on page 167. How are they alike? How are they different?

A mapmaker uses symbols to stand for real things. From high in the sky, a road looks like a narrow band or line. On maps, therefore, highways and smaller roads show up as narrow lines. More important roads are shown as thick lines.

Look at some of the symbols used on the Chicago area map. What does each symbol stand for?

Practice Your Skills

1. Find Grant Park on the map and on the photograph. Is the park circular in shape? How do you know?
2. Find the Merrill C. Meigs Airport in the photograph. What surrounds the airport? What is the name of the body of water? How do you know?

4 Buhler, Kansas

Buhler (**byoo**-lur) is a town that lies in the center of the state of Kansas. If you were to drive around Buhler, you would see many tall towers. Each of them holds tons of wheat. These towers are usually called **grain elevators.** But Kansans call them prairie castles.

grain elevator
a large tower for storing grain

Most of the farmers around Buhler grow wheat. Many of the people who live in Buhler work in a wheat-processing factory, called a mill.

Wheat can be made into many things. Have you ever pasted pictures in a scrapbook? Paste is made from wheat. Wheat is also used to make gasohol. Gasohol is cheaper to use than gasoline for running cars. But wheat is mostly used to make food, such as bread and cereal.

Because wheat is so often used to make bread, Kansas is called the Breadbasket of America. More wheat is grown in Kansas than in any other state.

Grain elevators in Kansas

A farmer working on a combine in a wheat field in Kansas

Processing Wheat

When wheat is ready to be gathered, farmers cut it and pick it up with a machine called a **combine** (**kom**-bine). This machine was invented by Cyrus McCormick, a Chicago inventor. It made wheat farming much easier.

combine
a large machine that cuts and gathers grain

Wheat is a grass. It grows on a long stem. At the top are nutlike grains. The grains are inside straw-like covers, or **husks.** The combine separates the husks and stems from the grain. Before McCormick's invention, much of this work had to be done by hand.

husk
the outer covering on grains such as wheat and corn

The husks and stems are separated from the grain. Then the grains of wheat are taken to the grain elevators. Some of the grains are stored. Some are cleaned and dried. When this is done, they are taken to the mill.

At the mill, the grains go through a machine that removes dust and dirt. Then the grains are soaked in water. The soaking loosens the bran or outer layer of grain.

The wheat then goes through another machine that removes the outer layer. Finally the inner parts of the grains are free of their coverings. These inner parts are ground into a powder, which is flour.

The flour has to be aged for a while. Vitamins are added to it. Then it is packed in containers and shipped out to buyers. Many of these buyers are large baking factories.

How Bread Is Made

Do you know how to make bread? Making one loaf of bread at home is similar to the way a baking factory makes many loaves. At a large factory, the flour is mixed with water and yeast. The three items are mixed together to make dough. Other things are mixed into the dough. Milk, salt, and more flour and water may be added. The dough is put in a warm room. The heat sets off an action in the yeast that makes the dough rise to a larger size.

Finally the dough is formed into loaves and put into pans. Again it is left to grow larger. At last, it is baked. You would use a kitchen oven for this step. But in a large factory, the loaves are moved through a heated tunnel where they bake. The loaves come out of the tunnel golden brown. They are cooled, sliced, and wrapped. Then they are shipped out to be sold.

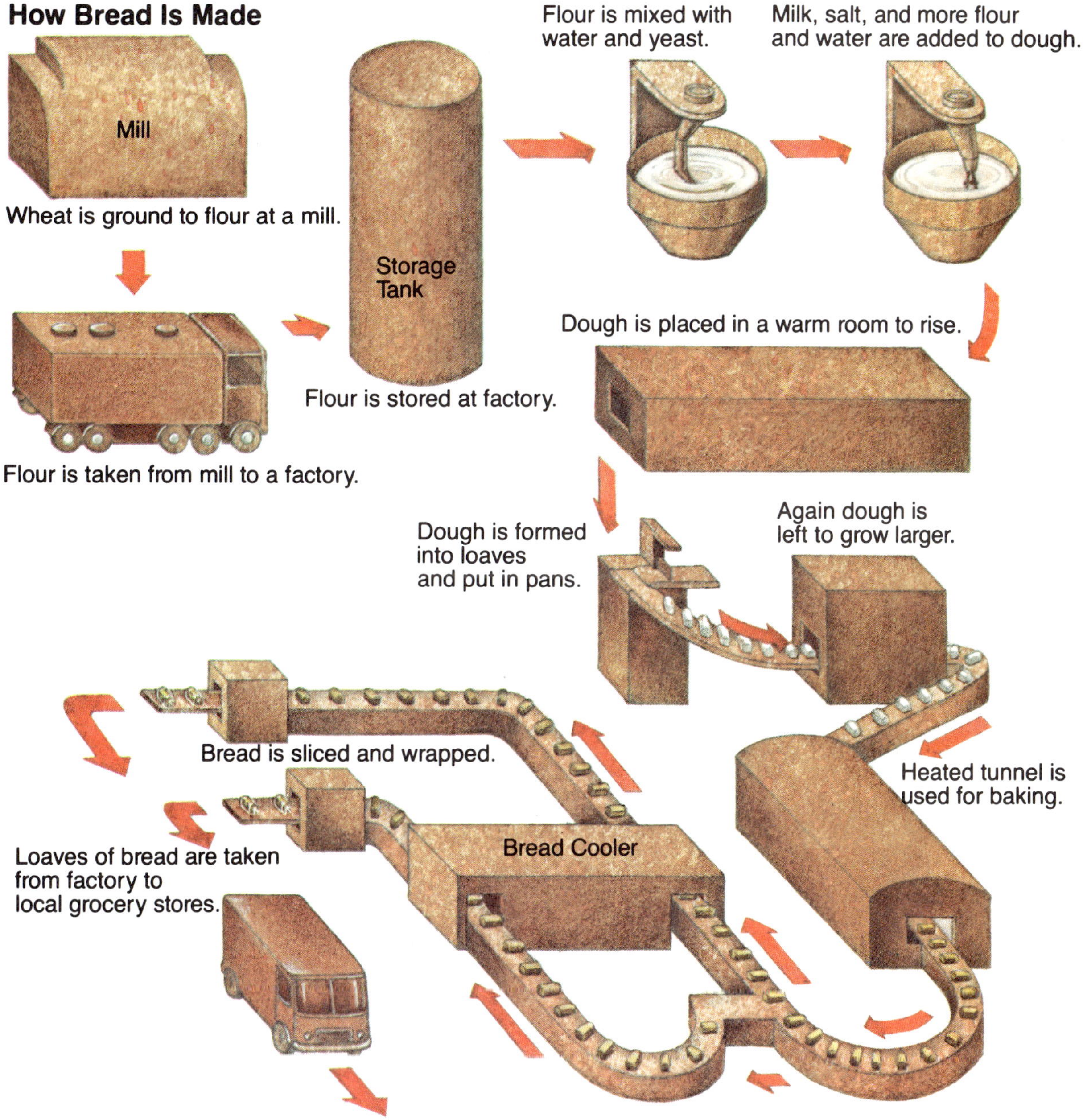

Section Review

Write your answers on a sheet of paper.

1. Why is Kansas called the Breadbasket of America?
2. What steps are taken to free the inner parts of the grains of wheat from their coverings?
3. What are the steps in making a loaf of bread?

Close-up on

Food Festivals In early times, each community grew its own food. When it came time to gather the crops, the community had a reason to celebrate. A good crop meant that people would have plenty to eat in the coming year. Today many communities hold festivals to celebrate the foods they produce. Around the United States, communities invite visitors to eat their own special foods. Food festivals are an American tradition.

Many of these food festivals are held in the Midwest, where much of our food is produced. Wisconsin sponsors a dairy festival. There people enjoy its wonderful cheeses. Iowa grows corn. At its festivals you can eat corn soufflé (soo-**flay**), a dish made with corn and eggs. In Indiana, one special dish is pudding made from persimmons (pur-**sim**-unz), a fruit grown there. With food festivals, these states show how proud they are of the foods they produce.

Other food festivals present the food of the people who first settled in the community. Decorah (duh-**kor**-uh), Iowa, was settled by people from Norway.

A Holiday Folk Fair, Milwaukee, Wisconsin

America

Kringlas *at the Nordic Festival in Decorah, Iowa*

The young woman is holding Armenian pastry called bourma.

If you went to Decorah's Nordic Fest in July, you would see Scandinavian food everywhere. You might want to taste goat cheese. Or you might stop to watch people twirling dough into fancy shapes for pastries called *kringlas.* You would want to save room for a slice of boiled beef and a plate of meatballs.

The Nordic Fest gives the people of Decorah a chance to remember their strong Scandinavian background. It gives people for miles around a chance to visit Decorah and taste the food of Norway.

A food festival is a celebration of many things. People enjoy sharing the food they produce. They also enjoy sharing their heritage. A food festival gives people a chance to share some very special dishes with their friends and neighbors.

UNIT REVIEW

Word Work

Write the sentences below on a sheet of paper. Fill in the blanks with the correct words from the list.

assembly line   pioneers   prairie   cargo

1. People who open the way for others to follow are ____.
2. A load that a ship carries is a ____.
3. ____ describes flat land covered with tall, thick grass.
4. The ____ is a way of manufacturing that moves work from one worker to another.

Knowing the Facts

Write your answers on a sheet of paper.

1. Why is corn grown in one part of the Midwest and wheat in another?
2. Why are many large midwestern cities on the Great Lakes?
3. How did transportation help the Midwest to grow?

Using What You Know

Choose one of the following activities to do. Follow the instructions given here.

1. Draw a map of a room in your home. How does the map compare to a photograph of the room?
2. How did the largest city in your state grow? How does it compare to the way Chicago grew?

Skills Practice

Use the following maps to answer the questions below. Write your answers on a sheet of paper.

1. What two states have no mineral resources or manufacturing centers?
2. What state has iron ore deposits and a major manufacturing center?
3. What two states have large coal deposits and many manufacturing centers?

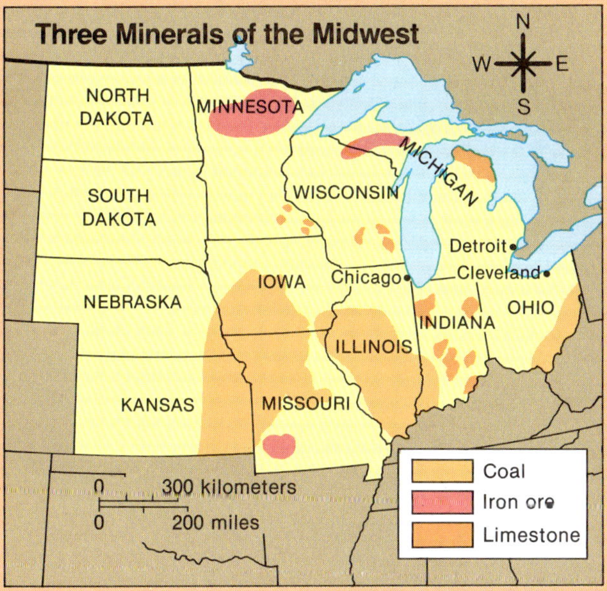

Your State

Do you know who the early settlers of your state were? Do some research in your library and write a report on these pioneers. Be sure to include information such as where they came from, how they traveled to your state, and what they found when they arrived.

UNIT 5 The Southwest Region

You have probably heard people talk about the Sun Belt. This expression is often used to refer to the Southwest region.

But the region offers much more than sun. It also has one of the country's largest ports—Houston (**hyoo**-stun), Texas. And it has one of the most beautiful natural land features in the world—the Grand Canyon. As you read this unit, think about some words you might use to describe the Southwest.

CHAPTER 9

The Southwest

Wheat field and oil refinery in Oklahoma

The Southwest is a region with many kinds of landforms. It is different from other regions of our country in one major way. The weather here is sunny more often than in any other part of the United States. In this chapter, you will see how land and climate affect the way resources are used in the Southwest.

At the end of this chapter, you should be able to:

- Name the four states that make up the Southwest region.
- Describe the land and climate of the Southwest region.
- Name the region's resources and industries.

1 The Land

The Southwest region makes up about one sixth of the land area of our country. Look at the map below. Name the states that are part of the Southwest. Which state is the largest? What body of water borders this state on the southeast? What river separates the Southwest from Mexico? What states border the region to the north?

Find the capital of Arizona on the map. Is Phoenix closer to Santa Fe or to Oklahoma City?

Plains, Mountains, Plateaus

More than half of the Southwest is plains. One part of the plains area is the coastal plain of Texas. Here the soil is good for growing crops. Find the coastal plain on the map on page 180.

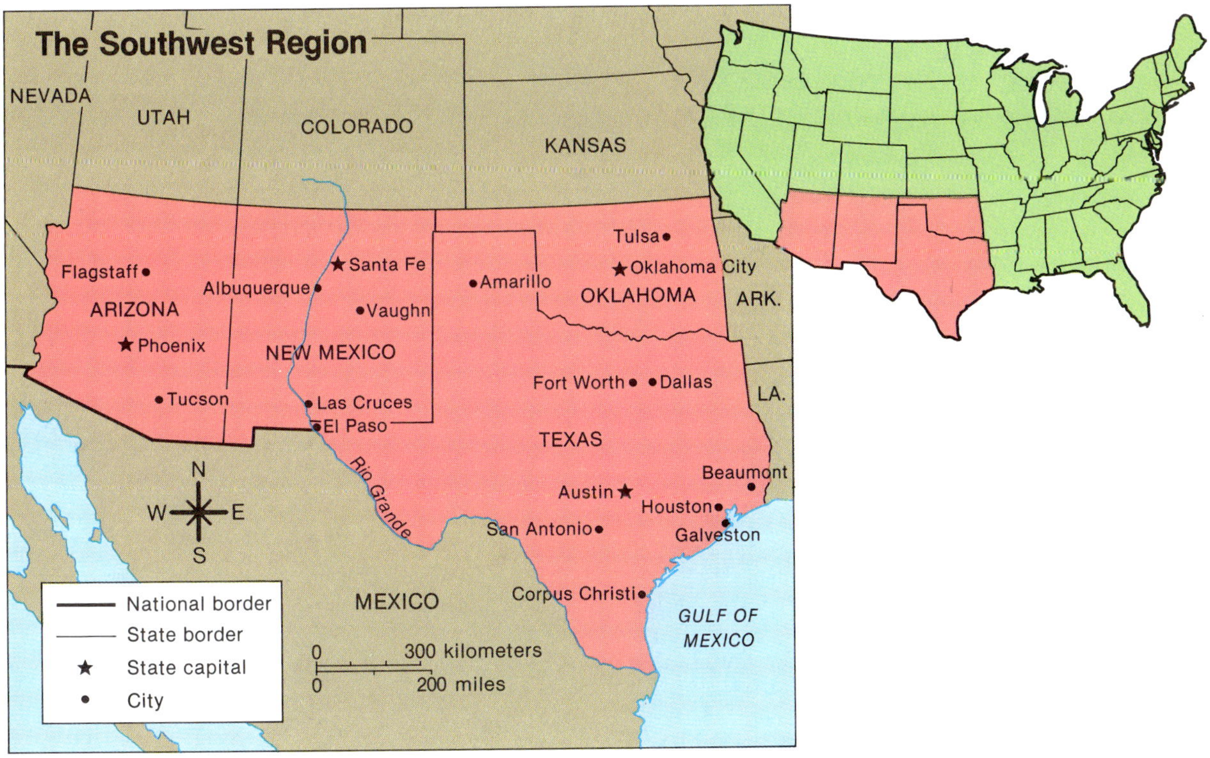

North and west of the coastal plain are somewhat higher plains. These make up the most southern part of the Interior Plains. Much of the land here, in Oklahoma, Texas, and New Mexico, is covered with grass. These grassy lands stretch as far as the eye can see.

Farther to the west, the land rises into mountains and plateaus. Find the mountains and plateaus on the map. Thick pine forests cover many of the mountains. Buried in the mountains are such minerals as silver and copper.

In the plateau areas of the Southwest, there are many valleys and canyons. The most famous canyon is the Grand Canyon. The Grand Canyon was formed by the waters of the Colorado River. Over many years, the river wore away at the rocks of northeastern Arizona. The river cut a deep gorge

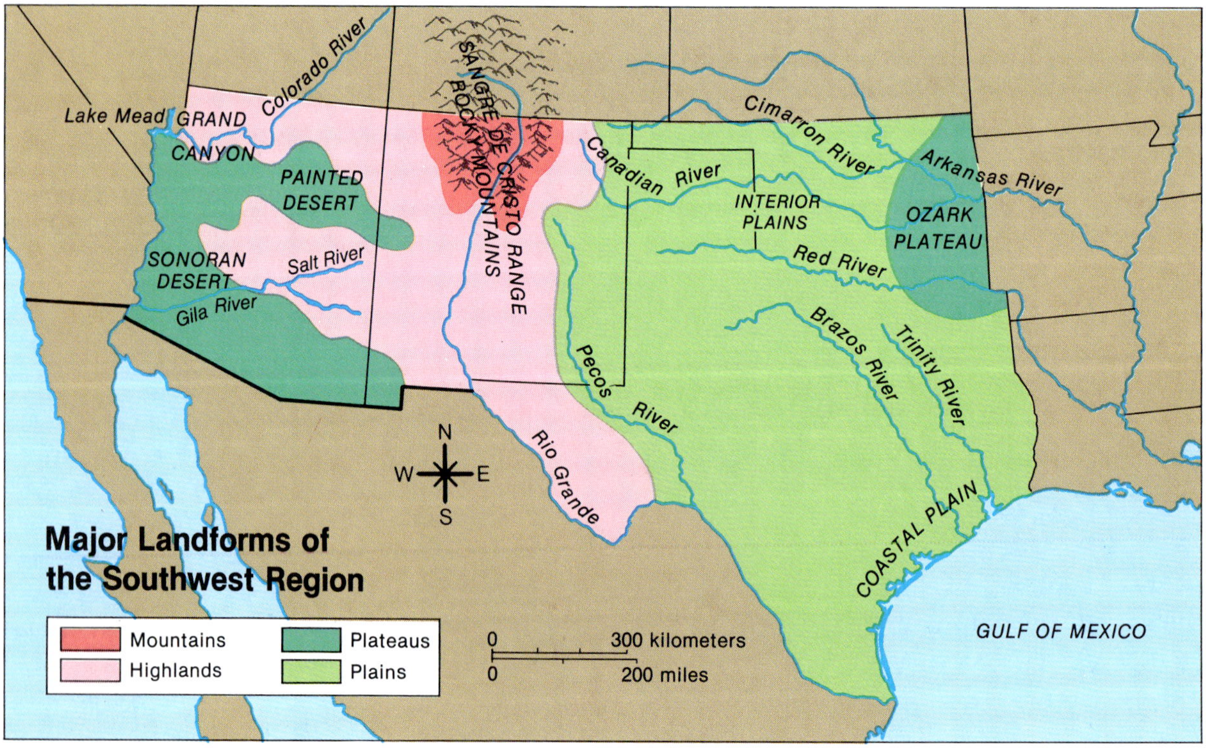

through them. The result was the Grand Canyon. Locate the Grand Canyon on the map on the facing page.

Water is one natural force that can wear away the land and change it. Wind is another natural force that can wear away the earth's surface. This process is called **erosion.**

erosion
the wearing away of land by water or wind

Deserts are another important part of the plateau areas of the Southwest. Find the deserts on the map on the facing page.

Rivers

Little rain falls in the Southwest. The people of the region have to make good use of the water they have. The water comes mostly from the rivers in the region. Two of the Southwest's most important rivers are the Rio Grande and the Colorado River.

The people of the Southwest gather water from their rivers and store it until it is needed. They have built dams along the rivers. Behind each dam, the water is held back. It then forms a lake, or a **reservoir** (**rez**-uv-wahr). The Hoover Dam, between Arizona and Nevada, has formed the reservoir called Lake Mead.

reservoir
a lake or pond where water is stored for use

Water from reservoirs makes it possible to farm land even though there is little rainfall. Pipes or ditches carry water from the reservoirs to the land. When the crops need watering, the farmers release water from the pipes. The water flows out into the fields. Or it sprays up and showers down on the crops.

Supplying water through pipes or by other means to dry lands is called **irrigation.** Irrigation makes it possible to farm millions of hectares of dry land.

irrigation
supplying water to dry land through pipes, ditches, or canals

Section Review

Write your answers on a sheet of paper.

1. Name three landforms of the Southwest.
2. Describe the process of erosion.
3. Why are the rivers of the Southwest important?
4. List some other places in the United States where you think people would use irrigation. Explain why you picked these places.

2 The Climate

Most of the Southwest gets an average of only about 25 to 50 centimeters (10 to 20 inches) of rain a year. That is only one third of the rainfall the Southeast gets. The driest parts of the Southwest are the desert areas of Arizona and New Mexico. Less than 25 centimeters (10 inches) of rain falls each year in these areas. The city of Yuma, Arizona, averages only a little over 7 centimeters (3 inches) of rain each year!

The Southwest gets so little rain because of its location. The air coming from the Pacific Ocean is full of moisture. But high mountains keep the Southwest from getting much moisture.

A desert in Arizona

There is one area of the Southwest that is generally humid. The southeastern part of Texas lies along the Gulf of Mexico. Winds blowing in from the Gulf bring moisture with them. There are no mountains to block the moisture. This southeastern area receives more rainfall than areas farther inland. As much as 130 centimeters (50 inches) of rain fall on it a year.

Summers in the Southwest are hot. Phoenix (**fee**-nicks), Arizona, which is in the desert, often has summer temperatures above 38° C (100° F). In general, the winters are mild, especially in the southern part of the Southwest. But in the northern part of Texas and Oklahoma, snow sometimes falls during the winter. There is also snow in the mountains of New Mexico and Arizona.

The fact that the Southwest gets so little rain helps explain why it is sunny. Rain-bearing clouds seldom pass overhead. Much of the Southwest is closer to the equator than most other regions of our country. Because of this, the sun shines longer here each day than in most other parts of the United States.

Section Review

Write your answers on a sheet of paper.

1. Describe the climate of the Southwest.

2. Why does the Southwest get so little rain?

3. The southern part of the Southwest is closer to the equator than many other regions in our country. How does that fact help to explain the climate of the Southwest?

3 Resources and Industry

The Southwest is one of the fastest-growing areas of our country. The many resources of the region help to account for this fact. Since resources are so valuable, they must not be wasted. Preserving valuable resources is called **conservation.** Minerals are one of the Southwest's greatest resources. The region is rich in copper. Arizona produces half of our country's copper. Arizona and New Mexico also produce gold and silver.

conservation
preserving valuable resources

Two minerals that are in great supply in the Southwest are **petroleum** and **natural gas.** Petroleum is an oily, liquid material buried in the earth. Natural gas is a lighter material often found near petroleum.

petroleum
an oily, liquid mineral

natural gas
a light mineral often used for fuel; often found near petroleum

Thousands of giant towers are scattered across Oklahoma and Texas. Machines inside these towers are used to drill holes into the earth to find petroleum and natural gas. Once these minerals

Oil rig in Texas

are found, they are brought to the surface. Then the petroleum or natural gas can be sent through pipes to places all over the country.

Manufacturing

After petroleum is taken from the ground, it is used as a raw material to make several useful products. These products are called **petrochemicals** (peh-troe-**kem**-ih-kulz). Human-made, or **synthetic** (sin-**thet**-ik), goods such as nylon, rayon, and some rubber are petrochemical products.

petrochemical
a product that comes from oil or natural gas

synthetic
human-made material

Before petroleum can be made into petrochemical products, it must go through a refinery. A **refinery** is a factory that cleans a raw material and makes it ready for use. In Texas and Oklahoma, there are many giant refineries.

refinery
a factory that cleans a raw material and makes it ready for use

Oil refinery in Texas

Producing petrochemical products is just one kind of manufacturing in the Southwest. Another kind is producing the machinery needed to drill for petroleum and natural gas.

Other products manufactured in the Southwest are cotton textiles, airplanes, and airplane parts. The clear weather of the region provides good conditions for testing new airplanes.

Farming

Raising horses, cattle, and sheep has long been important to farming in the Southwest. The region's wide-open spaces and grassy lands make it a good place for **ranching.** Huge herds of animals can graze on the grassy lands of the plains.

ranching
raising large herds of animals such as cattle, sheep, or horses

Beef cattle are raised in all the states of the Southwest. Texas is the center of ranching. A ranch there may spread out as far as the eye can see—and farther. The largest ranch in the Southwest, the King Ranch, covers nearly 334,000 hectares (about 825,000 acres) of land.

Even though the Southwest has little rainfall, the people have used their rivers to make the land fertile. Irrigation has made farming in the Southwest possible. Farmers in the valleys of the Rio Grande in Texas and New Mexico produce large crops of cotton, fruits, and vegetables. In Arizona, farmers use water from the Colorado River to irrigate their land. Because of this, they are able to raise cotton and vegetables. Farmers in Texas and Oklahoma raise wheat and other grains. Along the Texas coastal plain, rice is a major crop.

The Southwest also has many food-processing and meat-packing plants. Texas, New Mexico, Oklahoma, and Arizona all process the products of the farms and ranches.

Section Review

Write your answers on a sheet of paper.

1. Name one resource for each of the states in the Southwest.

2. What are petrochemicals?

3. Oil is often called black gold. Why do you think it was given this name?

FAMOUS AMERICANS

GEORGIA O'KEEFFE

Georgia O'Keeffe is known for her paintings of things such as rocks, bones, flowers, clouds, and the sky. But she paints them in a way that makes them look different from the way they usually look.

She does this by using close-ups of objects. For example, flowers in her paintings often appear to be large and mysterious.

Georgia O'Keeffe was born in Sun Prairie, Wisconsin, in 1887. She studied art in Chicago and New York. Later she became interested in the art of China and Japan. Her own work shows the clean and simple lines of Chinese and Japanese paintings.

In 1918, O'Keeffe moved to New York City. There she met Alfred Stieglitz (**steeg**-lits), a well-known American photographer. Stieglitz supported the work of modern painters. He helped to exhibit many of their paintings, including the work of O'Keeffe. O'Keeffe and Stieglitz were married in 1924.

After Stieglitz died in 1946, O'Keeffe moved to New Mexico. There, she painted things she saw in the desert, such as cows' skulls, bones, and flowers. She painted them using her special style of close-ups. In O'Keeffe's paintings, ordinary things in nature in the Southwest became very special.

CHAPTER 10 People and Places

This wall is in Santa Fe, New Mexico. Its style is a reminder that the Spanish settled here.

In the Southwest, you can see new homes built like American Indian houses of 500 years ago. You can hear people speaking Spanish, a language used by settlers 400 years ago. You can see people wearing clothes just like ranchers wore in the 1800's. The Southwest is a mixture of the old and the new.

At the end of the chapter, you should be able to:

○ Give reasons for the settlement of the Southwest region.

● Read a double bar graph.

○ Explain how resources help a city to grow.

○ Describe how wool is gathered.

1 The Early Settlers

American Indians were the first people to settle in the Southwest. Thousands of years ago, they lived in underground rooms. These rooms were dug out of the earth. The cool rooms protected them from the sun in this hot, dry region.

Many years later, the American Indians learned to build houses out of mud bricks. They made the bricks by mixing together hard, dry soil with water and straw. Their houses often were built on top of each other against the sides of cliffs. The houses were called **pueblos** (poo-**eb**-los). The people who built them are called Pueblo Indians.

pueblo
a house made of mud bricks and built into the side of a cliff

The Pueblos planted corn, squash, and beans in ditches near a river. When rains came, the river overflowed and the ditches filled with water.

Pueblos in Mesa Verde, Colorado

Dams at the end of the ditches kept the water from flowing away. Long before the region was settled by pioneers, American Indians knew how to live on the dry land.

The Spanish Settlers

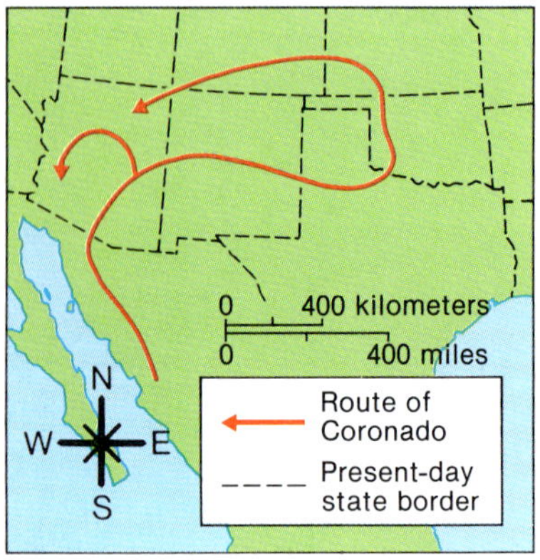

In 1540, a Spanish explorer named Francisco de Coronado (koe-ruh-**nah**-doe) came to the Southwest. Coronado and his soldiers were looking for seven cities of gold. They had heard stories about these cities. Of course, Coronado never found golden cities. But his search helped Spain learn about the lands that later became Arizona, New Mexico, Oklahoma, and Texas.

Because of Coronado's visit, Spain said it owned the lands of the Southwest. In 1598, the first Spanish settlement was built on the Rio Grande. It was called San Juan de los Caballeros (san **wahn** day los kah-bahl-**yair**-os). Soon other settlements were built. One was called Santa Fe (**san**-tuh **fay**). It became the capital of Spain's Southwest settlements. Today Santa Fe is the capital city of the state of New Mexico.

missionary
a person who teaches others about religion

Many early Spanish settlers were **missionaries** (mish-un-**err**-eez). These were people who came to teach Christianity. Their settlements were called missions.

The center of each mission was a church. Around it, the missionaries built storehouses, workshops, and usually a school. Many missions had farms or even ranches. You can still see some of these missions in the Southwest today.

More Settlers

Spain ruled the Southwest for hundreds of years. Then, in the early 1800's, Mexico fought a

A Spanish mission

war with Spain. Mexico won and took over the lands of the Southwest.

Few Americans were living in the region at that time. Spain did not want them to settle there. Also, the American Indians fought any new settlers who tried to take over their lands. But the Mexicans were eager to have new settlers come to the Southwest. They wanted Americans to move to the region and trade with Mexico.

Many Americans did come. Some fought the American Indians and began farming on Indian lands. Others traded cloth and tools with the Mexicans for silver and furs. Santa Fe grew into a center for trade.

But Texas was the place that grew the fastest. By 1830, more than 20,000 Americans lived there. Most worked as farmers. The Texans did not like being ruled by Mexico. In 1835 and 1836, they fought a war to become free.

Austin, the capital of Texas, in the 1840's

At the beginning of the war, a Mexican general attacked a fort in Texas called the Alamo. More than 100 Texans inside the fort died. One was the pioneer Davy Crockett. The Texans fought hard. They won the war, and Texas became a free country.

The States of the Southwest

In 1845, Texas joined the United States. Later that year, Mexico and the United States fought a war. They both wanted more land in the Southwest. The United States won the war and took over most of the region.

Many settlers then came to the Southwest. Cattle and sheep ranches grew. Big cotton farms were opened in Texas. When railroads were built in the late 1800's, even more settlers came to the region. In 1907, Oklahoma became a state. Five years later, New Mexico and Arizona became states. The huge Southwest region had been divided into the four states that we know today.

The Southwest Today

You can still see signs of the Southwest's Spanish and American Indian past today. Many cities and rivers have Spanish or Indian names. Houses and churches are usually built in a southwestern style. This is a mix of Indian and Spanish styles. Many southwestern people even wear Spanish- and Indian-style clothing.

Some of the land is still used as it was in the past. Sheep and cattle graze on the open grasslands. But much of the region's once wide-open spaces are now highways and cities. The Southwest's population has grown to more than 20 million. About two thirds of these people live in Texas. But the pleasant climate and growing industries of Arizona, New Mexico, and Oklahoma are attracting many people too. The populations of these states are also growing quickly.

The region is still the home of many American Indians. Over a third of the Indians in the United States live in the Southwest. Many Mexican Americans and Hispanics also make their homes here. Some of their families have lived in the region for hundreds of years.

Many different kinds of people live in the Southwest. Here are some people of the Southwest watching a street festival.

Maria Tallchief

Nancy Lopez

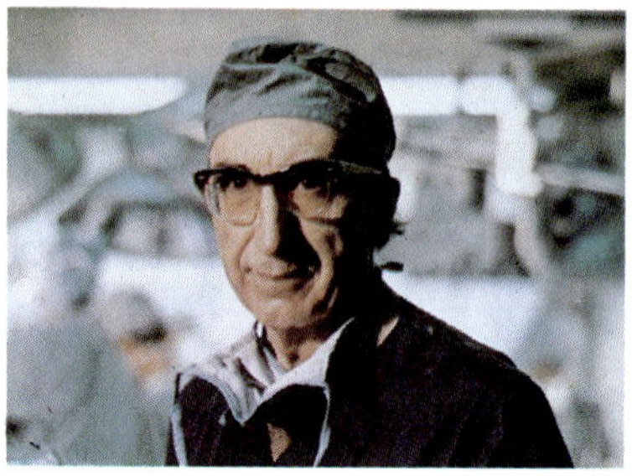

Dr. Michael De Bakey

Some Important People

The work of some people from the Southwest has become known around the world. Maria Tallchief is an Osage (oe-**sage**) Indian who was born in Oklahoma in 1925. As a girl, she studied piano and dance. A teacher told her to try to become an expert at one. Tallchief chose dance. She became one of the first American ballerinas to win praise all over the world. In 1980, she became the Artistic Director of the Chicago City Ballet.

Golfer Nancy Lopez (**loe**-pez) grew up in New Mexico. When she was 12 years old, she won a golf tournament. By 1980, she had won many more tournaments. She was elected to the All-American Collegiate Golf Hall of Fame. She is the first woman to receive this honor.

Michael De Bakey (duh **bake**-ee) is one of the world's most famous doctors. As a young man, he studied at Tulane University in New Orleans, Louisiana. In 1948, he went to work at the University College of Medicine in Houston, Texas. There he became interested in helping people who had heart diseases. In 1966, he invented a human-made heart that did the work of a real heart. Dr. De Bakey's work has saved many lives.

Section Review

Write your answers on a sheet of paper.

1. How did the American Indians farm in the hot, dry climate of the Southwest?
2. Why was the Southwest settled?
3. Make a list of things in your community that are a mixture of old and new.

Reading a Double Bar Graph

SOCIAL STUDIES SKILLS

Most bar graphs present only one set of information. A **double bar graph** compares two sets of the same kind of information. This graph compares the numbers of people living in four states during 1970 and 1980. The red bars show the numbers for 1970. The yellow bars show those for 1980. The numbers across the top of the graph stand for millions of people.

double bar graph
a graph that compares two sets of the same kind of information

Find the red bar for Arizona. Move your finger right to the end of the bar. Now move your finger straight up to the number at top. Do the same for the yellow bar. Compare the two numbers. As you can see, there were almost one million more people living in Arizona in 1980 than in 1970.

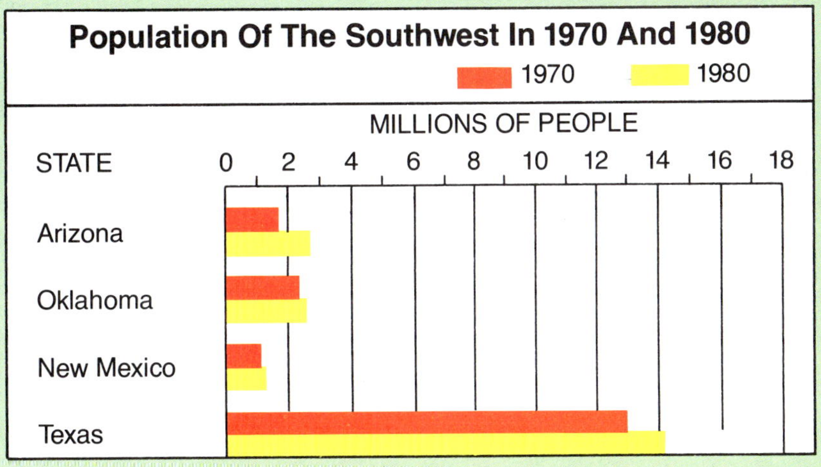

Practice Your Skills

1. What was the population of New Mexico in 1970? Was it larger or smaller in 1980?
2. Which two states were closest in population in 1970? Were they still close in 1980?
3. Which state's population grew the most? By how much did it grow?

2 Houston, Texas

Houston was founded in 1836. At that time, it was a small town with mud roads. A few farmers worked in nearby fields. Its downtown was one main street with a few wooden buildings. By 1926, Houston had become an important port city. Today it is the largest city in the Southwest.

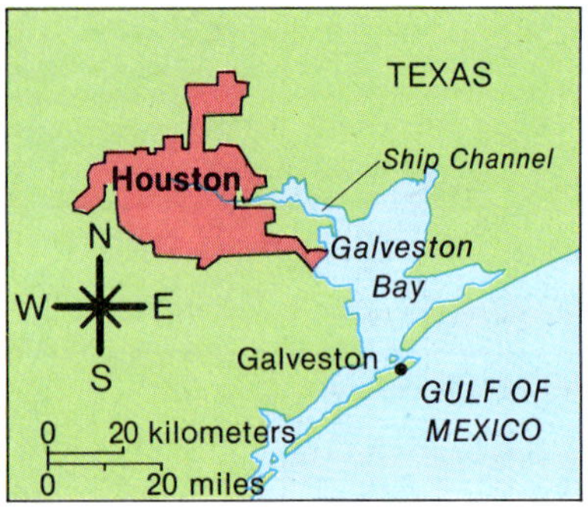

canal
a waterway dug across land for ships to go through

Shipping and Trade

Houston began growing in the late 1800's. At that time, people were building railroads across the nation. Houston's location in southeastern Texas made it a center for goods going from east to west.

Houston's real growth began because of ships. In 1914, a waterway, or **canal,** was dug across the land to join Houston with the Gulf of Mexico. This human-made waterway let ships from around the world sail into Houston. Today more than 4,000 boats use the 80-kilometer (50-mile) Houston Ship Channel every year. Many of them come to carry away valuable resources found near Houston.

The most important of these resources are oil and natural gas. The Houston area has more than 11,000 oil wells. The land is also rich in valuable minerals, such as salt and limestone. These resources are used in making fuel, building materials, medicine, food, and other products.

Houston has giant petrochemical factories. These factories turn oil into products such as nylon, rayon, and synthetic rubber. Thousands of people work in these factories. There are also

many other manufacturing companies in Houston where people work.

Houston Ship Channel

Ships and Outer Space

Through the years, Houston has kept growing. In the 1940's, shipbuilding became a big industry in Houston's harbor. In the 1960's, Houston became the home of the nation's rocket industry. Factories here make parts for rockets. The headquarters for astronauts, the Lyndon B. Johnson Space Center, is near Houston. Astronauts get ready for space flights in an area where cowhands once raised cattle.

Downtown Houston

The Future of Houston

Today more than a million and a half people live in Houston. Many of them have moved here in the past few years. Houston's leaders think that even more people will come to their city in the future.

Some of these people come because they enjoy the warm climate. But most people move to Houston to find jobs in its many industries. They often come from other regions of the country where business is not as good. The workers and their families know that Houston is a growing region. They believe that its industries will keep growing. The products these industries make are needed by everyone.

As more people come to Houston, new businesses open. Houston has many banks, department stores, theaters, and supermarkets. These new businesses also need workers.

Houston is the Southwest's biggest city. Its population comes from all over the nation.

Section Review

Write your answers on a sheet of paper.

1. What two natural resources are largely responsible for Houston's growth?
2. How did the Houston Ship Channel help the city to grow?
3. Why do you think Houston is the largest city in the Southwest?

3 Phoenix, Arizona

Phoenix, the capital of Arizona, is built on the edge of the Sonoran (suh-**nore**-un) Desert. Because of its location, Phoenix is one of the warmest cities in the nation. In the summer, the temperature is often above 38° C (100° F). Winter temperatures in Phoenix rarely go below 10° C (50° F).

Phoenix often gets more days of sunshine in a year than any other city in the nation. Since Phoenix lies in the Salt River Valley, people here call it the Valley of the Sun.

The sunshine and fine weather bring many people to Phoenix. It is one of the fastest-growing cities in the country. In 1970, there were 581,000 people in Phoenix. By 1980, that number had grown to more than 760,000!

Phoenix in the 1880's

Early Settlement

The first people to live in the Salt River Valley were the Hohokam (hoe-**hoe**-kum) Indians. They built canals from the river to help them water their fields. But the hot desert was not a good home. So the Hohokam Indians did not stay in the area.

For hundreds of years, the valley was empty. But in 1868, a group of settlers who wanted land came from the east. They found the old canals built by the Hohokam Indians. They believed that they too could build a settlement near the Salt River.

The people named their settlement Phoenix. The name came from an old story about a fabulous bird called a phoenix. The bird died in a fire. Out of its ashes, a new phoenix was born. The settlers hoped a new city would rise on the land where the Hohokam Indians once lived.

Phoenix was a small farming community. In 1911, a big dam was built on the Salt River. This supplied water for more farmland. In 1912, Arizona became a state. Phoenix was the state capital. The city began to grow.

From Farms to Industry

In the 1940's, the government opened two air force training bases near Phoenix. Thousands of soldiers came. After World War II, some moved to Phoenix with their families.

In the 1950's, air-conditioning helped the city grow quickly. A new and better way had been found to provide air-conditioning. Many people were able to have air-conditioning in their homes. They moved to Phoenix and did not have to worry about the hot climate. Many of the newcomers were people with health problems. The dry desert air is especially good for people who have problems with breathing.

As new businesses and industries opened, Phoenix's people needed more room. The city's leaders took over more desert land for building homes and factories. In 1950, Phoenix was less than 45 square kilometers (17 square miles) in area. Today it takes up more than 840 square kilometers (325 square miles).

As more people move to Phoenix, more houses are built.

Growing Pains

pollution
damage to air, water, or land by smoke or dust

This fast growth has brought some problems. Phoenix was once known for its pure, clean air. But smoke from factories and from cars causes **pollution** that is damaging to the air and land. This pollution sometimes falls on the nearby desert soil. The desert wind often blows the dirt back into the city.

Another problem for this desert city is finding enough water. The Salt River cannot supply water for all the people moving to Phoenix.

The people are working to solve these problems. Phoenix is expanding its public transportation system. Then people will not use their cars so much. When builders put up new houses, they water the dusty ground. This helps keep the dirt from blowing around and polluting the air. Canals are being built to carry water to Phoenix from the faraway Colorado River. The city leaders hope the things they are doing will cure their pollution problems.

Section Review

Write your answers on a sheet of paper.

1. Explain why Phoenix is well named.
2. Give one reason why people moved to Phoenix in the 1950's.
3. Are there pollution problems where you live? How are people working to solve these problems?

4 Vaughn, New Mexico

Vaughn (**vawn**), New Mexico, is a small town. Only about 750 people live here. But Vaughn is an important center for sheep ranching in the Southwest. In this area, there are many more sheep than people.

Vaughn has many sheep ranches, each with hundreds of sheep. The land around Vaughn is good for sheep ranching. Since Vaughn gets only 25 centimeters (10 inches) of rain a year, the grass is always short. This is just the way sheep like it.

A sheep roundup

Rounding Up the Sheep

Sheep ranchers work hard taking care of their flocks. Spring is the busiest time of year for the ranchers. In March and early April, most of the lambs are born. Ranchers take good care of the baby lambs to make sure they stay healthy. .

After the lambs are old enough to walk, the sheep ranchers begin to gather the flock. This is not an easy job. The sheep are spread over several square kilometers (square miles). The ranchers round up the flock on horses or in trucks. They ride around the sheep, bringing them closer and closer together. Dogs are also trained to help with this job. When the sheep have been gathered, ranchers drive them to fenced-in pens.

Gathering the Wool

Once the sheep are in the pens, the wool gathering can begin. A sheep's coat is called a **fleece.** The cutting of the wool is **shearing.**

fleece
the coat of a sheep

shearing
the cutting of a sheep's wool

Sheep are sheared in the spring when they no longer need their thick coats. Shearing is done by a team of people who travel from ranch to ranch. Workers use electric shearers that work like a barber's clippers. The fleece is sheared off in one piece. All the fleeces are rolled up and tied together with twine. Then they are packed in burlap bags. When the shearing is done, the ranchers take the wool to town to be sold. Most of the wool from Vaughn is of very good quality. New Mexico's clean air helps keep the fleeces fresh and clean.

After the wool is sold, it is cleaned and sorted. Machines comb out the knotty wool. Then the wool is spun and woven into cloth. It is just possible that you have a jacket or dress made of wool from the sheep in Vaughn.

Section Review

Write your answers on a sheet of paper.

1. Why is the area around Vaughn good for raising sheep?
2. Describe how ranchers round up their flocks.
3. Why are sheep sheared in the springtime?
4. In what other areas of the Southwest do you think sheep can be raised?

Close-up on

Sandpainting In the Southwest, an American Indian people called the Navajo (**nav**-uh-hoe) make paintings from sand. Many Navajos live in Arizona and New Mexico.

Since no water or oil is used in sandpainting, it is also called dry painting. The sand is used to make pictures of the sun, lightning, mountains, and rainbows. The sandpainters only use white, yellow, red, black, and blue. They make the colors by grinding different colored stones into the desert sand. Sometimes they mix in grain and soil to make the colors lighter or darker.

Navajos have made the same pictures for hundreds of years. No one knows who painted the first ones. Navajo legends say they were made by gods. Each painter has passed down the secret of how to make the sandpaintings.

The paintings are used in a ceremony to help sick people. The ceremony takes place in a large, earth-covered building. This building is called a hogan (**hoe**-gan). First an animal skin or a smooth layer of clean sand is put on the floor. Then the painters get on their knees. They carefully pour the colored sand into patterns to make the designs.

A Navajo sandpainter

When the sandpainters are finished, the sick person is seated on top of the picture. The colors in the pictures have special meanings to the Navajos. There are also different songs and chants for each picture.

After the ceremony, the painters gather up the sand. New paintings are made every time a ceremony takes place.

Other American Indians in the Southwest also make sandpaintings. But the Navajo artists are said to make the most beautiful ones.

Outside a hogan in Arizona

A Navajo sandpainting

UNIT REVIEW

Word Work

Write the sentences below on a sheet of paper. Fill in the blanks with the correct words from the list.

erosion petrochemical pueblos refinery

1. A _____ is a product that comes from oil or natural gas.
2. A place where oil is cleaned and made ready for use is called a _____.
3. _____ is the wearing away of land by water or wind.
4. Houses made of mud bricks that are built into the sides of cliffs are called _____.

Knowing the Facts

Write your answers on a sheet of paper.

1. What four states make up the Southwest?
2. Why is the land of the Southwest so dry?
3. What two industries helped Houston grow?
4. How are the people of Phoenix working to solve their problems?

Using What You Know

Choose one of the following activities to do. Follow the instructions given here.

1. Write a report describing how the United States gained Texas in 1845.
2. Make a time line of the history of the Southwest from 1540 to 1912.

Skills Practice

Use the following graph to answer the questions below. Write your answers on a sheet of paper.

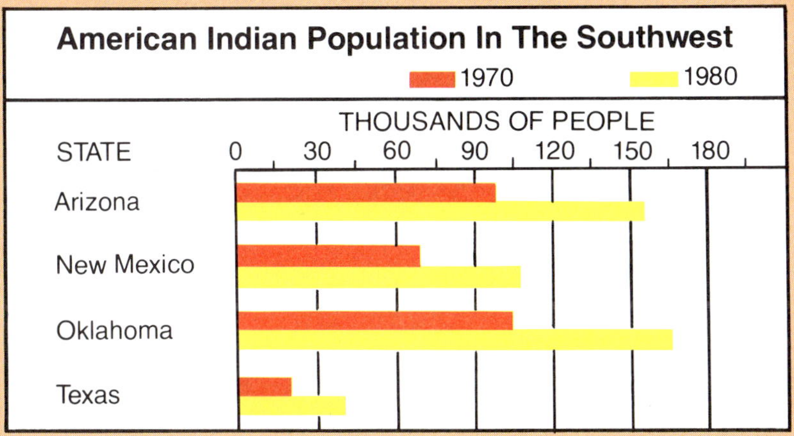

1. Which southwestern state had the largest American Indian population in 1970? in 1980?
2. Has the American Indian population of each state increased or decreased since 1970?
3. In which state did the American Indian population double between 1970 and 1980?

Your State

Every 10 years the United States government counts the population in each city and state. This count is called a census. Check the census of your state in 1970 and 1980. You can find this at your library, or your teacher can help you call the Census Bureau in your region.

UNIT 6 The Rocky Mountain Region

The Rocky Mountains are made up of more than 100 mountain ranges. They stretch from Alaska all the way down into Mexico. In the United States, these mountains and the area around them are called the Rocky Mountain region.

In this unit, you will read about this region of tall mountains, broad plains, and sandy deserts. You will also read about some of this region's busy cities.

CHAPTER 11

The Rocky Mountain Region

Tourists visiting the Great Sand Dunes National Monument in Colorado

The beauty of the Rocky Mountain region draws millions of tourists every year. Visitors come from all over the world to see the wonderful scenery. Many people like to camp, swim, and fish in the parks of this region.

At the end of this chapter, you should be able to:

- ○ Name the states that make up the Rocky Mountain region.
- ○ Describe the land and climate of the region.
- ○ Explain how altitude affects climate.
- ● Read an altitude diagram.
- ○ Name the major resources and industries of the region.

1 The Land

Find the Rocky Mountain region on the locator map in the margin below. In what part of the United States is this region found?

Look at the map below. How many states make up the Rocky Mountain region? What are their names? Find Wyoming on the map. Which state in the Rocky Mountain region is north of Wyoming? Which two states in the Rocky Mountain region are southwest of Wyoming? You can see that there are no large bodies of water in this region. This region borders on another country. That country is Canada. Find Canada on the map.

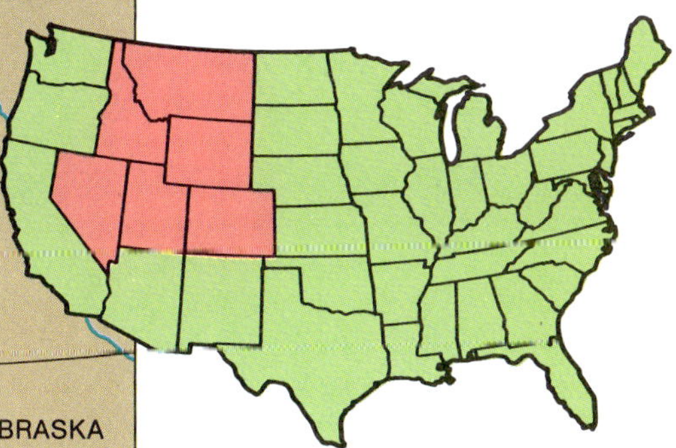

The map below tells you an important fact about this region. Even though it is called the Rocky Mountain region, it is not all mountains. What other landforms are in the Rocky Mountain region? Part of the Great Plains lies east of the mountains. To the west is an area of plateaus.

Plains and Plateaus

Which states in the Rocky Mountain region are partly covered by the Great Plains? Find the plateau area on the map below. This area is one of the driest in all the west. Much of the land is flat and covered with grass or pine forests.

In some parts of the plateau region, the land dips down and is surrounded by higher land. This

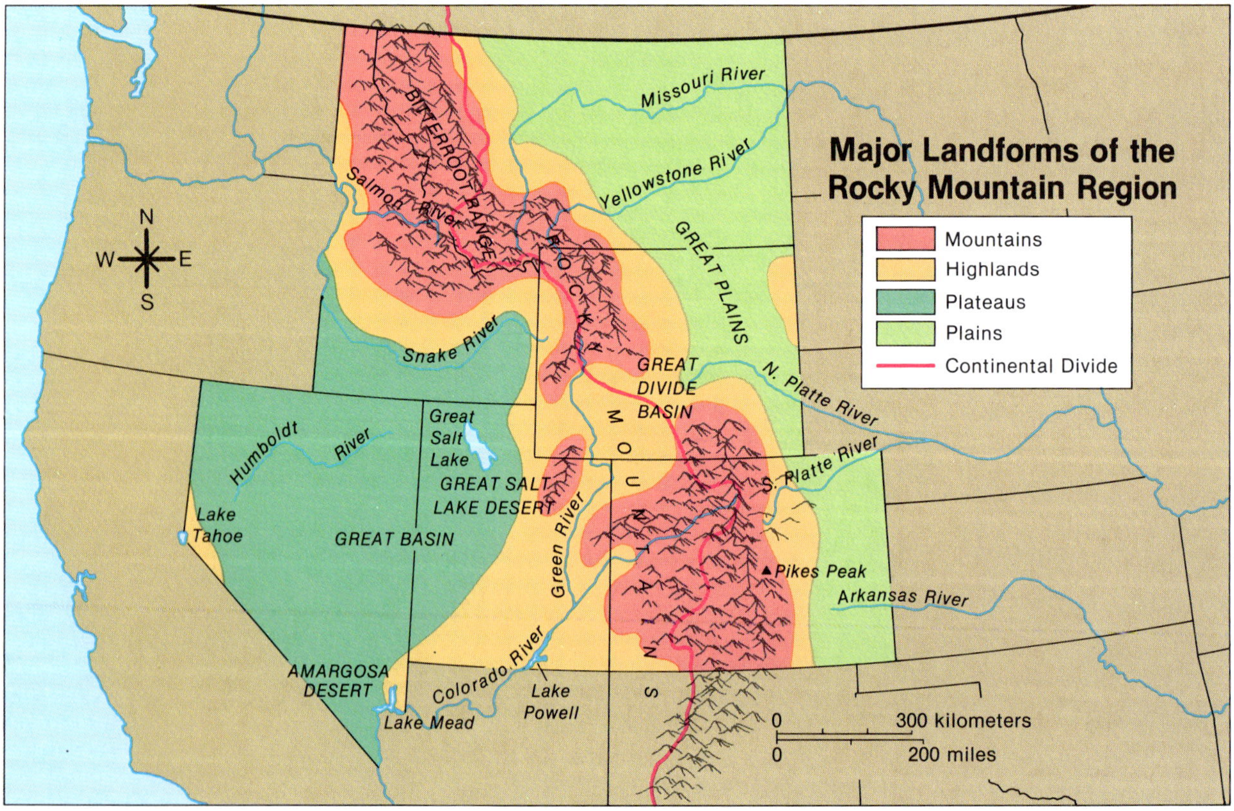

Major Landforms of the Rocky Mountain Region

is called a **basin** because it is shaped like a bowl. The basins in the Rocky Mountain region are so dry that only sagebrush or small shrubs grow on them.

basin
an area of land that is surrounded by higher land

Mountains and Highlands

The mountain area is one of snowy peaks and steep mountain slopes. Farther down the slopes are highland areas where cattle and sheep can graze. Still farther down, the highlands are covered with forests of pine trees.

Look at the map on page 216. The red line running through the Rocky Mountain states shows you where the **continental divide** is. This dividing line is a geographic area that separates the directions in which water currents flow. On the east side of this divide, water flows toward the Atlantic Ocean. On the west side, water flows toward the Pacific. Toward which ocean does the Arkansas River flow? Toward which ocean does the Colorado River flow?

continental divide
the geographic area that separates the direction in which water currents flow

Section Review

Write your answers on a sheet of paper.

1. Name three landforms found in the Rocky Mountain region.

2. Describe a basin.

3. Make a list of rivers that flow to the east and rivers that flow to the west in the Rocky Mountain region. Use the map on page 216.

2 The Climate

Three words describe the climate of the Rocky Mountain region—cold, hot, and dry. The temperatures in the high mountain area are very cold in the winter and cool during the summer. To the south, in the plateaus and plains, winters are milder than in the mountains. Summers in the plateaus and plains are warmer.

altitude
the height of land above the level of the sea

This difference in temperature is because climate is affected by altitude. The **altitude** of the land is its height above the level of the sea. The higher you climb, the colder it gets. It is colder at the top of a mountain than it is at the bottom.

Mountains affect climate in another way too. Because of the mountains, parts of the Rocky Mountain region are dry. The mountains block moisture from reaching lower land areas. For example, the Amargosa (am-ahr-**goe**-suh) Desert in Nevada gets less than 12.5 centimeters (5 inches) of rain a year.

Section Review

Write your answers on a sheet of paper.

1. Describe winters in the Rocky Mountain region. Describe the summers.

2. How do the mountains affect the climate of the Rocky Mountain region?

3. How does the climate of the Rocky Mountain region compare with the climate of the Southwest region?

Reading an Altitude Diagram

SOCIAL STUDIES SKILLS

The altitude of a place affects its climate. This diagram shows how climate changes on a mountain as altitude changes. The numbers on the left mark altitude in meters and feet. Each band shows different climate zones. You can see that the climate gets colder as the altitude gets higher. Plant life changes, too.

At the bottom of this mountain, you would be in a hot, desert climate where cacti and sagebrush grow. As you climb to a height of 1,500 meters (4,950 feet), the air would be colder. Grass would be growing on the ground. Above 2,500 meters (8,250 feet), you would find snow.

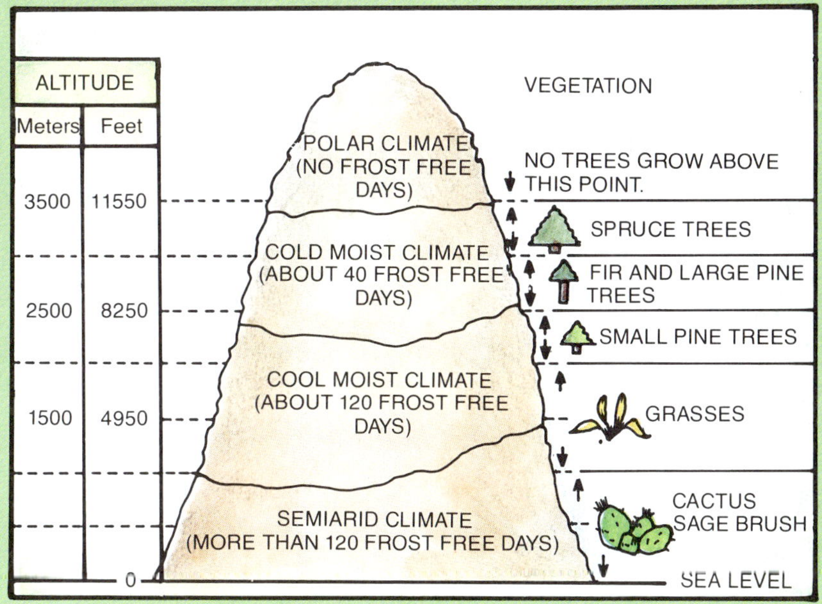

Practice Your Skills

1. How many climate zones does this mountain have?
2. In which two zones do trees grow on the mountain? In which zones are there no trees?
3. What is the climate like at 2,000 meters (6,600 feet)?

3 Resources and Industry

The land of the Rocky Mountain region is very dry. But snow that falls in the high mountains supplies some water. When the snow melts, it forms streams that feed several large rivers.

The people of the region have built reservoirs in which to store what water they can. Lake Powell and Lake Mead are both reservoirs that have been formed from the mighty Colorado River. Water from these reservoirs can be used farther downstream as it is needed.

Farming

The grassy mountain slopes and broad grasslands provide good areas for grazing. So there are many sheep and cattle ranches in the Rocky Mountain area, especially in Wyoming, Montana, Idaho, and Utah.

Irrigation in Idaho potato field

Because the region is dry, farmers use irrigation. With irrigation, the farmers of Idaho can produce one fourth of the nation's potatoes. And through irrigation, farmers of the region are able to grow two thirds of the country's sugar beets.

Wheat is another major crop here. It grows well in eastern Montana, Wyoming, and Colorado. Look at the map on page 216 and tell why.

Because of agricultural production, the Rocky Mountain area has developed a food-processing industry. Producing potato and meat products is important in Idaho, Colorado, and Utah.

Mining

The Rocky Mountain region is very rich in mineral resources. Gold and silver can be found in all of the states of the region. Nevada, Utah, Colorado, and Idaho are richest in these minerals. Copper is also found in the region, especially Montana. Lead and **zinc** are found here as well. They are used to make iron and steel.

zinc
a metal used in making iron and paint, and also used in electric batteries

A silver mine in Idaho

deposit
large area of a mineral deep in the earth

mining
the process of taking mineral deposits from the earth

ore
mixture of rock, soil, and minerals

Mineral resources are often found in large areas, or **deposits,** deep in the earth. Before these deposits can be used, they must be taken out of the earth. The process of doing this is called **mining.** Miners are people who dig the minerals out of the earth. Before the minerals are processed, they are found in the earth, mixed together with rock and soil. This mixture of mineral, rock, and soil is called mineral **ore.**

Each year millions of tons of mineral ore are taken out of the earth in the Rocky Mountain region. So are millions of tons of coal. Rich deposits of oil have been found in Colorado, Wyoming, and Utah.

With all the minerals being mined in the Rocky Mountain region, a large metal-products industry has developed. Copper wire and tubing, airplane parts, and electronic equipment are the major products manufactured here.

Section Review

Write your answers on a sheet of paper.

1. Name five resources of the Rocky Mountain region.
2. Why is the Rocky Mountain region ideal for cattle and sheep raising?
3. Tell how people of the region manage their water supplies.
4. Name four industries of the region.
5. If a freight train were leaving the Rocky Mountains for the east, what kinds of products could it be carrying?

FAMOUS AMERICANS

JIM BECKWOURTH

In the early days of the United States, the West was mostly wilderness. It was home to the American Indians. It was also home to the American mountain men. Mountain men were fur trappers who lived in the woods, far from cities or towns. They led lives of adventure.

Jim Beckwourth, a black trapper, became a famous mountain man. At 19, Jim Beckwourth quit his job in St. Louis and headed west. In his westward travels, he met some Crow Indians. They taught him their ways of hunting and trapping. They also taught him their language.

But a few years later, when Beckwourth was trapping in the woods, he was captured by Crow Indians who did not know him. They took him to their village. Beckwourth was afraid. But then an old Crow woman saw him. She thought he was her long-lost son and did not let anyone harm him. Beckwourth stayed on with the Crow Indians for 11 years. He was a good trapper and was brave in battle. For this, he was made a leader of the Crow people.

Jim Beckwourth had other adventures in the West. He operated a trading post and scouted for the United States Army. He also went to look for gold in California. On his way there, he discovered a pass through the Sierra Nevada range. Today it is known as Beckwourth Pass.

CHAPTER 12

People and Places

Virginia City, Nevada

The Rocky Mountain region was one of the last regions to be settled in the United States. Its high mountains and dry lands frightened settlers away at first. Today, it is a fast-growing region with a population of more than 7 million.

At the end of the chapter, you should be able to:

- ○ Give four reasons why people came to the Rocky Mountain region.
- ● Use a grid to locate places on a map.
- ○ Give examples of what happens when the population of a city grows.
- ○ List the steps in changing mineral ore into metal.

1 The Early Settlers

For years, people had looked for gold and silver in the Rocky Mountains. Then, in 1859, gold was discovered in the region of Pikes Peak in eastern Colorado. Within a short time, 50,000 gold seekers came. And more were on the way. Covered wagons heading toward Colorado carried signs that read, "Pikes Peak or Bust." In the same year, gold and silver were found near Virginia City in Nevada. Five years later, gold was found at Last Chance Gulch in Montana. With each new discovery, mineral seekers rushed to the new area, and a new town grew up.

Often towns would die out as soon as all the minerals were mined. Yet some mining towns became lasting settlements. Denver in Colorado is one. Last Chance Gulch became Helena, the capital of Montana.

A miner looking for gold in Montana

Farming Communities

Many lasting settlements were started by farmers who came west. One of these settlements became Salt Lake City, Utah's largest city. It was founded by the Mormons, a religious group. The Mormons came to the West to find religious freedom.

In the 1860's people began to build railroads in the Rocky Mountain region. The railroads made it easy to ship farm and ranch products to market. Farming and ranching grew. Settlements along the railroad lines, such as Pueblo, Colorado, and Cheyenne, Wyoming, became important cities in the region.

A Crow Indian reservation

American Indians

Long before other settlers came to the region, American Indians lived there. But the new settlers wanted more land for themselves. The government took away most of the Indians' land and gave it to the settlers. The government did set aside some areas of land as places for the Indians to live. Such areas of land are called **reservations.** Today there are more than 105,000 Indians living on reservations in the Rocky Mountain region.

reservation
an area of land set aside for a certain purpose, sometimes as a homeland for American Indians

Some Important People

The Rocky Mountain region has been enriched by the strength, courage, and hard work of its people. Some have been leaders in government. Others helped build the economy of the region. Still others fought for equal rights for all people.

Chief Joseph was a leader of the Nez Percé (nezz **purss**) Indians during the 1870's. He did not think it was fair for his people to be put on a reservation. He tried to convince the United States government to let his people keep their land and live as they wanted. He did not succeed. But Chief Joseph became an example of courage in the fight for human freedom.

Chief Joseph

Marcus Daly came to this country as a poor settler from Ireland. He arrived in Butte (**byoot**), Montana, in 1876. He bought a piece of land that everyone thought was worthless. But soon he discovered large deposits of copper beneath his land. Within 20 years, he built Butte into one of the world's leading copper producers.

Marcus Daly

Jeanette Rankin grew up in Missoula (muh-**zoo**-luh), Montana. In 1916, she became the first woman to be elected to Congress as a representative. At that time, most women in the United States were not allowed to vote. Rankin worked hard in Congress to win the right to vote for all American women.

Jeanette Rankin

Section Review

Write your answers on a sheet of paper.

1. Choose one group of settlers and tell why they came to the Rocky Mountain region.
2. How did the coming of the settlers affect the American Indians of the region?
3. Why do you think the population grew after the railroads reached the region?

SOCIAL STUDIES SKILLS

Using a Grid to Find Places on a Map

If you were planning a trip to a nature park, you might want to have a map like the one below. This map shows all the special places to see in the park.

grid
a series of evenly spaced lines used to locate places on maps

To help you find things quickly, the map has a set of lines that go up and down, left and right. These lines, which form squares, make a **grid.** Each square in the grid has both a number and a letter name.

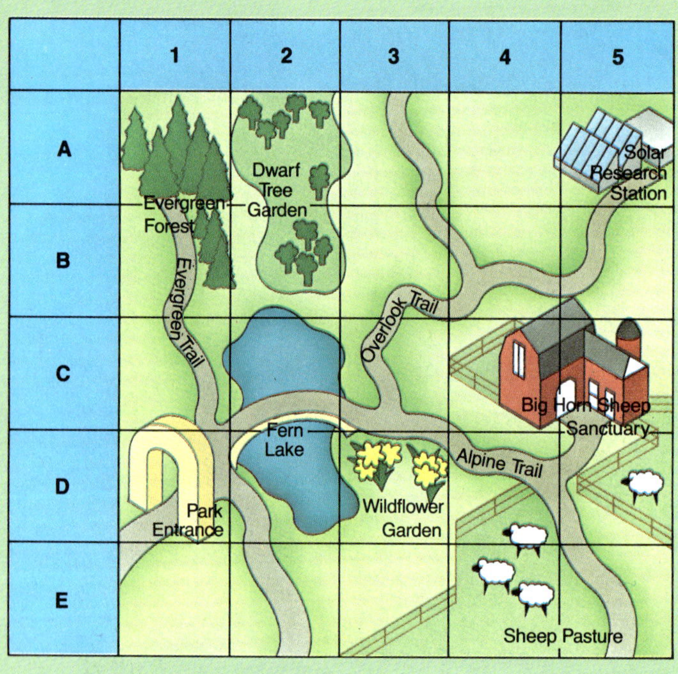

Suppose you wanted to locate the building in square A5. To do this, put your finger on the letter *A*. Now move your finger across the grid until it is below the number 5. You have located the Solar Research Station. It is in square A5.

Practice Your Skills

1. What is in square D1?
2. What is in square D3?
3. Across which two squares will you find the Dwarf Tree Garden?
4. In how many squares might you see sheep?
5. In which squares is the evergreen forest?

2 Cheyenne, Wyoming

If you have ever watched any westerns on television, you have probably heard of Cheyenne (shie-**an**), Wyoming. The Cheyenne you see in the westerns is the Cheyenne of a hundred years ago or more. At that time, it was a town of the "Wild West." There was very little law. People did pretty much what they pleased.

The Coming of the Railroad

Cheyenne became a town because of the railroad. In 1867, the builders of the Union Pacific Railroad needed a place for a shipping center. They chose the point at which Cheyenne now lies.

Cheyenne in 1867

With the coming of the railroad, Cheyenne became a center for ranching. It was also a center for shipping cattle to market. Cowhands bringing cattle to the railroad were often rowdy. Outlaws found the fast-growing town a good place to make money.

But within a few years, the growing town drew up strong laws. As families settled in and around the town, Cheyenne quieted down.

Cheyenne Today

Today Cheyenne is still a center for the ranching industry. It is also the largest city in Wyoming. Its population is more than 63,000. And it is the state capital.

Cheyenne also remains an important center for transportation. Its three railroads employ many people. But now the railroads ship coal as well as cattle. Two major highways serve Cheyenne. Today ranchers use trucks more than trains for shipping their cattle.

Cheyenne today

Cheyenne Frontier Days

The people of Cheyenne are proud of their history as a ranching center. So each year, they celebrate their past. They hold the Cheyenne Frontier Days.

For seven days, there are parades in which people dress in pioneer clothes. They ride in covered wagons and in old stagecoaches. At night, there are square dances, as there were in the Old West. American Indians from the area perform their dances. And there are plenty of riding, roping, and other events.

Section Review

Write your answers on a sheet of paper.

1. What first brought ranchers to Cheyenne?
2. Why is Cheyenne an important city today?
3. Why do you think ranchers use trucks more than trains to ship cattle today?

3 Denver, Colorado

Just about 160 kilometers (100 miles) to the south of Cheyenne lies Denver, Colorado. It is called the Mile-High City because it is a mile above sea level. It is located in the highland area, just east of the Rocky Mountains.

Only 150 years ago, Denver was a mining camp of 25 cabins. Miners made their homes there as they looked for gold. Today Denver has a population of 500,000. When you add the people who live in the suburbs, the population reaches more than 1.5 million.

Every day about 100 people move to the Denver area. This makes Denver one of the fastest-growing cities in the country. One thing that brings

people to Denver is its energy industry. Huge deposits of oil and coal are found in the Rocky Mountain region. The energy industry provides many new jobs. These jobs draw people from all over the country.

An Outdoor Paradise

People find Denver a good place to live because it offers many chances for recreation. The mountains are probably the greatest attraction. As you can see in the pictures, the mountains provide beautiful scenery. They are also good for skiing. Each year nearly 3 million visitors come to Colorado to ski. Many of them come to the Denver area.

But skiing is not the only mountain sport. Mountain trails draw hikers and backpackers. These mountains offer another attraction. Their steep sides are a challenge to skillful climbers.

Mountain climbing

Sports are just one major kind of recreation. Denver also has a fine symphony orchestra and the largest library in the Rocky Mountain region. An art museum, a summer theater, and the Denver Center for the Performing Arts provide enjoyment for thousands of people each year.

Denver is very proud of its park system. It is the largest one in the country. The system is made up of more than 200 parks within the city and 52 parks in the nearby mountains. Part of the park system is called the Greenway. It is a series of parks that runs along the South Platte River. This

Rafting along the South Platte River

river runs right through downtown Denver. Today it is possible to ride a kayak (**kie**-ack) right through the middle of downtown.

Looking to the Future

Denver once called itself the Climate Capital of the World. But now the many cars in Denver cause air pollution. Today a brown cloud of smog hangs over the city. The air is the second dirtiest in the country. Pollution from cars will have to be cut down to make the air clean again.

Lack of water is another problem for the people of Denver. Only 8 centimeters (15 inches) of rain fall on their city each year. So Denver must depend on the reservoirs filled with melting snow from the mountains. If the city keeps growing, these reservoirs will not be able to supply enough water for everyone. But there are ways to clean the water after it is used. If these ways are followed, there might be enough water for Denver in the future.

Section Review

Write your answers on a sheet of paper.

1. Why are so many people moving to Denver?
2. Name three kinds of recreation that Denver offers.
3. Describe two problems Denver has.
4. Many people in Denver do not want their city to grow any more. Why might they believe that growth is hurting Denver?

4 Butte, Montana

Like Denver, Butte, Montana, is a mile above sea level. It calls itself the City That Is a Mile High and a Mile Deep. That is how deep miners have dug under the city to remove the mineral deposits below it. The people of Butte say that they live on "the richest hill on earth."

Butte is on the western slope of the Rocky Mountains. It is not a large city. The population is only about 40,000 people. Yet the people of Butte work to provide nearly one tenth of all the copper mined in the United States. Butte is also a leading producer of other valuable metals, such as gold, silver, and zinc.

Mining Copper Ore

Most copper ore is found either in beds of rock or in deposits that are surrounded by rock. Often mineral ore is buried very far under the ground. The purpose of all mining is to separate the ore from the rock and to get the ore above ground.

One way to do this is to dig deep holes, or **shafts,** into the earth. Once the shafts are dug, miners can go down into them. Next they remove the ore from the rock. The ore is sent up to the surface in carts that look like small railroad cars.

shaft
a deep passage dug into the earth to remove mineral ore

Another way to mine ore is to dig a huge pit from above ground. The picture below shows this way. Huge power shovels pick up the rock containing the copper ore. Then the shovels dump the rock into trucks or railroad cars that move it from the mine. The miners in Butte have been using this method more and more.

A copper furnace

Processing Ore into Copper

Once the rocks with the copper are taken from the mine, they are sent to a mill. At the mill, the rocks and ore are crushed. The waste rock is then removed. Water is added to the crushed ore. This mixture is placed in giant containers that are half filled with iron balls. Powerful machines turn the containers. As the containers turn, the iron balls grind the copper ore into small bits.

slurry
copper ore and water ground up in a mixture

This ground-up mixture of ore and water is called **slurry** (**slur**-ee). It is next placed in other large containers, and a churning process begins. Paddles or air jets mix the slurry and make it bubbly. A chemical is added that coats the mineral bubbles. It causes them to stick together. The mineral bubbles rise to the top, and the unwanted material falls to the bottom. The bubbles are skimmed off and dried. The result is copper that is almost pure.

To make the copper still purer, workers put it into a furnace and heat it. The heat burns off any of the remaining noncopper materials. The copper is at last ready to be turned into useful items.

Some of the copper may become copper wire. Copper wire is used in television sets, motors, and electrical equipment. Some of the copper may be combined with zinc. This mixture produces brass for doorknobs, candlesticks, or clocks. Or maybe the copper will become something you have with you right now—a penny.

How Copper is Made

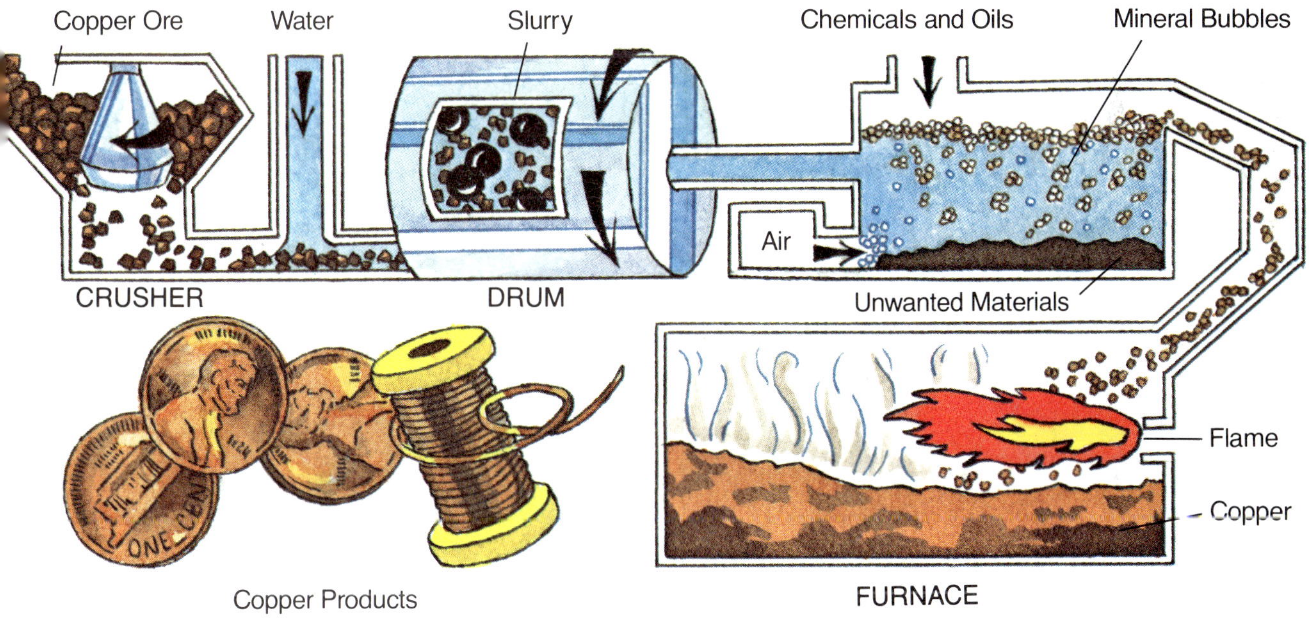

Section Review

Write your answers on a sheet of paper.

1. Name three minerals that Butte has in large supply.
2. Describe how ore is mined from an open pit.
3. List in order the steps needed to turn copper ore into pure copper.

Close-up on

Rodeo In the days of the Old West, cowhands often held contests with one another. They might have had a roping contest. Or they might have seen who could stay on a bucking horse the longest.

Nearly 100 years ago, a small town in the West decided to hold such a contest. There were races and riding and steer roping. The event was so popular that other towns decided to have contests too. Soon, towns all over the West were holding these events. This was the beginning of rodeo.

Rodeo is still a big sport today. People continue to come from all around to see cowboys and cowgirls hold their contests.

The biggest rodeo event is saddle bronc riding. A horse and a rider wait in a closed-in stall. The door is flung open. The bucking horse rushes out. The rider holds onto the

(left) Barrel Racing: Horse is steered through pattern of barrels as fast as possible. (right) Bull-riding event

saddle with only one hand. While the rider is getting bounced up and down, judges are watching. They rate how well a rider sits on the horse and how calm the rider stays. A rider must stay on a bronco for eight seconds. Cowhands say that eight seconds can seem like the longest time in the world.

Another big event is riding a bucking bull. In bull riding, the rider has only a rope to hold on to. If a rider is thrown off the bull, the rodeo clowns run out. It is their job to keep the bull busy so the rider can get out of the way. If things start to look rough, the clowns must get out of the way too. They have a big padded barrel to hide in.

Most rodeo events have a history. They were once part of the cowhands' work. When you go to a rodeo, you can relive some of the days of the Wild West.

Rodeo clowns keeping the bull busy

UNIT REVIEW

Word Work

Write the sentences below on a sheet of paper. Fill in the blanks with the correct words from the list.

continental divide mining reservation basin

1. A ____ is a piece of land set aside for a certain purpose.
2. The ____ separates the rivers that flow east from those that flow west.
3. A ____ is an area of land that is surrounded by higher land.
4. Taking natural materials out of the earth is called ____.

Knowing the Facts

Write your answers on a sheet of paper.

1. How does altitude affect the climate of the Rocky Mountain region?
2. Why did people move to the Rocky Mountain region?

Using What You Know

Choose one of the following activities to do. Follow the instructions given here.

1. Make a list of products that might be made from minerals from the Rocky Mountain region.
2. Make a picture poster of the places you would like to visit in the Rocky Mountain region.

Skills Practice

Use the following map to answer the questions below. Write your answers on a sheet of paper.

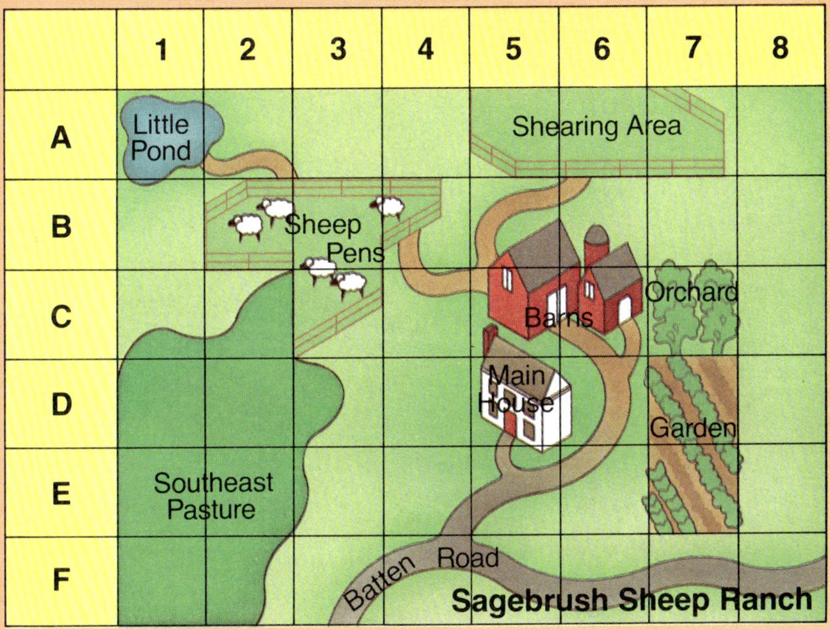

1. In which square is the main house?
2. What would you find in squares C5 and C6?
3. Across how many squares is the shearing area?
4. Which is bigger—the orchard or the garden?
5. Where is Batten Road located?

Your State

There probably is some mining in your state. Remember that oil and natural gas are also taken from the ground. Use an encyclopedia to find out about the minerals that are mined in your region. Compare these minerals with those mined in the Rocky Mountain region.

UNIT 7

The Pacific Region

Our country's largest state is in the Pacific region. So is one of the smallest states. The state with the most people is there. So is the state with the fewest. Our only island state is also in the Pacific region.

In this unit, you will learn why people from all over the world have moved to the Pacific region of our country. You will also learn about the region's industries, land, and history.

CHAPTER 13 The Pacific Region

Imagine long, sandy beaches and tall mountains covered with snow. Think of green mountain ranges and wide plains covered with ice. These landforms are found in the Pacific region.

In this chapter, you will learn about these landforms. You will also learn how the people of this region live and work.

At the end of this chapter, you should be able to:

- ○ Name the five states that make up the Pacific region.
- ○ Describe the climates of the Pacific region.
- ○ Identify the chief resources and industries of the Pacific region.
- ● Read an ocean currents map.

1 The Land

All of the states in the Pacific region have at least one border on the Pacific Ocean. One state, Hawaii, is completely surrounded by the Pacific Ocean. It is the only state that is not on the North American continent.

Three states in the Pacific region border other countries. Look at the map on this page. Which states border other countries?

The Pacific region includes Alaska. What body of water borders Alaska to the north?

Mountains, Plains, Valleys

Look at the map on page 248 and find the mountain ranges. There are mountains all along the Pacific coast. Thick forests of fir, pine, and redwood

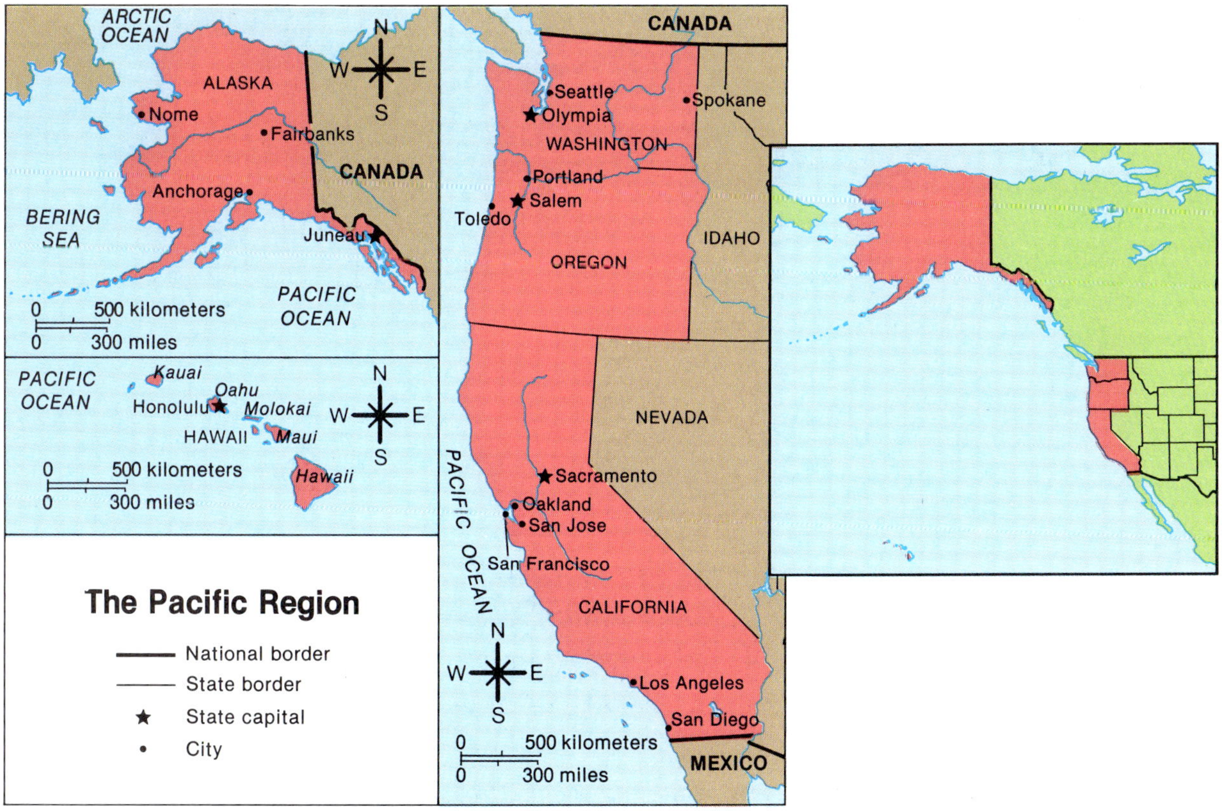

trees cover most of these mountains.

In Alaska, many of the mountains are in cold places. Mount McKinley, a peak in the Alaskan range, is the highest mountain in North America.

Another range in a cold part of Alaska is the Brooks range. Find the Brooks range on the map.

The Cascade range extends through Washington and Oregon. Name the mountain range in the eastern part of California.

Most of the land between Alaska's mountains is too rocky and hilly for farming. But in the valleys of Washington, Oregon, and California, much of the land is flat and fertile. Puget (**pyoo**-jit) Sound Lowland in Washington and the Willamette (wih-**lam**-it) Valley in Oregon are important farming areas. California's Central and Imperial valleys are among the best farming regions in the nation. Find these valleys on the map below.

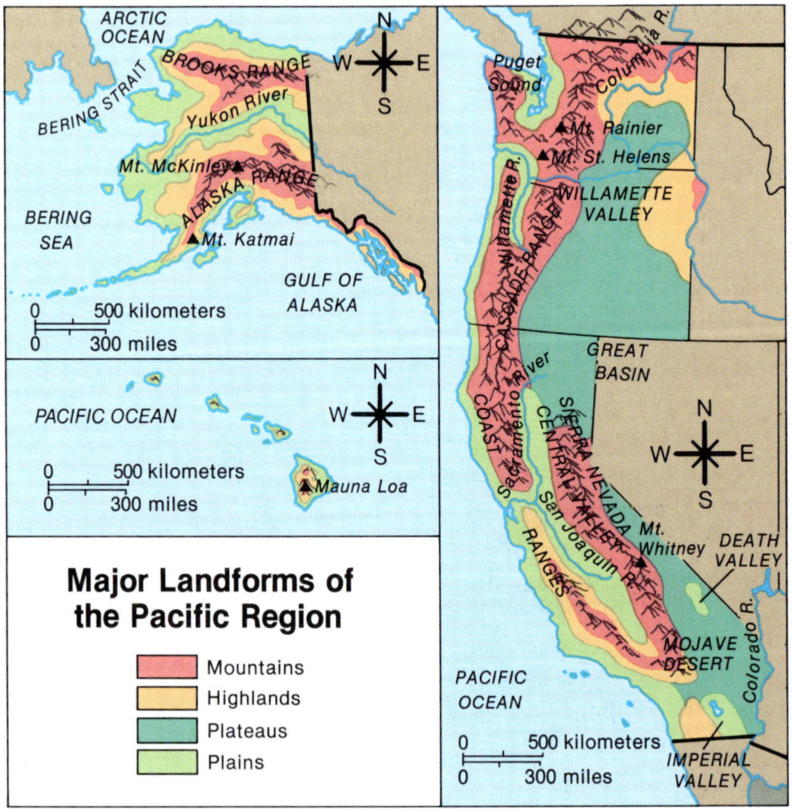

Waterways

The land east of the Pacific region's mountains gets little rain. Farmers in parts of California, Washington, and Oregon use rivers to irrigate their crops.

California farmers irrigate their land with water from the San Joaquin (**san** waw-**keen**), Sacramento (sack-ruh-**men**-toe), and Colorado rivers. In Oregon and Washington, the Willamette and Columbia rivers are used for irrigation. People in Washington also use the Columbia River to produce hydroelectric power.

Desert and Tundra

East of the Sierra Nevada mountain range is California's huge, hot Mojave (moe-**hah**-vee) Desert. It is 65,200 square kilometers (25,000 square miles) in area. In the same region is Death Valley. It is one of the hottest and driest places in the world. Almost nothing grows in these dry desert lands.

Another nearly empty land is a wide, cold plain in northern Alaska. It is called a **tundra.** Some of the tundra is frozen beneath the surface. Plants cannot grow roots in this frozen soil.

tundra
wide, treeless plain where few plants or animals live

Imperial Valley in California

Mount St. Helens in Washington

Volcanoes

lava
hot, liquid rock

volcano
an opening in the earth's surface through which hot, liquid rock, and other materials are forced out

The state of Hawaii is actually a chain of mountains whose tops stick out of the ocean. Gases and hot, liquid rock erupted through the ocean floor thousands of years ago. Liquid rock is called **lava** (**lah**-vuh). As the lava spread and cooled, it formed mountains.

Mountains that were slowly formed by explosions in the ocean floor are called **volcanoes.** Some volcanoes are still active. The largest active volcano in the world is Mauna Loa (**mow**-nuh **loe**-uh) in Hawaii. Another active volcano in the region is Mount St. Helens, in Washington. There are many volcanoes in Alaska. But most of them no longer erupt.

Section Review

Write your answers on a sheet of paper.

1. What state in the Pacific region is completely surrounded by water?

2. Describe how a volcano is formed.

3. Why do you think Alaska has the smallest population?

2 The Climate

You can find just about any kind of climate in the Pacific region. Northern California and the western parts of Washington and Oregon are very wet. Moist air from the Pacific Ocean blows over the Cascade Mountains. When the air hits the mountains, rain falls. The diagram below shows this. The western side of the Cascade Mountains gets more than 250 centimeters (100 inches) of rain each year. The land on the eastern side of the Cascade Mountains gets very little rainfall. Only about 13 to 38 centimeters (5 to 15 inches) of rain fall a year.

The Pacific region states are affected by warm waters of the Pacific Ocean. Because of this, most of the Pacific region has a mild climate. The

A glacier in Alaska

southern part of California is warm and dry. The pleasant climate makes southern California a popular place to visit and to live.

The southern part of Alaska near the ocean also has mild temperatures. In the summer, the temperature is usually about 20° C (68° F). In winter, the temperatures usually range from −10° C to 0° C (14° F to 32° F). In northern Alaska, temperatures are cold all year round. In winter, the temperature is usually −24° C (−11° F). Summer temperatures are around 7° C (43° F). This is the land of the tundra. In many areas, large masses of ice called **glaciers** (**glay**-shurs) cover the land.

glacier
large, thick mass of ice

How different the climate of Hawaii is! There the temperature ranges from 20° C to 30° C (68° F to 86° F) all year long. Winds from around the equator blow toward Hawaii. These winds make the temperature moderate. Some parts of Hawaii are very wet. They get more than 200 centimeters (80 inches) of rain a year. A mountain on the island of Kauai (**kow**-ie) often gets more rain in a year than any other place on the earth. This is caused by moisture from the winds that blow from the equator toward Hawaii.

Section Review

Write your answers on a sheet of paper.

1. Compare the climate west and east of the Cascade Mountains.
2. Describe the climate in northern Alaska.
3. Why do you think Hawaii has some of the thickest forests in the United States?

3 Resources and Industry

The map below shows some of the resources of the Pacific region. Which states have many forests? What minerals lie beneath the ground? What kind of crops are grown? As you can see, the Pacific region is rich in many kinds of resources.

Farming

The Pacific region is a leading farming area. The fertile soil and warm climate of most of the region contribute to its large agricultural and food-processing industries. California is the leading agricultural state in the country. It produces nearly 70 kinds of fruits, as well as vegetables and grain. What are the chief crops of Washington, Oregon, and Hawaii?

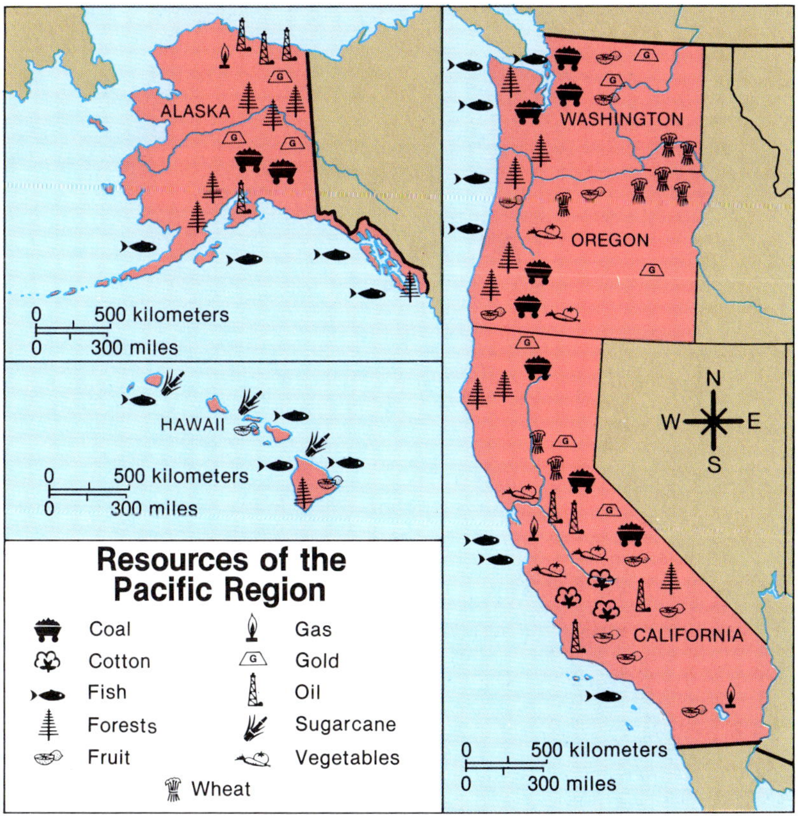

Lumber

The forests of the Pacific region are large and thick. Oregon, California, and Washington lead in the production of lumber in the western United States. Their factories make paper, lumber, pencils, and other wood products.

Fishing

Since all of the states in the Pacific region border the Pacific Ocean, fishing is a large industry. Tuna, salmon, and many other kinds of fish are plentiful in Pacific waters and in rivers that flow to the Pacific. Alaska produces more salmon than any other state in the United States.

Mining

Alaska's natural resources include many kinds of minerals. Oil, natural gas, and gold are among

Salmon fishing in Alaska

them. Mining companies drill deep into the ground to mine these resources. Look at the map on page 253. What other states are rich in these resources?

Factories in the Pacific region turn the minerals into many different kinds of products. Chemicals, machinery, gasoline, and airplane parts are made in many Pacific region factories. This is done especially in California, Washington, and Oregon.

Tourists on Waikiki Beach on the island of Oahu in Hawaii

Tourism

More than 9 million people visit the Pacific region each year. They enjoy the pleasant climate and the beautiful scenery.

Many people like to visit places of interest in the Pacific region. In California, many people go to Hollywood, where television shows and movies are often made. Hawaii's warm climate attracts many people. Tourists in Alaska visit Mount McKinley and enjoy every kind of winter sport. Thousands of visitors a year view Oregon's beautiful coastal scenery. And the wilderness of Washington is used for hiking, fishing, and camping.

Section Review

Write your answers on a sheet of paper.

1. Name three industries that have grown in the Pacific region because of natural resources.
2. Name five agricultural products of the region.
3. Make a list of the products that you think Alaska has to bring in from other places.

SOCIAL STUDIES SKILLS

Reading an Ocean Currents Map

current
a fast-moving stream of water in the ocean

Within our oceans are fast-moving streams of water called **currents.** The rotation of the earth and strong winds cause the ocean currents to move constantly. Some currents carry warm water from the equator north toward the cold waters near the North Pole. As cold currents flow back toward the warm waters near the equator, they become warm again.

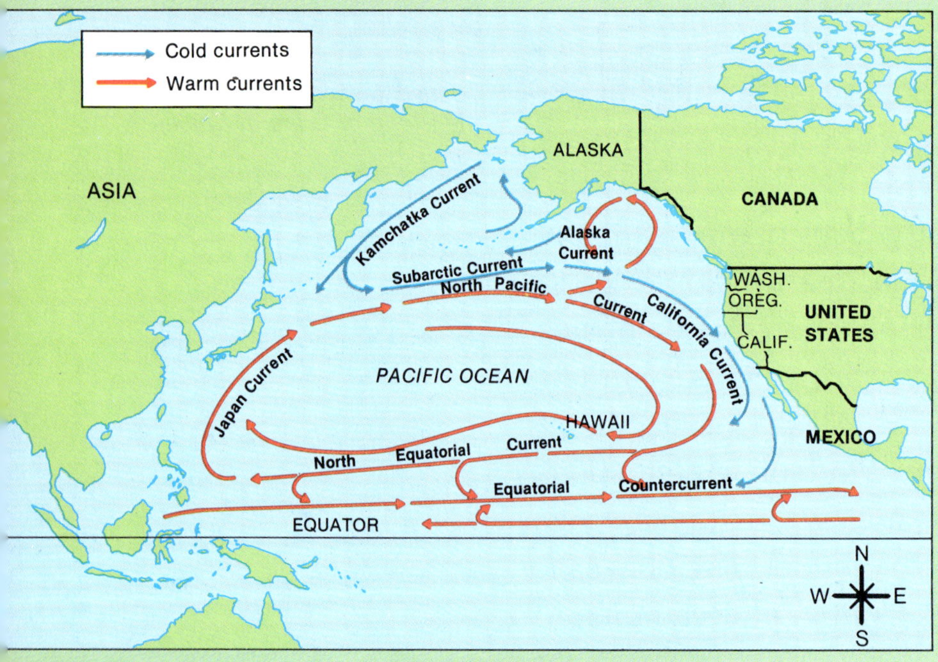

This map shows some cold and warm currents in the Pacific Ocean and the direction in which they flow. The arrows show the direction of currents.

Practice Your Skills

1. In which direction does the California current flow? Is it a warm or cold current?
2. Which current carries cold water directly into the California current? Why does that current cool the California current?
3. Which current splits in two as it flows west around Hawaii? Is it a warm or cold current?
4. Which current runs along the equator? Is it a warm or cold current?

FAMOUS AMERICANS

NARCISSA WHITMAN

Narcissa Whitman was one of the first women to cross the Rocky Mountains. In the early 1800's, only a few explorers, trappers, and traders had made that journey. But Narcissa Whitman had a dream. She wanted to bring Christianity to the American Indians. In 1836, she and her husband, Marcus, left New York and headed west.

In those days, many areas had no roads. There were few stores in which to buy food and supplies. Many people did not want to cross the Rocky Mountains. But the Whitmans were not afraid of hardships. Finally they arrived in what is now the state of Washington. They set up a mission near present-day Walla Walla.

Narcissa Whitman and her husband lived among the Cayuse (**kie**-yooss) Indians. She started a school where she taught English and singing. The Whitmans also planted crops and built a mill to grind corn and wheat.

More and more people were encouraged by the Whitmans' example. Pioneers began moving into the area, then called Oregon Country. Many bought food and fixed their equipment at the mission. The Whitmans helped Oregon Country become a settled area.

The Whitmans died in 1847. The mission they had founded was closed. Today the spot where the mission was located is preserved as a historic landmark.

CHAPTER 14 People and Places

Seattle, Washington, today

"Go west, young man, and grow up with the country." This saying was very popular in the 1850's. People are still going west today. The Pacific region is one of the fastest growing parts of our country. In this chapter, you will read about the Pacific region of yesterday and today.

At the end of this chapter, you should be able to:

○ Describe the settlement of the Pacific region.
○ Explain how the location of a city affects its industry.
○ Explain how wood is used to make paper.
● Read a time zone map of the United States.

1 The Early Settlers

Long before pioneers settled in the Pacific region, American Indians lived there. The Indians fished in the coastal waters. They hunted for deer and bear in the forests. Eskimos were also one of the first groups of people who lived in Alaska. Animals of the land and sea were the Eskimos' source of food and clothing.

Heading West

Europeans explored the Pacific coast for more than 200 years before starting permanent settlements there. In the late 1700's, the Spanish began building missions and towns in southern California, just as they had done in the Southwest region. Father Junípero Serra (hoo-**nee**-puh-roe **ser**-uh) established a mission in San Diego (**san** de-**ay**-goe) in 1769. Within 13 years, he started eight more along the California coast. In all, the Spanish founded 21 missions in California.

American Indians of the Pacific Northwest in the 1800's

Oregon City was the last stop on the Oregon Trail. This is the way it looked in 1857.

To the north, merchants from Russia, Great Britain, and the United States traded with the American Indians for furs. As time passed, Great Britain and the United States began to argue over who would control the Pacific region. In 1846, these two countries signed a treaty. In the treaty, they agreed to divide a large region of land in the northwest between them. From the American part, the states of Oregon, Washington, Idaho, and part of Montana were formed.

At about the same time, the United States gained a large amount of land in the Southwest from Mexico after a war. From this land, the state of California was formed. Nevada, Utah, and parts of four other states were also formed from this land.

Thousands of pioneers moved to the Northwest in the 1840's. Many traveled by way of the Oregon Trail. This trail extended for 3,200 kilometers (2,000 miles) from Missouri to the Pacific Northwest. Some came because of the fertile soil. Others came in search of adventure on the frontier. Then, in 1848, gold was discovered in California. Thousands of people rushed to California

Looking for gold in Alaska in the 1890's

from the United States and other countries, including China. They traveled by land and by sea. Between 1847 and 1852, California's population grew from 15,000 to 250,000!

Settling Alaska

Russia is only about 90 kilometers (56 miles) away from Alaska, across the Bering Strait. Russian traders established the first European settlements in Alaska in the 1700's. In the following years, Russia and other European countries were interested mainly in Alaska's furs. Then, in 1867, Russia sold Alaska to the United States for a little more than $7 million. Many Americans thought this was a waste of money. They believed Alaska was a worthless wilderness. But they changed their minds when gold was discovered there in 1896. This discovery brought in many new settlers. In 1959, Alaska became our forty-ninth state. Today the state's oil and natural gas industry is bringing many more people to Alaska.

Pineapple fields in Hawaii

Settling Hawaii

In 1778, British explorer James Cook became the first European to go to the Hawaiian islands. Then, in the 1800's, Americans began settling there. Some went to spread Christianity among the Hawaiian people. Others wanted to profit from Hawaii's sugarcane business and later from its pineapple plantations. People came to Hawaii from China, Japan, and other countries to work in these fast-growing industries. In 1959, Hawaii became our fiftieth state.

The Pacific Region Today

The Pacific region today has much in common with its past. Fishing, farming, and gold mining are still important activities of the region's people. But there are many other industries as well. For example, the Pacific region's thick forests have led to the building of lumber mills and wood-processing plants.

Many small towns of the past are now large cities. More than 29 million people live in the Pacific region today. About three quarters of these

Population of the Pacific Region (1960-1980)

State	1960	1970	1980
Washington	2,853,214	3,409,169	4,130,163
Oregon	1,768,687	2,091,385	2,632,663
California	15,717,204	19,953,134	23,668,562
Alaska	226,167	302,173	400,481
Hawaii	632,772	769,913	965,000

people live in California. That state has the largest population in the country. Alaska—the largest in area of our 50 states—has the smallest population. About 400,000 people live in Alaska. Fewer people live there than in Seattle, Washington.

The Pacific region's people come from a variety of backgrounds. Some are the great-grandchildren of settlers who traveled the Oregon Trail. Others come from Asian, Canadian, or Spanish backgrounds. California has a large Mexican population. And Alaska has a large Eskimo population. This mixture of Americans from different backgrounds makes the Pacific region one of many cultures.

Some Important People

Many people from the Pacific region are well-known for their contributions to our country. In 1973, Thomas Bradley became the mayor of Los Angeles. He was the first black mayor of an American city with a mainly white population. As mayor, Bradley worked to make Los Angeles a good city for all its people.

Patsy Mink was born in a tiny village on the Hawaiian island of Maui (**mow**-ee). Mink later became a congresswoman. In Congress, she supported education and women's rights.

Thomas Bradley

Patsy Mink

As a young man in Alaska, William Oquilluk (oe-**kwill**-luk) was concerned about his people, the Eskimos. He wanted to make sure that people in the future would know how the Eskimos had lived in the past. Oquilluk began collecting stories about Eskimo history. In 1973, these stories were published. Through the work of William Oquilluk, the history of the Eskimo people has been preserved for all people to read.

Abigail Scott Duniway (**dun**-uh-way) led the fight for women's rights in the northwestern United States in the early 1900's. Her efforts helped women gain the right to vote in Washington, Oregon, and Idaho.

(left) William Oquilluk
(right) Abigail Scott Duniway

Section Review

Write your answers on a sheet of paper.

1. What caused the sudden growth of California's population in the mid-nineteenth century?
2. Describe some of the reasons Americans settled in Alaska and Hawaii.
3. What country established the first European settlements in Alaska? Why do you think this country was first?

2 Seattle, Washington

Seattle is one of the chief cities of the western United States. Find Seattle on the map below. What body of water borders it on the west? Now find the Strait of Juan de Fuca (**hwahn** day **foo**-kuh). What two bodies of water are connected by this strait?

Gateway to the Orient

Seattle's location has helped make it one of the most important port cities of the country. Ships sail through Puget (**pyoo**-jit) Sound and the Strait of Juan de Fuca to reach the Pacific Ocean. From there, they go across the ocean to the cities of Asia. For this reason, the port of Seattle is sometimes called the Gateway to the Orient.

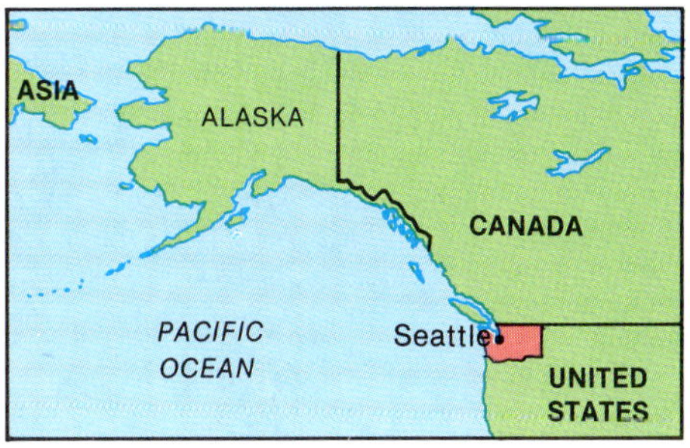

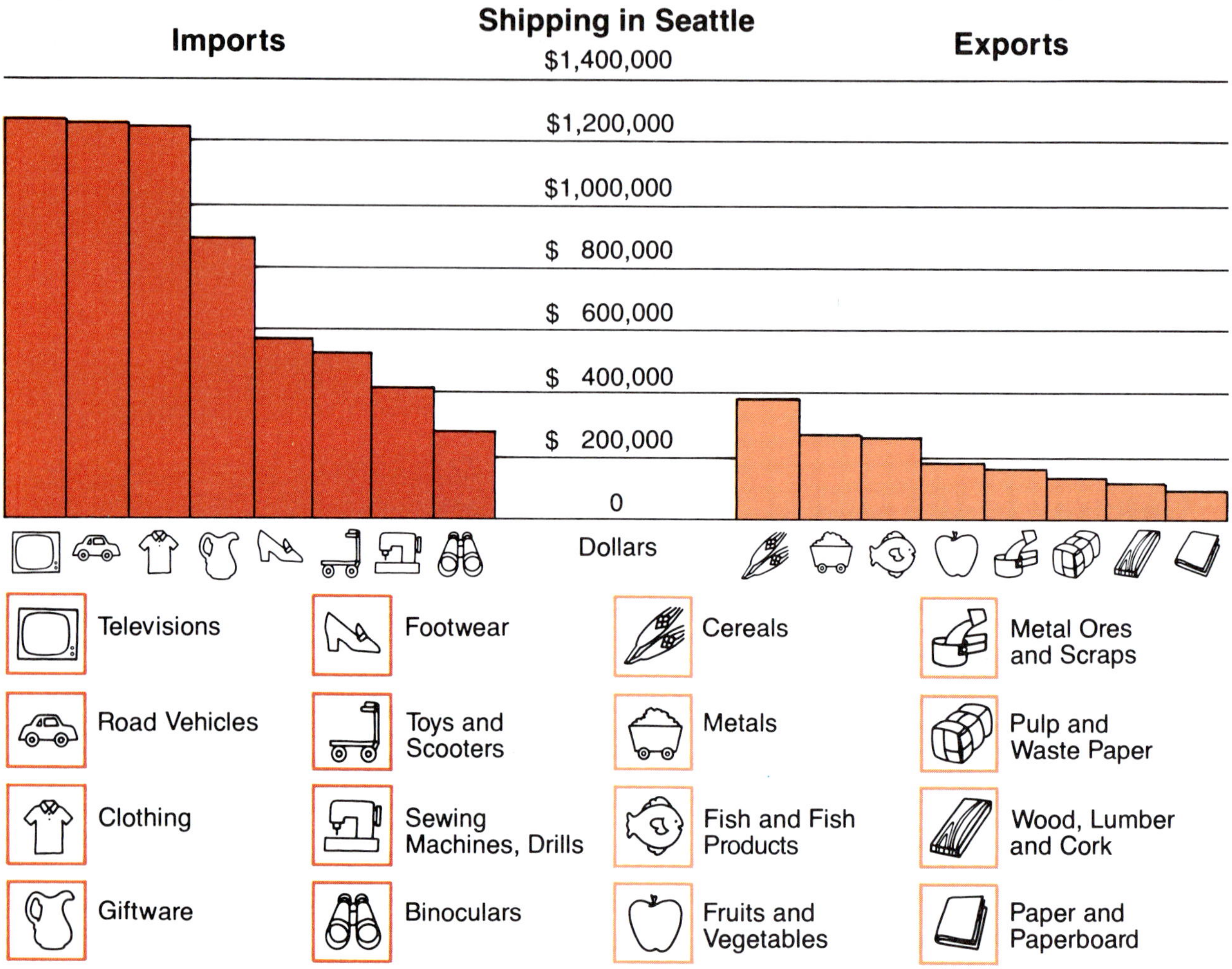

export
product sent from one country to another

Goods of all sorts are sent out through the port of Seattle. These goods are called **exports.** More than 70 countries receive products from the United States through the port of Seattle. These countries are in Asia, South America, and other parts of the world.

import
product received by one country from another

The United States also receives goods from other countries through the port of Seattle. These goods are called **imports.** Mexico, Japan, and Canada are some countries the United States imports goods from. The graph above shows you the products that go in and out of Seattle.

Gateway to Alaska

Seattle has another nickname: Gateway to Alaska. Seattle is the chief port for ships carrying

The busy port of Seattle

goods to and from Alaska. This has been true ever since gold was discovered in Alaska in the late 1890's. As stories of gold strikes spread, thousands of people rushed to Seattle. There they bought food and supplies. Then they boarded ships sailing north to the Alaskan goldfields. New buildings, factories, and stores were built. By 1910, Seattle's population was three times what it had been in 1900. This was because the gold rush created so many businesses and industries.

Shipbuilding and airplane manufacturing are two of Seattle's key industries today. Seattle's coastal location has made it one of the Northwest's busiest cities.

Section Review

Write your answers on a sheet of paper.

1. How has Seattle's geographic location been important to its growth?

2. Why is Seattle called the Gateway to the Orient? the Gateway to Alaska?

3. Do you think the business people of Seattle thought the discovery of gold in Alaska was a good thing? Why or why not?

3 Los Angeles, California

What was the name of the last movie you saw? Was it a western or a movie about invaders from outer space? Did you go to a movie theater, or did you watch it on television?

Whatever movie you saw, it was probably made in Los Angeles (**laws an**-juh-luss), California. About 7 out of 10 motion pictures made in the United States are produced in this city. Most movies are made in the part of the city known as Hollywood.

An Entertainment Center

Los Angeles is in southern California on the Pacific coast. It is one of the largest cities in the world. It covers 1,202 square kilometers (464 square miles) of land.

Los Angeles leads California in manufacturing and shipping. But movie making is probably the city's best-known activity. That is why Los Angeles is often thought of as the entertainment capital of our country.

Birth of an Industry

Filmmaking became popular in Los Angeles in the early 1900's. One reason for this was California's mild, dry climate. This made it easier to make movies outdoors. Another reason was the scenery around the city. High mountains, forests, rocky canyons, and the Pacific Ocean are all near the city. Such varied scenery could be used for many different movies.

In 1911, Hollywood's first motion-picture studio was built. In the years that followed, other studios were built in Hollywood. These studios made films for movie theaters. Later they made films for television. Writers, actors, and musicians came to

Making a film in Hollywood in the late 1920's

Inside a television sound studio today

live and work in Los Angeles. Music recording has also become an important part of this entertainment center. The music is recorded for movies and television.

Today many films are made inside soundproof buildings. Because of air travel, films can also be made anywhere in the world. The climate and scenery around Los Angeles are not as important to the movie maker as they once were. But the city is still considered the country's movie and television capital.

Section Review

Write your answers on a sheet of paper.

1. Name three important industries in the city of Los Angeles.

2. Why did filmmaking become popular in the city of Los Angeles?

3. How did the filmmaking industry contribute to the growth of Los Angeles' population?

4 Toledo, Oregon

Each year, thousands of books, magazines, and newspapers are printed in the United States. Many of these are used in schools and libraries. Others are sold in bookstores and at newsstands.

Do you know where the paper for these publications comes from? The answer is trees.

Logs are taken from the forests to be shipped to the paper mill.

From Forest to Paper Mill

Earlier you read about the Pacific region's dense forests. Much of our paper comes from those forests. Toledo (tuh-**lee**-doe), Oregon, is a town of about 3,000 people. It is in the heart of papermaking country.

Toledo is in the northwestern part of Oregon. This is an area of forests and mountains. Mild climate and heavy rain help trees grow 60 to 90 meters (200 to 300 feet) tall. Mild climate also means that lumber workers can work year-round. Using power saws, tractors, and trucks, workers cut and transport logs to the region's paper mills. One of Oregon's largest paper mills is in Toledo.

Making Wood into Paper

wood pulp
ground-up wood fibers from logs

In order to make paper, logs must first be made into **wood pulp.** This is ground-up wood fibers from logs. One way to make logs into pulp is by simply grinding them up. Another way to make wood pulp is by a chemical process. Most paper comes to us through such a chemical process. This happens because chemically treated pulp is cleaner than pulp that has only been ground up. Paper made from chemically treated pulp also lasts longer.

Processing wood into pulp and then making the pulp into paper involves several steps. First a tree is cut down and sawed into logs. The logs are taken to the paper mill. There the bark is removed. This is done by first cutting the log into pieces. Then the pieces are passed through a large iron cylinder. This cylinder turns around and around. The pieces bump against one another until the bark is knocked off.

Next the wood is put into a chipping machine, or chipper. The chipper has a revolving steel disk with several sharp blades. The blades cut the wood into chips about 2 centimeters (less than an inch) long.

The chips are then put into a huge iron tank. Inside this tank, the wood is cooked in a chemical

The fourdrinier—the last step in the paper-making process

solution until wood pulp is formed. This pulp is then washed to remove the chemical.

The wood pulp, mixed with water, is cleaned some more. This is done by passing it through a series of screens. These screens take out any dirt or other matter. Next chemicals are used to bleach the pulp. Then the pulp is washed again. Next the wood pulp is passed through other machines that break down the pulp's wood fibers.

Finally the pulp goes to a huge machine called a fourdrinier (foohr-**drih**-nee-ur). The fourdrinier is a long paper-making machine that presses the pulp into a sheet. Air suction pumps and heavy rollers take out water and flatten the sheet. Sometimes a large roller presses a design into the paper. This design is called a watermark. The watermark tells who manufactured the paper.

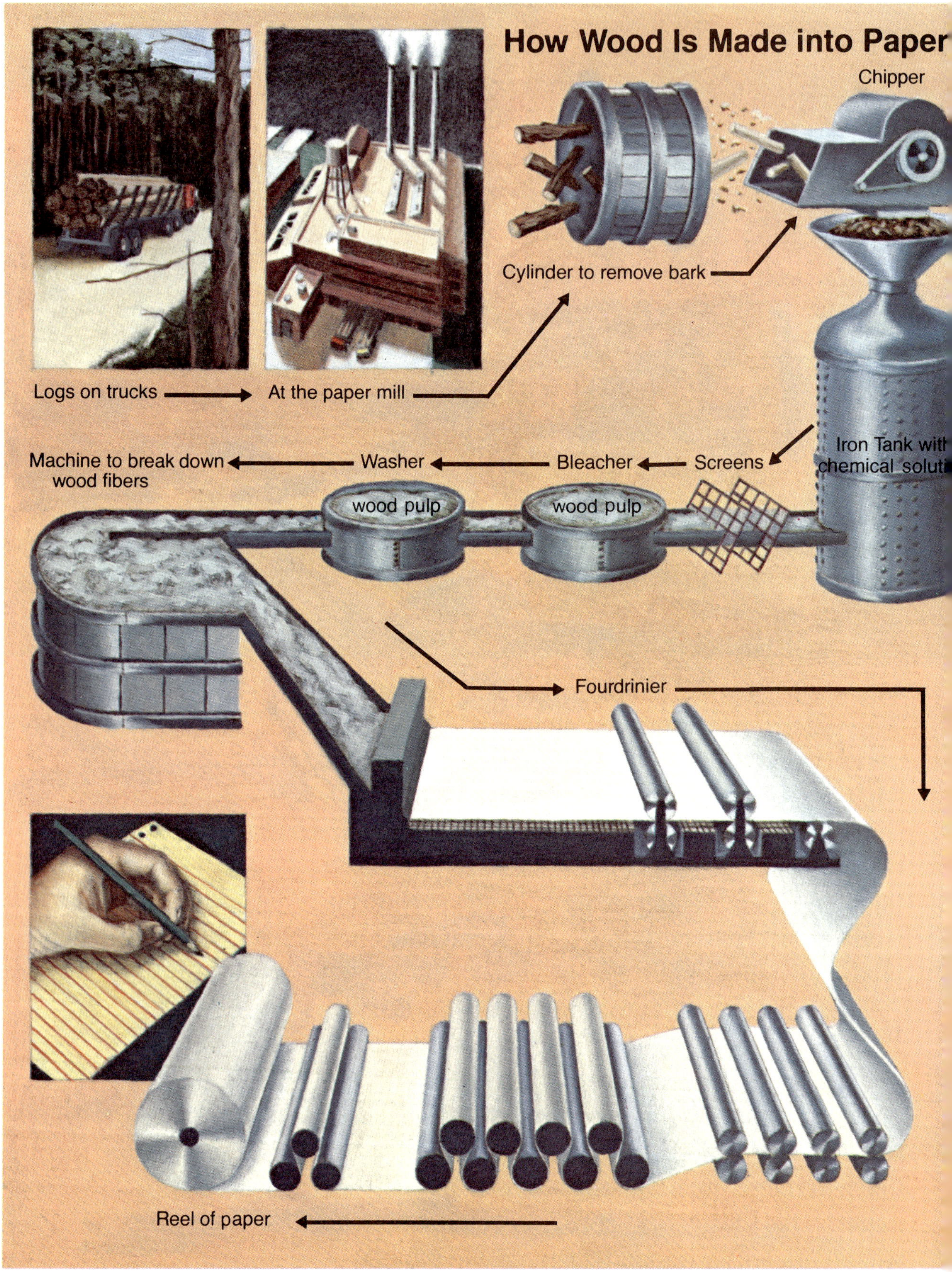
How Wood Is Made into Paper
Chipper
Cylinder to remove bark
Logs on trucks
At the paper mill
Machine to break down wood fibers
Washer
Bleacher
Screens
Iron Tank
wood pulp
wood pulp
Fourdrinier
Reel of paper

Finished reels of paper

As the sheet moves through the fourdrinier, rollers continue to flatten, dry, and smooth it. A set of cast-iron rolls at the end of the machine gives the paper a smooth finish. Finally the paper is wound onto large reels. Many of these reels are sold to printers. Then printing presses make the paper into book pages—just like the one you are looking at right now.

Section Review

Write your answers on a sheet of paper.

1. How does Oregon's climate help make lumbering an important industry in that state?
2. What is wood pulp?
3. What is a fourdrinier?
4. Make a list of the steps by which wood is processed into paper.

SOCIAL STUDIES SKILLS

Understanding Time Zones

time zone
one of 24 areas or zones of the earth in which the time is one hour earlier than the zone to its east

As you have learned, the earth turns on its axis once every 24 hours. As it turns, the side facing the sun has daylight. The side facing away from the sun has night. That is why all the clocks in the world do not show the same time. If they did, one side of the world would be dark at midnight, while the other side would be light at midnight.

So instead of one world time, there are local **time zones** for each part of the earth. In the 48 United States with connecting borders, there are four time zones. In each zone, the local time is one hour earlier than the zone to the east.

Look at the map on page 277. Find the Eastern Time Zone. At about 6:00 in the morning, this part of the world is just beginning to face the sun. It will take almost three hours for the places in the Pacific Time Zone to face the sun. According to the clock labels on the map, what time is it in Washington, when it is 6:00 A.M. in Massachusetts?

Practice Your Skills

1. How many states are located in the Pacific Time Zone? in the Eastern Time Zone? in the Hawaii-Aleutian Time Zone?
2. What is the time difference between the Central Time Zone and the Pacific Time Zone? the Eastern Time Zone and the Central Time Zone?
3. When it is 4:00 P.M. in Utah, what time is it in Georgia? in California? in Arkansas? in Hawaii?

CANADA
WASH.
OREGON
CALIFORNIA
NEVADA
IDAHO
MONTANA
WYOMING
UTAH
COLORADO
ARIZONA
NEW MEXICO
NORTH DAKOTA
SOUTH DAKOTA
NEBRASKA
KANSAS
OKLAHOMA
TEXAS
MINN.
IOWA
MO.
ARK.
LA.
WIS.
ILL.
MISS.
ALA.
TENN.
KY.
MICHIGAN
IND.
OHIO
W. VA.
VA.
N.C.
S.C.
GA.
FLORIDA
PA.
N.Y.
N.J.
DEL.
MD.
CONN.
R.I.
MASS.
VT.
N.H.
ME.
PACIFIC OCEAN
ATLANTIC OCEAN
MEXICO
0 600 kilometers
0 400 miles
N
S
E
W
ALASKA
CANADA
PACIFIC OCEAN
HAWAII
Eastern time zone
Central time zone
Mountain time zone
Pacific time zone
Alaska time zone
Hawaii-Aleutian time zone

Close-up on

Cartoons Have you heard of Mickey Mouse? How about *Bugs Bunny*™ or Snoopy? To millions of people around the world, these names are as familiar as they are to you. Imagine—cartoon characters more famous than most real people!

Movie cartoons date back to the time when motion pictures were first made. Like motion pictures, cartoons did not have sound in the beginning. Then, in the 1920's, Walt Disney worked to make movie cartoons something special. In 1927, sound was added to the movies. And, in 1928, Disney produced the first sound cartoon called *Steamboat Willie.* Its star was Mickey Mouse. Disney gave Mickey Mouse a voice and a personality. The first

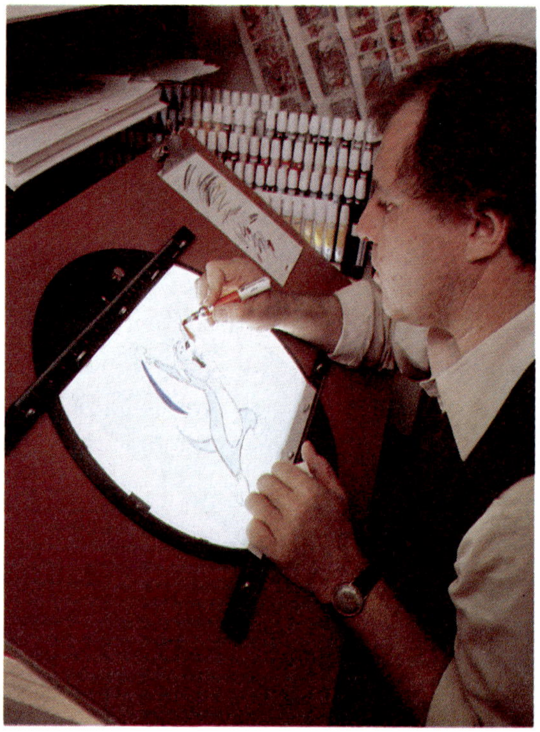

A cartoon artist at work

audiences that saw him loved him, and audiences today do too!

From Mickey's first speaking part in 1928, Disney Studios grew. And many other cartoon stars, such as Minnie Mouse, Pluto, Donald Duck, and Goofy, were created. Longer cartoons, such as *Snow White and the Seven Dwarfs* and *Dumbo,* proved that cartoons could be as popular as live-action movies.

It takes many people to make a cartoon. Authors write the words that the cartoon characters say. Musicians write and record the music. Artists draw the characters' actions to go with the sound. Many artists may work on one cartoon. This is necessary because 24 drawings must be created for just one second of a cartoon! Each drawing is just a tiny bit different from the one before it. The finished drawings are photographed by a special camera. The developed film is shown on a screen at a very fast speed. Your eye blends the drawings together. The drawings then seem to move! A character laughing may actually be more than a dozen separate drawings blended together.

So, the next time you see *Road Runner*™ or Yogi Bear dash across your television screen, just think— it takes over 7,000 drawings to make one five-minute cartoon.

Bugs Bunny © *Warner Bros., Inc. 1966*

UNIT REVIEW

Word Work

Write the sentences below on a sheet of paper. Fill in the blanks with the correct words from the list.

imports glacier time zones volcano

1. A large, thick mass of ice is called a ____.
2. A ____ is an opening in the earth's surface through which hot, liquid rock is forced out.
3. At 5 P.M. in Oregon, it is 7 P.M. in North Dakota because of different ____.
4. ____ are goods brought into a country.

Knowing the Facts

Write your answers on a sheet of paper.

1. How do the mountains of the Pacific region affect that region's climate?
2. Name three industries of the Pacific region.
3. Why is Seattle known as the Gateway to the Orient?
4. What is wood pulp and for what is it used?

Using What You Know

Choose one of the following activities to do. Follow the instructions given here.

1. Write a report on the role the resources played in the settlement of the Pacific region.

2. Imagine you are a pioneer in the 1850's. What area of the Pacific region would you settle? Explain why.

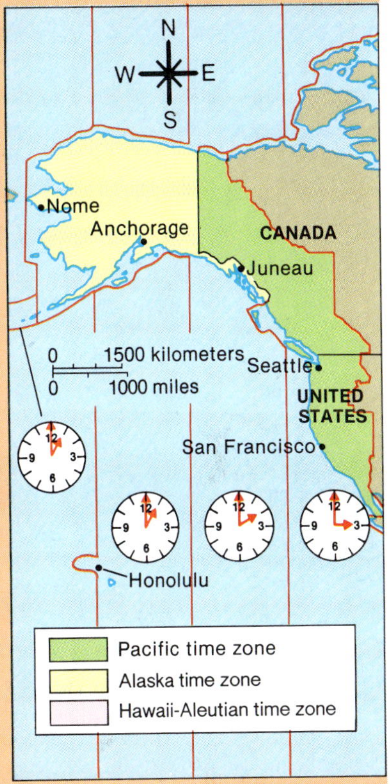

Skills Practice

Use this map to answer the questions below. Write your answers on a sheet of paper.

1. What city on the map is in the same time zone as Seattle? What cities are in the same zone as Anchorage?
2. What is the time difference between the Pacific Time Zone and the Hawaii-Aleutian Time Zone?
3. When it is noon in San Francisco, what time is it in Juneau? in Nome? in Honolulu?

Your State

The location of a state affects its industry and the kind of work people do. Where in the United States is your state located? Is it bordered by any bodies of water? How does your state's location affect its industry? How does it affect the kind of work the people do?

UNIT 8 World Regions: Mountains and Grasslands

Mountains and grasslands are found all over the world. They provide us with beautiful scenery. They also offer us many rich resources.

In this unit you will learn about the resources of mountains and grasslands. You will read about the land, plants, and animals of these regions. You will also read about the people and cities that are found in them.

CHAPTER 15

Mountain Regions

Mount Rainier, Washington

Mountains cover about one fifth of the earth's surface. People have lived in some mountain regions for thousands of years. But only a few plants and animals can live in other mountain regions. In this chapter you will learn about life in some of the mountain areas of the world.

At the end of this chapter, you should be able to:

- ○ Name some of the resources found in mountain regions.
- ○ Name some of the different kinds of plants and animals found in mountain regions.
- ○ Describe how people live in two of the world's mountain regions.
- ● Use latitude and longitude to locate places on a globe.

1 Land and Climate

Mountains are found on every continent. They affect the climate of a region. They also affect the way people live in a region.

A mountain is an area of land that is at least 610 meters (2,000 feet) above the land around it. The lowest part of a mountain is called the **foot**. A **peak** is the pointed top of a mountain. Mountains can have more than one peak. The **summit** is a mountain's highest peak. Valleys are the lower areas between mountains.

Most of the earth's mountains are found in large groups called mountain ranges. Look at the map on this page. It shows the main mountain ranges of the world. Where are mountain ranges found in the United States?

foot
the lowest part of a mountain

peak
the pointed top of a mountain

summit
a mountain's highest peak

Mountain Ranges of the World

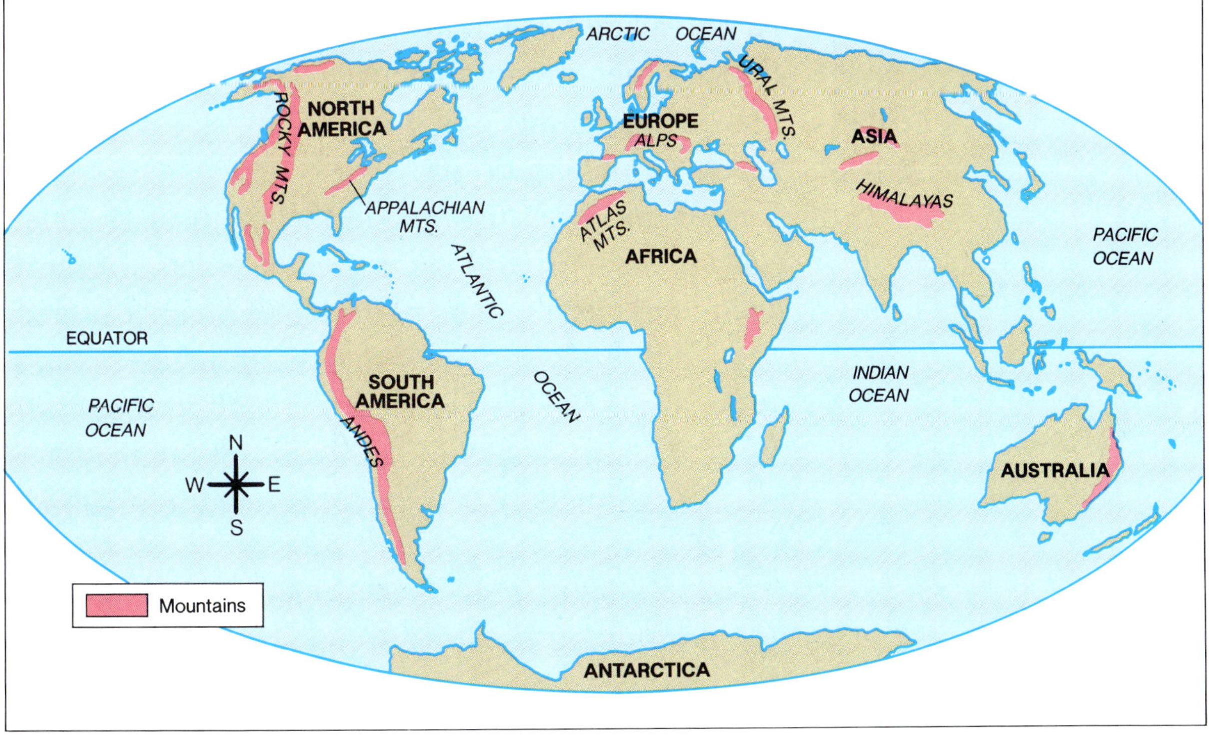

How Mountains Are Formed

magma
the hot, melted rock inside the earth

plate
a section of the earth's crust

Scientists believe that the inside of the earth is made of hot, melted rock, called **magma**. They also believe that only the outer layer, or crust, of the earth is solid. Most scientists think that the crust is divided into sections, or **plates**. These plates rest on top of the magma.

Heat inside the earth causes pressure to build up. Sometimes this pressure causes the magma to move. As the magma moves it presses against or between the plates. In this way the plates move. The movement of plates builds mountains. The Black Hills of South Dakota were formed when the moving magma made bulges in part of a plate.

A Volcano Erupts

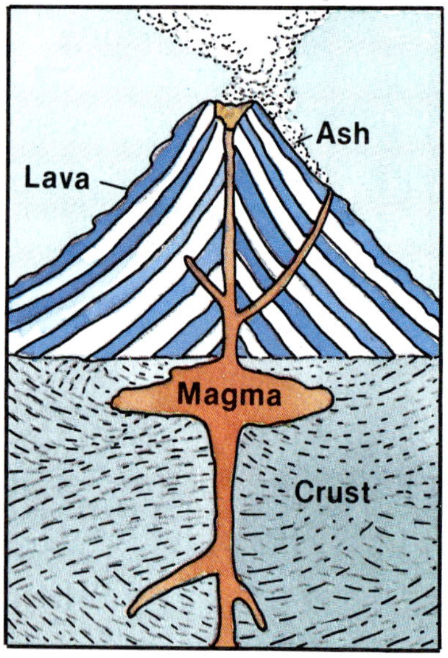

Mountains are also formed when ash and magma break through the surface of the earth. The magma that breaks through the surface is called lava. The opening through which the lava explodes is called a volcano. Over thousands of years cooling lava from a volcano builds up into a mountain. Scientists believe that the Hawaiian Islands were formed from volcanoes on the ocean floor. Other mountains have also formed under the ocean. In fact, long chains of mountains run along the ocean floor.

Heat and pressure inside the earth also cause earthquakes. Earthquakes occur when pressure inside the earth makes plates slide against or past one another. Volcanoes and earthquakes sometimes affect the lives of people living in mountain regions. Earthquakes in the Andes of South America, for example, have often caused much damage and loss of life.

The forces that make mountains are active all the time. And many mountain ranges are still growing.

Mountains and Climate

In Chapter 13 you learned how mountains affect climate. When wind blows over a mountain range, air is pushed up the slopes. As air rises it gets colder. Cold air cannot hold as much moisture as warm air. So this moisture falls as rain or snow. When a moist wind blows from the east, most of the rain falls on the eastern side of the mountain range. The mountains block moisture from reaching the other side. This leaves the western side of the mountains very dry.

How high a mountain range is also affects the climate. The temperature gets colder as you climb up a mountain. Even at the equator it is cold high in the mountains.

(above) A tropical rain forest in Peru (below) Atacama Desert, Chile

The Himalayas (him-uh-**lay**-uhz) are the highest mountains in the world. Mt. Everest, the world's highest peak, is in the Himalayas. Mt. Everest and the other high Himalaya peaks are covered with snow all year.

Weather affects mountains too. The water that falls as rain and snow runs down mountain streams and rivers. It wears away the soil and rock. Wind can break down the rock even more. Where slopes are steep, this erosion happens more quickly.

The higher slopes of mountains are often rockier than the lower slopes. The soil on the higher slopes may be very poor. It is richer and thicker farther down the mountain. People often grow crops or raise animals on the lower slopes.

Mountains and Resources

Many mountain regions contain important resources. The forests of the Rocky Mountains and other mountain ranges are used for lumber. In Chapter 11 you learned that many minerals are also found in the Rockies.

A village in the Urals

Hikers in Great Smoky Mountains National Park, Tennessee

The Ural Mountains have many important minerals too. These mountains form part of the boundary between the continents of Europe and Asia. Some of the minerals mined in the Urals are coal, copper, diamonds, iron ore, and nickel. **Gems** have been mined in the Urals since the 1800's. A gem is a precious stone used to make jewelry.

gem
a precious stone used to make jewelry

Mountain regions are also areas of beautiful scenery. Tourists enjoy visiting many of these regions. The Alps in western Europe are a famous tourist area. People also visit the many national and state parks in the Rocky Mountains of the United States.

Section Review

Write your answers on a sheet of paper.

1. What is magma?
2. What happens when a moist wind blows over a mountain range?
3. Name three resources of mountain regions.
4. Why do you think fewer people live on the higher mountain slopes than on the lower slopes?

2 Plant and Animal Life

The plants and animals that live at the foot of a mountain are often different from those that live much higher up. The climate at the foot of a mountain is often warmer than the climate higher up. Plants and animals that need a warm climate live on the lower slopes. Those that can live in a colder climate live higher up the mountain.

Mountain Plants

Different plants grow best in different places. Some plants need more water. Many plants need certain types of soil. Some plants grow best in the rocky soil of the higher mountain slopes. Others grow best on the lower slopes where the soil is richer.

deciduous tree
a tree that sheds its leaves each fall

In some mountain regions **deciduous** (dih-**sihj**-uh-wuhs) **trees** grow on the lower slopes. A deciduous tree sheds its leaves each fall. The

(left) A tropical forest at the foot of the Himalayas, Nepal
(right) Conifers in winter

Rocky Mountains, Colorado

dead leaves enrich the soil. When the trees lose their leaves, more light can shine onto the forest floor. Then many other smaller plants and bushes can grow.

At higher altitudes **conifers** grow. A conifer is a tree that has cones. It also has thin, needlelike leaves. Conifers have thick bark to protect them from the cold. Conifer roots can take moisture from the soil even when the ground is frozen. Most conifers are **evergreens**. An evergreen tree keeps its leaves all year. Some examples of conifers are pines, firs, spruce, and redwoods.

conifer
a tree that has cones and thin, needlelike leaves

evergreen
a tree that keeps its leaves all year

There is a point very high in the mountains above which trees cannot grow. This point is called the **timberline**. Above the timberline the ground may often be frozen and covered with snow and ice. The soil may be too rocky for any plants to grow. But in some places mosses, grasses, and some flowers are able to grow above the timberline.

timberline
the point on a mountain above which trees cannot grow

Mountain Animals

tropical
hot and wet

Many kinds of animals live in the mountain forests of the world. Animals such as leopards, rhinoceroses, and elephants live in even the highest mountains. The lower slopes of the Himalayas, for example, have a hot and wet, or **tropical**, climate. In these areas you find the same animals and plants that live in tropical forests.

Some animals can live at many levels in the mountains. Animals such as deer, chipmunks, and rabbits feed in mountain meadows. Birds, squirrels, and other small animals eat seeds and buds at different altitudes. Others eat insects. Some animals eat other animals. These include coyotes, bears, weasels, eagles, and mountain lions.

Some animals live high in the mountains only during the summer. Plenty of grass and other food to eat may be found here at this time. But in the winter it is harder to find food at these altitudes. So the animals move to lower levels. Elk and sheep are two animals that live this way.

(left) Mountain lion
(right) Mountain goat

(left) Llamas in Peru (below) A yak in the mountains of Nepal

Some animals live on the highest rocky slopes all year round. Certain things help them live in these places. The feet of mountain goats are shaped to help them climb around on the rocks. Yaks, llamas, alpacas, and other animals have thick, woolly coats to keep them warm.

Some birds that live at high altitudes, such as eagles, are very strong fliers. Their sharp eyes can spot prey far below. A bird must be able to fly down quickly to catch a meal. Then it must fly up again to its nest to feed its young.

Other birds can live high in the mountains because of their small size. They can find homes, food, and protection in the cracks between rocks.

Section Review

Write your answers on a sheet of paper.

1. What are two things that help conifers survive in cold places?
2. What plants can grow above the timberline?
3. Name four animals that live in mountains.
4. Why would elephants not be found on the higher slopes of the Himalayas?

3 The Alps

The Alps are the highest mountains in Europe. Look at the map. Which countries do the Alps run through? These countries make up the Alpine region. This region is famous for its beautiful scenery.

Most of the people of the Alps live in small villages. Many village people herd cows and goats. They move the animals up the mountains to graze in the lush mountain pastures during the summer. In the fall the herds are brought down to the villages. During the long, snowy winter, the herds are fed crops such as hay. These crops have been grown during the summer and stored for winter use.

Cheeses are made from goat's milk and cow's milk throughout the year. Famous cheeses such as Swiss cheese and Italian Gorgonzola (gore-gun-**zoe**-lah) were first made in the valleys of the Alps.

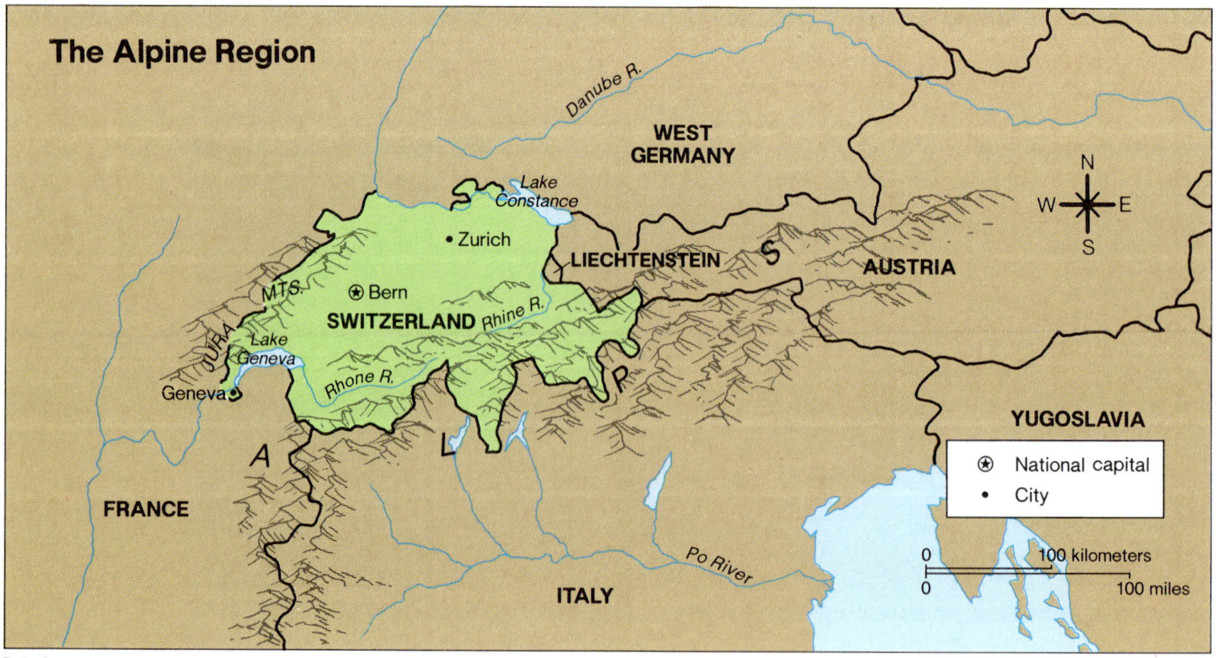

During the winter the cold, snowy climate of the Alps keeps the farmers and herders indoors. But millions of people from other countries come to the Alps in the winter to ski. The warmer summer climate of the Alps melts the snow. During the summer months tourists come to the Alps to hike and climb the high peaks. They also come to view the scenery.

Rain adds to the melting snow during the warmer months and makes many waterfalls. All this water is a good source of power. The water is carried from dams through pipes. It is then used to make electricity.

Switzerland—An Alpine Country

Switzerland is a small country in the middle of the Alpine region. Almost two thirds of the country is covered with mountains. The southern part is in the Alps. The Jura (**joor**-uh) Mountains run along the northwest border with France. The cold climate during winter makes life in the mountains difficult. So most Swiss live on a fertile plateau between the mountain ranges.

Making clothing in Basel, Switzerland

Two of the great rivers of Europe begin in the Swiss Alps. These rivers begin near each other. But the rivers flow in different directions. The Rhine River empties into the North Sea. The Rhone River flows south to the Mediterranean Sea.

The valleys of the Rhine and Rhone rivers are good for farming. Wheat, vegetables, and hay for dairy animals are grown here. Still, Switzerland does not have much farmland. The winters in Switzerland are too cold to grow most crops. Much food must be imported from other countries.

The main food the Swiss can export to other countries is cheese. Swiss cheese can be made at any time of the year. Its special flavor has made it famous.

The Swiss are also famous for the watches and clocks they make. These are made in many small factories. These factories are in the towns and cities between Zurich and Geneva. Most factories use hydroelectric power to run their machinery. This power comes from streams and rivers in the Alps. The mountain waters provide plenty of clean, inexpensive energy for the factories.

Swiss factories make many things besides watches and clocks. Some make fine machinery and tools. Others produce chemicals and textiles. As factories have grown, towns have grown into busy cities around them.

Each large city in Switzerland is different. This is partly because different languages are spoken in different parts of the country. German is spoken in northern and most of eastern Switzerland. Some people in eastern Switzerland speak a language called Romansh (roh-**mahnch**). French is spoken in the western part of the country. Italian is the language of the south.

German is spoken in Zurich (**zoor**-ik). Zurich is Switzerland's largest city. It is also an important banking center. Many factories here make textiles and fine machinery.

Geneva is southwest of Zurich. It is a French-speaking city. Many countries meet in Geneva to discuss world problems.

Bern is the capital of Switzerland. It is near the center of the fertile plateau. Government work is the main activity in this city. But many small watch and tool factories are nearby.

Geneva, Switzerland

The Swiss people work hard to live as well as they do. Work of some sort begins early in life. Most children in Switzerland start school when they are six years old. Both school and work begin at seven o'clock in the morning.

But the Swiss take time off for fun too. Every day most schools and factories stop work from noon until two o'clock. During this time the people take walks or play sports. Then the Swiss return to work or school.

These large chess games are popular in Zurich, Switzerland.

Section Review

Write your answers on a sheet of paper.

1. Through which countries do the Alps run?
2. What do the villagers of the Alps do with their herds of cows in summer?
3. What type of power do Swiss factories use?
4. If you visited Geneva and Zurich, what is the first difference you would notice?

4 The Andes

The Andes extend all along the western side of South America. Look at the map. Follow the Andes through the countries of South America. Notice that the mountain chain is widest in its central section. Here a high plateau separates two ranges of the Andes.

Most moist winds come to northern South America from the east. Rain falls on the east side of the Andes in Peru and Colombia. The west side of the range here is often dry.

An Indian herder with llamas near Cuzco, Peru

In the southern Andes the moist winds come from the west. In southern South America the heavy rains fall on the western mountainsides. The dry lands here are east of the Andes.

Many Indians live in the high Andes. Their houses are simple and are made of mud bricks or stone. There are few schools and no school buses. Students sometimes walk for two hours to get to school.

The Indians grow potatoes, beans, and squash on small farms. These crops have been grown here longer than anywhere else on earth. The Indians are careful when they plant in the thin mountain soil. They do not want the soil to wash away. So they use only hand tools to work with it.

Other Indians care for herds of llamas, sheep, and alpaca. The animals provide milk and meat for food. Wool from these animals is woven into beautiful cloth.

Peru—A Country in the Andes

Peru is on the west coast of South America. It has three different regions. These are the coastal, mountain, and tropical forest regions. The coastal region is a narrow desert. It lies between the Andes and the Pacific Ocean. Almost half of the people in Peru live near the coast. Most of the country's business is done in this region.

The mountain, or sierra (see-**air**-uh), region is where most of the small Indian villages are found. Some villages and towns are higher than 3 kilometers (about 2 miles) in altitude. No trees grow this high in the mountains because the climate is so severe. Even grass is scarce here.

The tropical forest, or selva (sel-**vuh**), region is east of the Andes. This region is hot and wet all year. It is covered with tall trees. Here small Indian tribes live in huts. They get most of their food by hunting animals, gathering fruits, and fishing. The Indians travel on the rivers of the region. These rivers include the Amazon and Ucayali (ook-uh-**yah**-lee) rivers.

Peru has many natural resources. Gold and silver were first mined by the Incas, the Indians who ruled Peru long ago. Now copper, lead, and iron ore are also mined. Oil has been found off the northern coast. It has also been found under the selva region of eastern Peru.

Huge schools of fish are found in the Pacific Ocean off Peru. Tuna are caught and shipped to canneries. They are also sold fresh. Anchovies (**an**-choh-veez) are used to make oil or are canned. These tiny fish are made into fish meal as well. Fish meal is fed to cattle in Peru and other countries.

Fishing for anchovies off the coast of Peru

Hardwood trees are harvested from the selva region of Peru. They are used to make furniture. Other plants are used to produce medicines and rubber.

Only a small portion of the land in Peru is fertile. Still, most of the people work either at farming or herding. In the Andes farmers can produce only enough for themselves. But on the coast there are large irrigated farms. Cotton, rice, and sugarcane are grown on these farms. Farmers on the coast produce enough crops to sell to other countries.

Much of the industry of Peru is found in a few large cities. One of these cities is Lima (**lee**-muh). Lima is the capital of Peru. It is also an important manufacturing center. Over 3 million people live in Lima.

Cuzco, Peru

Cuzco (**koos**-koh) is a small city high in the Andes. It is very different from Lima. Cuzco was the capital of the Inca empire. Some beautifully made Inca buildings still stand in this city.

In the 1500's, the Spanish conquered Cuzco and the Inca empire. Spanish people came to live in Peru. This Spanish population has been very powerful in the government and business of Peru.

A traditional weaver near Cuzco, Peru

Spanish is now the official language of Peru. It is the language of government, business, and trade.

A large part of Peru's population is still Indian. The Spanish taught the Indians about the Catholic religion. Yet the Indians still keep many of their ancient ways. Schools teach reading and writing in Spanish. But some Indians know only their own language, called Quechua (**kech**-oo-wuh).

Many people in Peru have both Spanish and Indian ancestors. These people are called **mestizos** (meh-**stee**-zohs). In the past Spanish people kept the mestizos out of Peru's government and business. However, today mestizos are taking a more active part in running the country.

mestizo
a person who has Spanish and Indian ancestors

Section Review

Write your answers on a sheet of paper.

1. What divides the central section of the Andes?
2. Where do most of Peru's people live?
3. Why do you think it is hard for farmers in the Andes to grow much food?

SOCIAL STUDIES SKILLS

Using Latitude and Longitude

Suppose you were asked to tell where Lima is. One correct answer would be Peru. But there is another way to tell where a place is located.

Mapmakers have created a way of using imaginary lines to help locate places on a map or globe. The equator is an imaginary line that runs east-west around the middle of the globe. Other imaginary east-west lines that are drawn north and south of the equator are called lines of **latitude**, or parallels. Lines of latitude are numbered from 0° to 90°. The lines located north of the equator are labeled **N** for north. The lines located south of the equator are labeled **S** for south. For example, a label for a line of latitude might be 90° N or 90° S.

latitude line
an east-west line drawn parallel to the equator on a globe

Another set of imaginary lines is drawn north-south from pole to pole. These north-south lines are called lines of **longitude**, or meridians. The **prime meridian** is a special line of longitude. It is the starting point for measuring all other lines of longitude. Lines of longitude are numbered from 0° to 180°. Lines located west of the prime meridian are labeled **W** for west. Those east of the prime meridian are labeled **E** for east. For example, a label for a line of longitude might be 90° W or 90° E.

longitude line
a line drawn from north to south from pole to pole on a globe

prime meridian
a special longitude line that is the starting point for measuring all other lines of longitude

When both sets of lines are drawn across a globe or map, they form a pattern called a grid. These lines make it easy to locate places.

Look at the largest globe on page 305. On what line of longitude is San Juan, Peru, located? Ottawa, Canada, is also located along this line. How do you tell them apart? You must name their latitudes as well as their longitudes. San Juan is near 15° S latitude and 75° W longitude. Ottawa is near 45° N latitude and 75° W longitude.

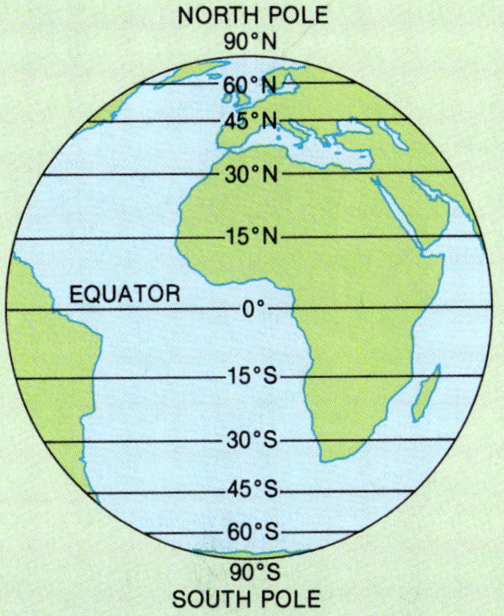

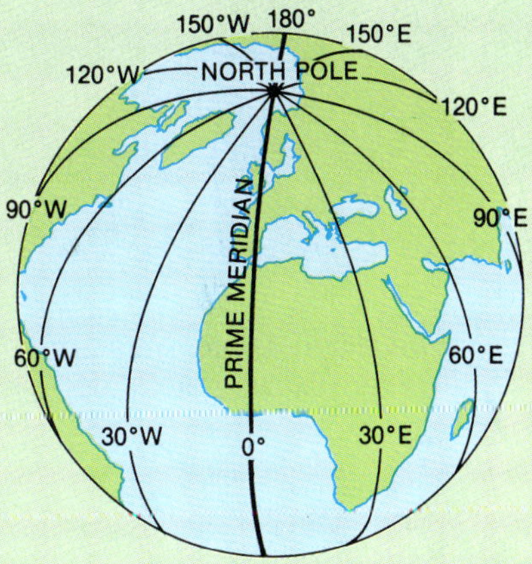

Practice Your Skills

1. What town in Brazil is near 15° S, 60° W?
2. What is the latitude of Salem, Oregon?
3. What is the longitude of New Orleans, Louisiana? Ruidosa, Texas?
4. What is the approximate location of Quito, Ecuador? Anchorage, Alaska?

CHAPTER 16 Grassland Regions

Wheat harvesting, New South Wales, Australia

Most of the food people eat is grown on the world's grassy plains. The flat land, good soil, and moderate climate make them the best land for farming and ranching. In some grasslands many kinds of animals feed on the grasses and other plants that grow there.

At the end of this chapter, you should be able to:

- Describe the kinds of plants and animals that live in grassland regions.
- Describe the ways people use grassland regions.
- List some of the products of grassland regions.

1 Land and Climate

Plains are low, flat land areas. You have read about plains in parts of the United States. Many other parts of the world have plains regions too.

Different types of plants may grow on plains in different regions. The plains you will read about in this chapter are grasslands. A **grassland** is an area where grasses are the main form of plant life. But forests are also found on plains.

grassland
an area where grasses are the main form of plant life

Much of the population of many countries lives on grassland plains. More people live on plains because it is easier to build houses and roads on flat land. The soil is often rich. Grassland plains are good for growing crops.

Types of Grasslands

Most large grasslands are located between forests and deserts. Some are near hot, tropical rain forests. Others are near forests where the climate is **temperate**. Temperate means neither very hot nor very cold.

temperate
neither very hot nor very cold

Prairies are one of the many kinds of grasslands. Prairie soils have thick, dark, fertile upper layers. Deep plant roots hold the soil together. When plants die, the decaying roots provide food for living plants.

The prairie of North America is the largest prairie in the world. Prairie lands are found in other countries too. In South America they are called **pampas** (**pam**-pahs). *Pampas* is the Spanish word for plains. The term pampas refers to the grassy, treeless plains of southern South America. Most of these plains are in central Argentina.

pampa
a grassy, treeless plain of southern South America

The **High Veld** (velt) is the prairie land of southern Africa. The term *veld* comes from a Dutch word for field. The High Veld is at an altitude of 1,200 to 1,800 meters (4,000 to 6,000 feet).

High Veld
the prairie land of southern Africa

Savannas (suh-**van**-uz) are the grasslands of tropical climates. They are usually found between rain forests and drier areas and include some trees as well as grasses. Savannas are in South America, Africa, India, southeast Asia, and northern Australia.

savanna
a grassland of tropical climates

(left) A giraffe on the African savanna (right) Kansas prairie grass

The Russian steppes

Steppes are grasslands that are drier than prairies. But they are not as dry as deserts. The grass on steppes often grows in clumps. The interiors of North America, Europe, and Asia have large steppes.

steppe
a grassland that is drier than a prairie but not as dry as a desert

Grassland Climates

The climate of a grassland area depends partly on how close it is to the equator. Savannas are closest to the equator. So it is hot all year in these grasslands. Most savannas get between 75 and 100 centimeters (30 to 40 inches) of rain a year. Some get less, but some get even more. Savannas have a wet and a dry season. During the wet season the grass is tall and green, but there may be floods. Fires often burn the yellowed grass during the dry season.

Prairies and steppes are found farther away from the equator. They have hot summers and cold winters. Most prairies get from 51 to 89 centimeters (20 to 35 inches) of rain and snow a year. Less rain falls on the steppes. Steppes get 25 to 51 centimeters (10 to 20 inches) of rain each year. Most of the rain in these grasslands falls in summer. So warm days and rainfall make summer the best growing season for plants.

Look at the map on this page. It shows the main grassland regions of the world. Find the prairie of North America. Find the savannas of Africa. What other grasslands do you see? Notice how far each kind of grassland area is from the equator.

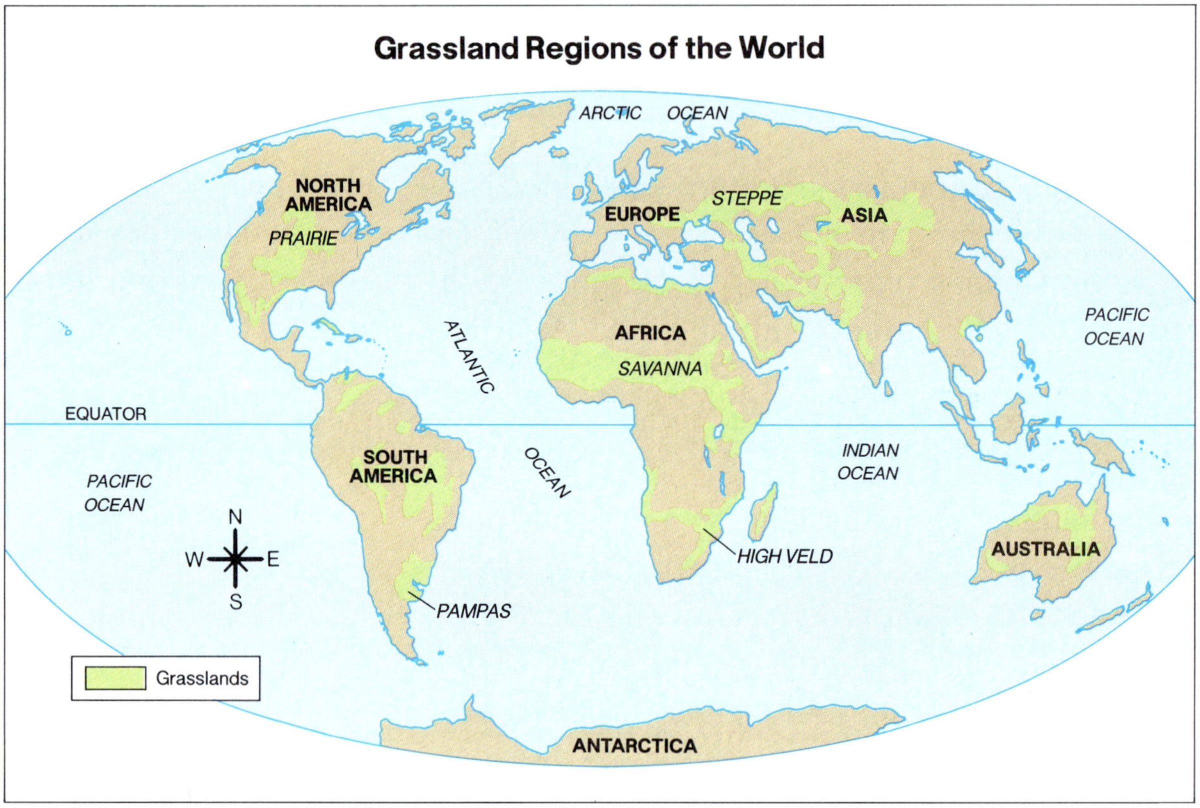

Section Review

Write your answers on a sheet of paper.

1. Name three types of grasslands.
2. What kind of grassland is closest to the equator?
3. How do you think the climate of the savanna of Africa differs from the climate of the Great Plains of the United States?

2 Plant and Animal Life

Grassland plains are much more than flat land with lots of grass. Many different plants and animals live on grasslands. They are homes for many things, from tiny wildflowers to giraffes.

Grassland Plants

Grasses are the main plant life of grasslands. Prairies have thick, tall grass. Many kinds of grasses grow on the prairie. Some grow best in marshy places. Others grow best in drier areas.

Flowers grow on the prairie too. They usually bloom in the spring. They add color to the beautiful scenery. A few woody shrubs also grow on the prairie. The prairie rose is one kind of woody shrub.

Very few trees grow on prairies because it is sometimes too dry. Winters are often too cold. Some trees grow on the North American prairie. But these grow mostly in river valleys. They are cottonwoods, oaks, and willows.

Prairie land is good for farming. Wheat, corn, oats, rice, and other crops are grown on many prairies.

Blooming flowers on the prairie, Illinois

A storm is about to break over this dry riverbed on the savanna of southern Africa.

The steppe areas have shorter grasses than the prairies. The grass is also not as thick. Grains such as wheat, barley, oats, and rye are grown on steppes.

Tall savanna grass is also different from prairie grass. It often grows in clumps. Savanna grasses have large root systems. For this reason they can live through the dry season and fires. The grass grows back quickly once the rains come. But in some areas too many grazing animals have eaten too much of the grass. The grass cannot grow back. So some savanna land is turning into desert.

Unlike the prairie, some trees are found on the savanna. Examples of these are baobabs (**bay**-oh-babz), acacias (uh-**kay**-shuhz), and palms. Many trees on the savanna lose their leaves during the winter dry season.

drought
a long period of time with little or no rain

Overgrazing is not the only problem on some grasslands. Sometimes plowing can cause problems too. After plowing the soil is bare. At this time strong winds can blow the soil away. This is especially true during a **drought** (drout).

Droughts are long periods of time with little or no rain. This happened in parts of the United States during the 1930's.

Grassland Animals

Many of the animals that live on grassland plains are grazing animals. They eat the grasses and other plants. Usually it is easy for them to find food in the rainy season. It is harder in the dry season.

Huge herds of buffalo used to roam the North American prairie. Rabbits, pronghorn, and wild horses still live there. Many birds nest in the thick plants of grassland regions all over the world. Grasshoppers and other insects also thrive. On the African savanna, antelopes, giraffes, zebras, and other animals live as well. Some unusual animals are found on the Australian grasslands. One of these animals is the kangaroo.

Some plains animals are **carnivorous** (kahr-**niv**-uh-rus). This means that they eat other animals. Some carnivorous animals that live on the North American prairie are coyotes, foxes, and hawks. Others, such as lions, cheetahs, and hyenas, live on the African savanna. Wild tigers are found only in Asia. Many tigers live in tropical forests and in mountains. But some live on Asian grasslands.

Animals that are hunted by carnivorous animals have to protect themselves. There are few places to hide in grasslands. So some animals travel in large herds. Many have strong legs and feet. This helps them run fast. Very small animals, such as mice and prairie dogs, hide in holes in the ground called burrows. Very large animals, such as elephants, are protected by their size.

carnivorous animal an animal that eats other animals

A pronghorn buck

Cattle, sheep, and goats are also found in some grassland areas. These animals are raised on ranches. Ranching is an important activity on grasslands because some grasslands are too dry for farming. Ranches on grasslands are usually very large. A lot of land is needed to feed the animals. Some products that come from these animals are meat, wool, and leather.

nomad
a person who has no permanent home

In some parts of Asia and Africa, there is very little plant life in the grasslands near deserts. Here, **nomads** raise herds of sheep, goats, and camels. A nomad is a person who has no permanent home. Nomads travel in search of food for their herds.

Masai cattle traders, Kenya

Section Review

Write your answers on a sheet of paper.

1. Why are there few trees on the prairie?
2. Describe some traits of grassland animals.
3. What is the difference between ranchers and nomads?

3 Grasslands of the Soviet Union

The largest plains in the world are in the Soviet Union. They cover more land area than all of the United States. If these plains were all fertile grasslands, the Soviet Union could grow food for the whole world. But the country lies so far north that much of it is frozen for most of the year. Most of its plains are too cold to be fertile.

Only the steppes in the southwestern Soviet Union are fertile. The rick, dark soil of the steppes is the best farming land in the country. The steppes take up a little more than one tenth of the Soviet Union's land. But most of the country's farm goods come from this region.

Ukrainian farm workers, Soviet Union

The crops of the fertile steppes are grown on large government farms. These farms are much larger than most American farms. The government provides huge tractors to work the farms.

Most workers on government farms are paid wages. These workers do not earn money from the sale of crops, as do farmers in the United States. The crops are sold by people appointed by the government.

Farm workers live in government houses on the farms. They use government schools, doctors, and theaters.

The Soviet government does let workers own half-hectare ($1\frac{1}{4}$ acre) gardens. Farmers work these gardens by hand. They work hard to grow crops they can sell.

Soviet farmers seem to tend their own gardens more carefully than the farms controlled by the government. The gardens make up only 3 percent of the farming land in the Soviet Union. But they produce almost 30 percent of the food.

Whether large or small, the farms of the steppes are the most productive in the Soviet Union. They have helped the country to produce more wheat, barley, rye, potatoes, and sugar beets than any other in the world.

A Look at the Soviet Union

The Soviet Union is the largest country on earth. It is bigger than some continents. It has many different landforms.

The steppes extend from Europe to a plateau in central Siberia. Siberia is a region that covers much of the eastern part of the Soviet Union. The Ural Mountains run north and south across the country. The Urals are old mountains that have been worn down over thousands of years. Other higher mountain ranges are located in the south and in Siberia. The Soviet Union also has deserts in the south. Much of the northern part of the country is a frozen plain.

It is very hard for people to live in the cold northern part of the Soviet Union. In many areas the soil is always frozen. This frozen soil is called **permafrost**. It makes farming impossible. Many of the rivers in the Soviet Union are frozen most of the year. This makes water transport impossible. In some southern areas where it is warmer, very little rain falls. Farmers must get water for their crops from far away.

permafrost
soil that is always frozen

However, the Soviet Union has great natural resources. It has more forests than any other country. Many other resources have helped the Soviet Union to become an industrial nation. The country is the leading producer of coal, iron ore, and oil. It is second in the world in the production of many minerals. Some of these minerals are gold, lead, and nickel.

Winter on the tundra of the Soviet Union

Leningrad, Soviet Union

Moscow is the capital and largest city in the Soviet Union. It is also a transportation center. Textiles, steel, machinery, cars, and trucks are all produced in Moscow.

Leningrad is the best port in the Soviet Union. It is kept free of ice for 10 months of the year. Leningrad is also a center for art, education, and industry. Fine tools, machinery, and ships are made here.

The people of the Soviet Union are from many different cultures. They speak many different languages. But the Soviet government has tried to strictly organize everyone under one system. For example, many of the buildings in Soviet cities are built in the same way. The government provides everyone with food and clothing. But only one kind of a good may be sold in government stores.

The Soviet system often does not work very well. People often cannot get good housing. Shortages of goods are common. There may be only a few different things in a whole market. People must wait in long lines for meat and fresh fruit.

The Soviet government also controls schools throughout the country. Some children go to nursery school and kindergarten. Most children start school when they are seven years old. They stay in school for several hours a day while both parents work. They go to school six days a week. They study Russian as well as the language of their republic, or state. They also study mathematics, science, and music.

At the age of 14, Soviet students can go to a school to learn a trade. Or they can go to a school for gifted children. To enter such a school, they must first pass a test. Older students can then go on to a trade institute or to a university to learn a profession.

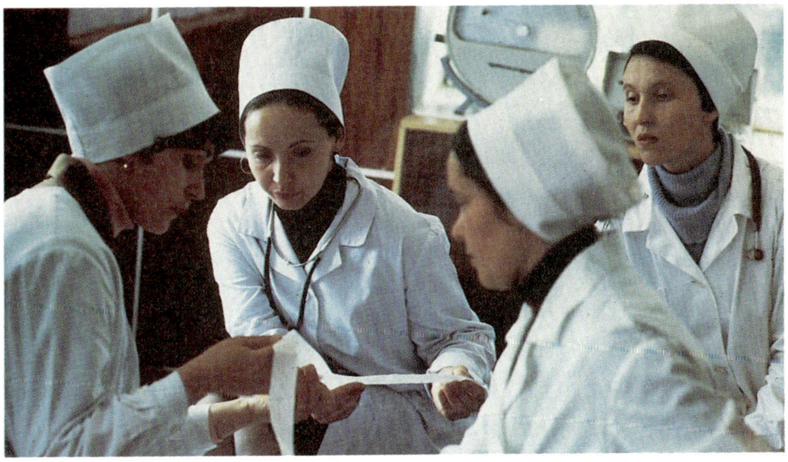

Doctors in a Russian hospital

Section Review

Write your answers on a sheet of paper.

1. Where are the steppes in the Soviet Union?
2. Why are there no farms on the northern plains of the Soviet Union?
3. Compare everyday life in the Soviet Union to life in your community.

FAMOUS PEOPLE

Leo Tolstoy was one of the greatest Russian writers. His two most famous books are *War and Peace* and *Anna Karenina.* He was born in 1828. He was part of a wealthy family. His parents died when he was a child. But he received a good education and studied at a university. Then he spent a few years in the army. While in the army he wrote stories about his home.

Tolstoy believed that the way poor people had to live was unfair. At that time many of the people of Russia were forced to live and work on the large estates of the nobles. Tolstoy freed his own workers. His writings showed an understanding of the suffering of the poor. He wrote about many of the unfair things done by the government and Russian society.

Tolstoy's writings made him well-known. But in 1880, he decided to work in his fields as the farm workers did. In 1890, he gave all his wealth and lands to his family. He accepted no money for the writing he did. Instead, Tolstoy made his living by farming and making shoes. He spent most of his time with the farm workers.

Leo Tolstoy lived the rest of his life simply and peacefully. He lived as he believed everyone should live.

4 The Pampas of Argentina

Look at the map. Find the pampas in the middle of Argentina. Much of the pampas is covered by rich, deep soil. The soil has been washed down from the slopes of the Andes. The pampas soil also includes dust blown onto the land by storms. These storms blow loose soil from the bare plains to the south.

Two kinds of climate are found on the pampas. The western part is dry and hot. Deserts are located here. The eastern part has more rain and cool breezes. The temperature here is comfortable all year. Grass grows in this part of the pampas.

gaucho
a South American cowhand

Most of the ranches and farms of Argentina are on the pampas. Cowhands, or **gauchos** (**gow**-chohz), once herded cattle across the plains. Today tractors plow rich farms.

Argentina— Land of Plains and Mountains

Argentina has five land regions. The Andes Mountains run along the western border of the country. East of this region is the Gran Chaco (grahn **chah**-koh). Stunted trees and patchy grassland cover this rugged region. Few people live here or in the Andes. Most people in Argentina live and work in the pampas region.

Farmland in Argentina

A region called Mesopotamia (mes-uh-puh-**tay**-mee-uh) lies between the Paraná (par-uh-**nah**) and Uruguay (**oor**-uh-gwy) rivers. Mesopotamia means "between rivers." This region has dense forests and grasslands.

Patagonia (pat-uh-**goh**-nee-uh) is a windy, dry region in southern Argentina. Much of the land is not fertile. The soil has been blown away. Few plants can grow here. However, South American Indians live among lakes near the Andes.

Each land region of Argentina has a different climate. The Gran Chaco and Mesopotamia are closest to the equator. So the climate in these regions is hot. Mesopotamia has tropical storms all year. The pampas has warm summers and mild, cool winters. Enough rain falls in this region for many crops to grow.

Patagonia is far from the equator, so it is cool all year. Much of this region is dry. However, some rain falls near the Andes. The whole Andes region is cold and wet or snowy all year.

La Casa Rosada in Buenos Aires houses the office of Argentina's president and other government offices. Guards protect the entrance to this building.

Argentina has a number of different resources. Oil and gas are found in Patagonia and the Gran Chaco. Lumber comes from Mesopotamia. The Andes region is rich in undeveloped resources of coal and minerals. But Argentina's greatest resource is the fertile soil of the pampas. Much of the land can be farmed year after year. Nothing is needed to make the soil richer.

Various types of animals and crops are raised on the pampas. These animals and crops are used to make many different products. Cattle and sheep provide meat products and leather goods. Sheep are also a source of wool. Cotton is grown on huge farms on the pampas. Wool and cotton are sent to textile mills to be made into cloth. Wheat is grown in huge amounts. It is one of the main exports of Argentina. Corn, barley, and rye are also grown for trade.

Buenos Aires (**bway**-nohs **i**-rays) is the most important city on the pampas. Buenos Aires is also the capital and largest city in Argentina. Several good ports have been dug in the Río de la Plata (**ree**-oh deh lah **plah**-tah), the river that flows past Buenos Aires. Ships are loaded with the many goods from farms and ranches on the pampas. These goods are sold all over the world.

Ships unloading in a harbor at Buenos Aires, Argentina

Factories in Buenos Aires make many things by using the resources of the pampas. Paper mills and car factories are also found near the city. Buenos Aires has beautiful parks and buildings, as well as industry. It is a center for art and music. Students from all over Latin America study at Buenos Aires University.

Rosario (roh-**zahr**-ee-oh) is the second largest city in Argentina. It is farther inland, on the Paraná River. Trains bring wheat, hay, and meat from the western pampas to export through Rosario. Farm equipment is brought up the Paraná River to Rosario. It is then taken to farms in the pampas.

The people of the cities and countryside of Argentina are mostly of Spanish and Italian descent. Some American Indians live in the southern mountains.

Some of the Spanish and Indians in Argentina are descendents of gauchos. The gauchos were among the early settlers of the pampas. They were good horse riders. They were able to withstand the rough life of the open plains. The gauchos wore special clothes. They wore loose

A gaucho rounding up cattle on the pampas, Argentina

pants that were tucked into their boots. They also wore round, flat hats. The gauchos often wrapped wide belts or sashes around their waists. These belts had silver sewn through them. Wool **ponchos** (**pon**-chohz), or capes, kept them warm and dry. A rope with a ball attached to each end was used as a lasso. Such a rope was called a **bola** (**boh**-lah).

poncho
a wool cape

bola
a rope with a ball attached to each end, used as a lasso

Today few people in Argentina wear clothes like those of a gaucho. In school, for example, students dress much as do students in the United States. School is free for all students up to the age of 19. Most people in Argentina can read and write. At 14 boys and girls may go to a trade school to learn a skill. Or they may go to schools to prepare for college. Several large universities are found in the cities of Argentina.

Section Review

Write your answers on a sheet of paper.

1. What is Argentina's greatest resource?
2. What did a gaucho use for a lasso?
3. Name products you use that might have been made from animals and crops raised on the pampas.

Close-up on

Inca Stonework Long before Europeans came to the Americas, the Incas of Peru had a great civilization. They built roads, palaces, and waterways out of stone. These structures lasted for hundreds of years.

The Incas did not know how to use the wheel. But they still were able to move huge blocks of granite stone. They shaped the stone with tools made of stone harder than granite. The shaped pieces of granite fit together very well. No cement or mortar was needed to make walls. Even after many earthquakes, some of the Inca stone buildings are still standing.

Some of the stone roads built by the Incas are also still used today. They are found in parts of Peru and Bolivia. The roads were built so that Inca soldiers could march several across. This allowed the soldiers to move more quickly than their enemies. The other armies had to march in single file on narrow, winding paths.

the World

The Incas knew how to prepare for the heavy tropical rains. Inca roads were made so they would drain water quickly. Rope bridges were also built high over the Andes rivers. This kept the bridges from being washed away.

The Incas also knew how to help the dry parts of their land. They built long, stone canals. These canals carried water from the mountains to farms along the coast. Parts of these canals are still used today.

The Incas were known to be strict rulers. Their stonework has a stern look to it. But art work made of other than stone shows that the Incas also had a sense of humor. Much of the drawing on their pottery shows that joy and laughter were important to the Incas.

UNIT REVIEW

Word Work

Write the sentences below on a sheet of paper. Fill in the blanks with the correct words from the list.

timberline peak savanna permafrost

1. The pointed top of a mountain is its ____.
2. Soil that is always frozen is called ____.
3. Trees cannot grow above the ____.
4. The ____ is the grassland of tropical climates.

Knowing the Facts

Write your answers on a sheet of paper.

1. How does the weather affect mountains?
2. Why do fewer plants grow on the upper slopes than on the lower slopes of mountains?
3. How have people used much of the world's prairie and steppe land?
4. Compare the resources of the Soviet Union with those of Argentina.

Using What You Know

Choose one of the following activities to do. Follow the instructions given here.

1. Make a poster that shows the animals that live in one of the regions discussed in this unit.
2. Pretend you are a Swiss student from Zurich on a visit to Argentina. Write a letter home telling about how life in Argentina is different from life in your homeland.

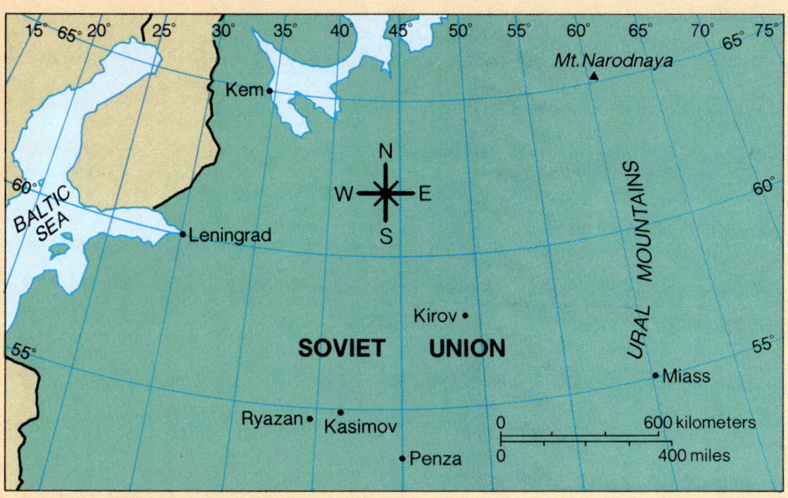

Skills Practice

Use the above map to answer the questions below. Write your answers on a sheet of paper.

1. At what latitude is Kasimov? Kem?
2. Along what longitude are the Ural Mountains? Near what longitude is Penza? Kirov?
3. What is located at 65° N, 60° E? What is near 55° N, 40° E?
4. What is the location of Leningrad? Miass?

Your State

More people live on the pampas of Argentina than live in the Andes. More people live on the plateau of Switzerland than high in the Alps. In what area or areas of your state do most of the people live? What resources or industries draw them there? Does the climate have any effect on why many people live in these areas?

UNIT 9 World Regions: Deserts and Forests

You may think of deserts and forests as being very different. One kind of region is bare and open. The other is crowded with very large plants. But both deserts and forests are rich in their own ways.

In this unit you will learn about the plant and animal life of deserts and forests. You will read about the people who live in deserts and forests. You will also learn how the resources of these regions are used.

CHAPTER 17

Desert Regions

Damascus, Syria

Deserts are usually described as hot, dry, sandy places where nothing can grow. But many kinds of plants and animals live in deserts. They must be very good at making a little bit of water go a long way.

People live in deserts too. In this chapter you will learn about some of the plants, animals, and people in deserts.

At the end of this chapter, you should be able to:

- ○ Describe some of the plant and animal life of deserts.
- ○ List some of the products of desert regions.
- ○ Describe how different people live in the desert.

1 Land and Climate

Not all deserts are alike. Some deserts are hotter than others. More rain falls in some deserts than in others. How hot or wet a desert is depends on where it is located.

Find the equator on the map on this page. Deserts that are closest to the equator are the hottest. Ones farthest from the equator are the coldest. The coldest deserts are near the North and South poles. Find these deserts on the map. Moisture falls on these deserts mainly as snow. However, as little as 0.5 to 2.5 centimeters (0.2 to 1 inch) of rain or snow may fall in a year! Low altitude deserts, such as the Sahara (suh-**har**-uh), are hotter than high altitude deserts, such as the Gobi (**goh**-bee).

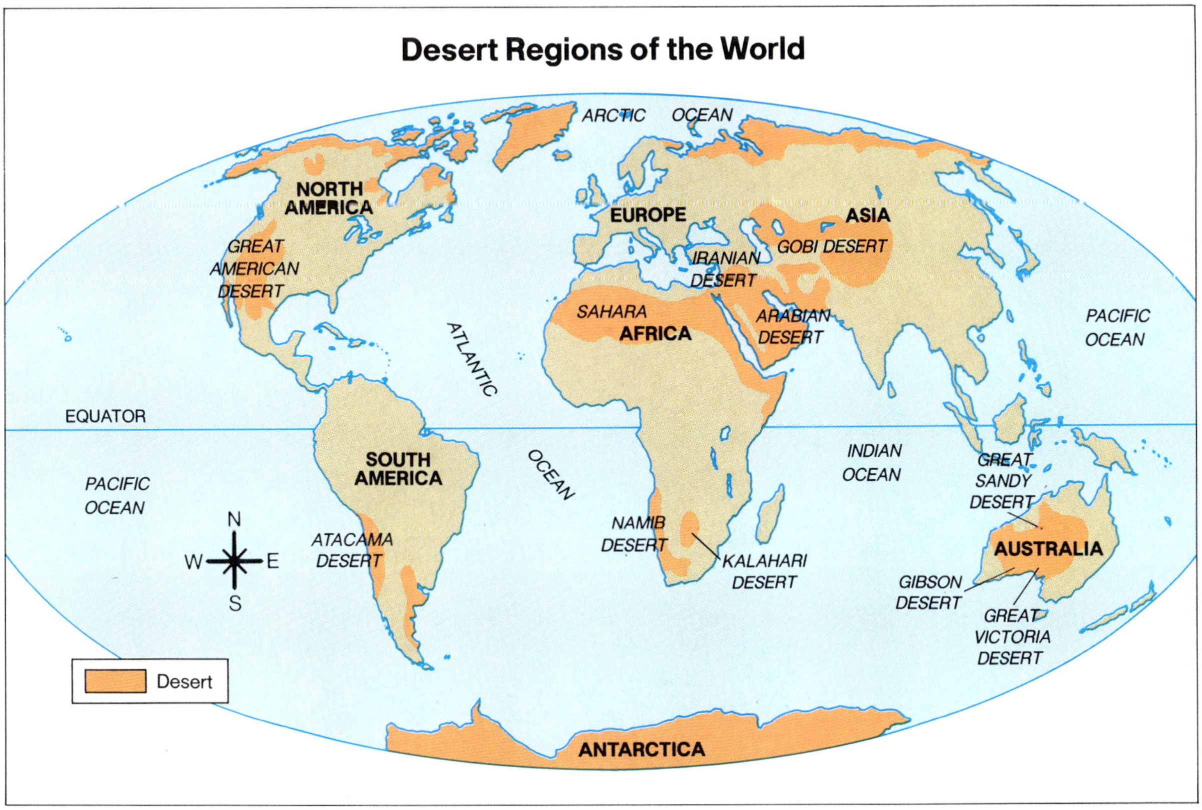

Desert Climates

Deserts have winter and summer seasons. The coldest deserts have long, dark, cold winters. They have short, barely warm summers.

Some deserts are very hot. But the dry desert air does not hold heat. At night the temperature can drop as much as 38° C (100° F)!

Deserts have wet and dry seasons too. But deserts get less than 25 centimeters (10 inches) of rain a year.

Why are deserts so dry? Some deserts are found on the dry sides of mountain ranges. Others are near the middle of a continent. Winds pick up moisture mainly over the oceans. By the time these moist winds reach inland deserts they are dry. And the air above the deserts is usually too dry for rain clouds to form.

Sometimes rain does fall in the desert. But the air is so hot and dry that any falling rain dries up quickly. A light rain might dry up before it hits the

An arroyo on the Black Rock Desert, Nevada

These tanks in Saudi Arabia are used to store oil.

ground. However, a heavy rain might cause flooding. This happens because the ground cannot soak up all the rain at once. Much of the water flows away quickly. The fast-moving flood water washes away some of the rocks, sand, and soil. This creates ditches called **arroyos** (uh-**roy**-ohs).

Wind can affect deserts too. It often blows desert sand into piles. These sandy hills are called **dunes**.

arroyo
a ditch formed by flood water

dune
a sandy hill formed when wind blows sand into piles

Resources and Desert Life

Some deserts contain precious resources. Much of the world's oil is found in deserts. The Arabian and Iranian deserts have rich oil fields. Copper is found in the desert area of northern Chile. Some other minerals found in deserts are iron ore, silver, and gold.

It is difficult to live in a desert. But nomads have lived in some deserts for thousands of years. The Berbers (**bur**-burz) of North Africa herd sheep and goats. Some desert nomads use camels, llamas, horses, or other animals to carry their goods. The natives of the Australian desert live by hunting and gathering their food. They eat roots, fruits, insects, reptiles, and other animals.

Cairo, Egypt

oasis
a place in the desert with enough water for many plants to grow

Not all desert people are nomads, however. Permanent settlements in the desert have been started in places where water is always found. Such a place is called an **oasis** (oh-**ay**-sus). An oasis is a place in the desert with enough water for many plants to grow. One city that has grown at an oasis is Cairo (**ky**-roh), Egypt. The Nile River provides the area with water throughout the year. People have been growing crops along the Nile banks for thousands of years.

In some parts of the deserts, water is found deep under the ground. Sometimes the water rises to the surface in a spring. In other places people can dig wells to reach it. If the amount of water is large enough and the soil is fertile, crops can be grown in the desert.

Section Review

Write your answers on a sheet of paper.

1. Why are deserts cold at night?
2. What is an arroyo?
3. Why do you think desert areas with water have larger populations than other desert areas?

2 Plant and Animal Life

The desert is a hard place for people to live. But plants and animals are found in even the driest parts of a desert. They have certain traits that help them live without much water.

Desert Plants

Desert plants have root systems that let them live in dry places. Some have roots that stretch out far around them to gather as much moisture as possible. Others have very deep roots that can reach water far under the ground. Some mesquite (meh-**skeet**) roots go down more than 12 meters (40 feet)!

Other plants have thick roots that store water. Cactuses have thick stems that store water after a rain. These plants do not lose water through their leaves as other plants do. They have no leaves. The leaves of **succulents** (**suhk**-yuh-luhnts) store water just as cactus stems do. A succulent is a plant with thick, waxy, or leathery leaves. The waxiness helps hold moisture in the leaves. The yucca (**yuhk**-uh) is a succulent.

succulent
a plant with thick, waxy, or leathery leaves

Mesquite trees, Death Valley, California

Desert tree in bloom, Namibia

Some desert trees and bushes simply lose their leaves when it is dry for a very long time. These desert plants are still alive. But they do not grow larger during dry times. One such plant is the creosote (**kree**-uh-soht) bush.

Still other desert plants sprout from seed only when there is water. They have tough seeds that may last for years. When it rains, the seeds sprout. Soon the plants bloom, grow seeds, and die. All this may happen in only two weeks! Some of the seeds are eaten by animals. But some lie in the ground until the next rain.

Very few plants are found in cold deserts. Most of the water is frozen, so plants cannot use it. But during the short summer, mosses, grasses, and some flowering plants can grow.

People have irrigated some warmer desert land. Farmers grow cotton in California deserts. Alfalfa is grown in the desert of Nevada. Wheat is grown in the Arabian Desert. Dates and other crops are grown in many other desert areas.

Desert Animals

Animals need water just as plants do. They must keep their bodies from getting too hot. Some animals are small. Their bodies lose heat quickly. Many desert animals live in burrows. The air is cool and damp in a burrow. Some desert animals, such as scorpions, stay in their burrows during the day. They come out at night to hunt.

Other desert animals, such as lizards, hunt smaller animals during the day. But they stay in the shade during the hottest hours. Some, such as the ground squirrel, sleep, or **hibernate**, during the hottest part of the year. At this time their body temperatures drop. Their breathing and pulse rates slow down.

hibernate
to spend winter or summer sleeping

Some desert animals can stand high body temperatures and the lack of water. Antelopes, certain birds, and camels are examples of such animals. Camels sweat very little. This allows them to go a long time without water. The scaly skin of reptiles keeps them from losing water quickly. Ostriches can drink salty water. Their bodies have a way of getting rid of the extra salt. The American mourning dove can fly long distances to find water.

Many animals get moisture from the food they eat. Some birds and spiders eat juicy insects. Kangaroo rats and gerbils get water from seeds and other dry foods. Other animals get water from the plants they eat.

King penguin colony, South Georgia, Antarctica

Cold deserts do not have as much animal life as do hot deserts. Penguins live near the shore in Antarctica. They depend on the sea for food. Some types of ducks and **ptarmigans** (**tahr**-mih-gunz) live near the Arctic Ocean. A ptarmigan is a type of bird with feathered feet. It is found in mountainous and cold regions. Other birds, such as geese, loons, and falcons, nest near the Arctic Ocean during the summer.

ptarmigan
a type of bird with feathered feet, found in mountainous and cold regions

Many animals graze on the spring and summer plants in the Arctic. Some of these are caribou, reindeer, and musk ox. Arctic polar bears eat fish and seals. Wolves prey on other animals. In the winter the fur of Arctic foxes and hares turns white. The white fur helps to hide these animals from other animals.

Section Review

Write your answers on a sheet of paper.

1. What is the main problem of desert plants?

2. How do animals get water in a desert?

3. How is a cactus like a camel?

3 The Kalahari Desert of Africa

The Kalahari (kal-uh-**hah**-ree) Desert is in southern Africa. Sand dunes are found in the southwest Kalahari. In the northern and eastern parts, some grasses and deep-rooted trees can grow. The eastern part has the best soil.

The summer in southern Africa is very hot. Heavy rains may fall at this time. The dry winter has cold nights and sometimes droughts.

Some pastures and farms are on the eastern side of the desert. But even the eastern part of the desert is often too dry for most plants to grow. A dry year can kill the crops and livestock.

The people of the Kalahari have learned to live with the harsh, dry climate. Two groups of people who live in the Kalahari are the San, or Bushmen, and the Hottentots (**haht**-en-tahts). Both of these groups have lived here for hundreds of years.

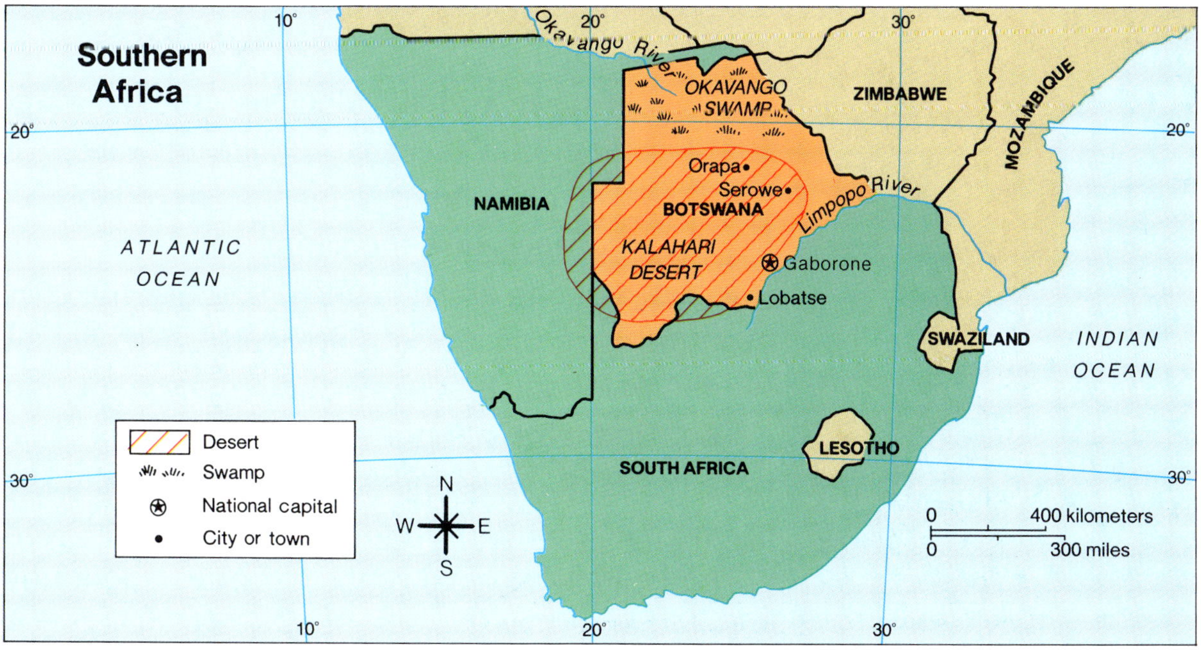

San cave painting, South Africa

The San are nomadic hunters and food gatherers. They move when they need to find water and food supplies. They live in small grass shelters. The San build these shelters out of grasses and other materials found nearby. They abandon the shelters when they move to a new place.

The San have a great talent for finding water. It might seem that there is no sign of water. Yet the San can often find water just by pushing a hollow reed deep into the sandy soil.

In the past San artists painted some of the most beautiful cave paintings in the world. We can still see the paintings that were done many years ago.

The Hottentot people are nomads too. They raise herds of cattle and sheep. They usually stay in one place longer than the San.

The Hottentots have very clear rules about how people should treat each other. Each member of a family must treat the other family members in certain ways. Everything from water to cattle is shared. Their rules help the Hottentots to live in peace with each other.

Botswana—A Country in the Kalahari

Find Botswana (bot-**swah**-nuh) on the map on page 341. Note that most of the country is covered by the Kalahari Desert. Botswana is in a large, level basin. Low, rocky hills are in eastern Botswana. The only large lakes found in the country are dry most of the year. The only big rivers run along the north and east borders. The largest river in Botswana is the Okavango (oh-kuh-**vang**-oh). This river branches out and disappears into a swamp.

The climate of Botswana is dry all year. It is very hot in the summer and mild in the winter. Since Botswana is south of the equator, its summer comes when the United States has its winter. Its winter comes when the United States has its summer.

The dry desert of Botswana has valuable resources. Diamonds, coal, copper, and nickel are mined in the east-central part of the country.

In some parts of Botswana there are farms. But the soil is often too poor for farming. Most of the people herd cattle, sheep, and goats. They move when the pasture land or water gives out. Good pasture land is found among the eastern hills of the country, such as near Serowe (suh-**roh**-ee). Some meatpacking and leather production is done in towns such as Lobatse (loh-**bat**-see). But often the herds are used for both food and clothing by the people that tend them. Nothing is wasted. Little is left to trade with others.

The National Assembly meets in this building in Gaborone, Botswana.

Some trading does take place in Botswana's tribal towns. These towns also have small schools. Often the children learn as much from the work and the music of their tribes as they do in school. They grow up close to their families. They always help tend their families's herds.

In some modern cities, such as Gaborone (gahb-uh-**roh**-nee), life is different. Here children can go to one of several schools. Paved streets, buildings, and businesses are found in the city. The growing mining towns, such as Orapa (ohr-**ah**-puh), also have schools and shops. They are very much like modern towns all over the world.

Section Review

Write your answers on a sheet of paper.

1. In what part of the Kalahari are pastures and farms found?
2. How do the San reach underground water?
3. Compare how a child in a city and a child in a tribal town learn their ways of life.

4 The Gibson Desert of Australia

Look at the map. Find the Gibson Desert. It is between the Great Sandy Desert and the Great Victoria Desert. These deserts are on the Western Plateau. One road crosses the Gibson Desert. It is so straight that it is called the "Gunbarrel."

Only small shrubs and grasses grow on the desert. The few lakes turn into dry, salty basins during droughts.

Droughts are common on the Gibson Desert. The average rain per year is less than 25 centimeters (10 inches). Sometimes no rain falls for three years or more. Some of the deserts of Australia are windy and dust-blown. But the Gibson has little wind. During winter the weather is mild.

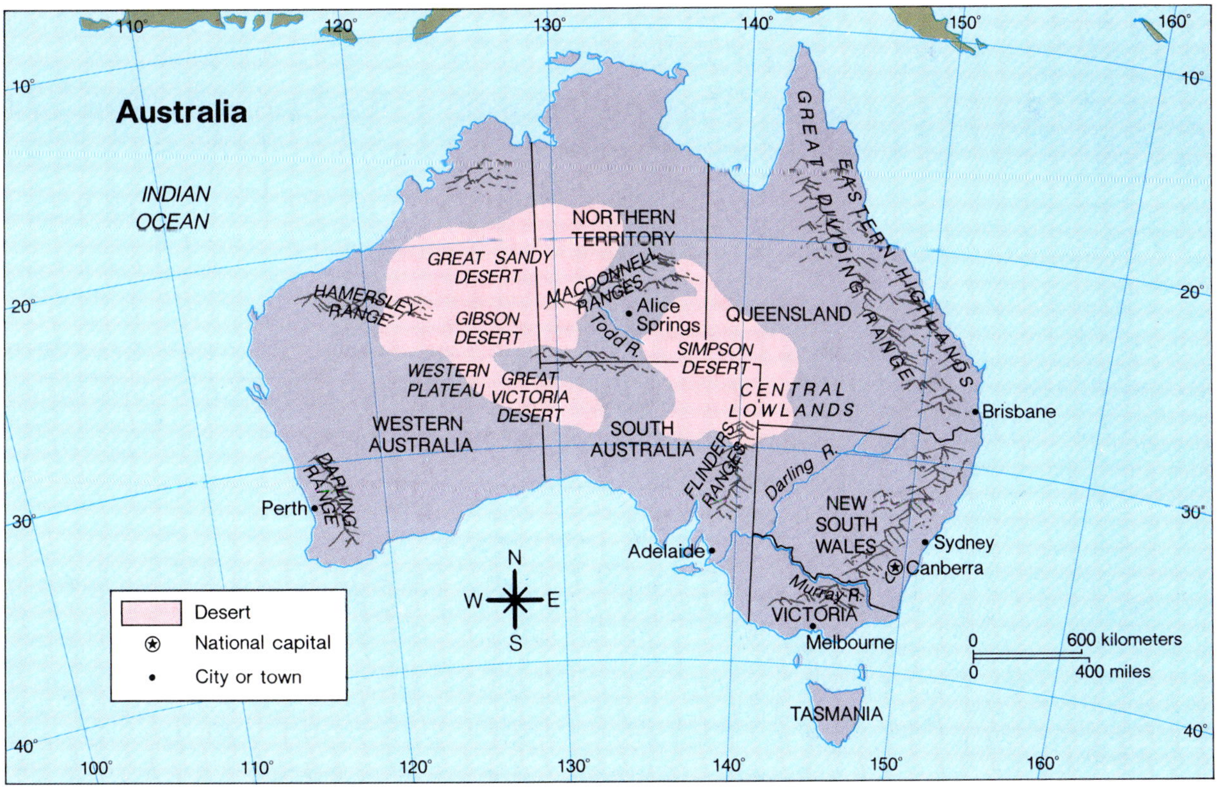

Australian Aborigines with boomerangs

No people live in the center of the Gibson Desert. There is no water there. But near the eastern edge of the desert some water can be found. This is where the **Aborigines** (ab-uh-**rij**-un-neez) live. The Aborigines were the first people to live in Australia. They had been living in central Australia for thousands of years before the Europeans arrived.

Aborigines
the first people to live in Australia

The Aborigines hunt desert animals. They also seek out rare plants with roots that can be eaten. Most important, the Aborigines are very skilled at locating water in the desert.

The Aborigines use a variety of spears, nets, and traps to hunt animals. They also use a special weapon called a **boomerang** (**boo**-muh-rang). Boomerangs are curved or bent throwing sticks. Some boomerangs are made to return to the thrower.

boomerang
a curved or bent throwing stick

Today not many Aborigines still live in the desert. Many have gone to government schools. Some have found jobs on ranches. Others have moved to Australia's cities and learned modern ways of life.

A Look at Australia

Australia is a country in the Southern Hemisphere. It is also a continent.

The continent has three main land regions. The Eastern Highlands rise from a narrow plain on the coast up to mountain ranges. This part of Australia is green with grass and forests. Most of the rivers of the country are in this region.

The Central Lowlands are flat grasslands. They stretch from the west side of the mountains to the center of the continent.

The Western Plateau is almost completely flat and dry. It is higher than the central part of the country. The land is mostly sandy or rocky. In the southwestern corner grass and trees grow.

Long, dry summers are common in many parts of Australia. Most of the country has mild weather in the winter. Only a few of the mountains in the east get snow.

This mild climate is good for farming. If water is available, good crops can be grown. Rich soil and fine pasture land are found in the wetter eastern and southern parts of Australia. Australians raise many farm animals and crops in these areas. Wool, meat, cotton, and wheat are exported to other countries.

Rounding up cattle, New South Wales, Australia

bauxite
an ore used to make aluminum

Australians make use of the many other rich resources of their continent. They mine coal, copper, gold, iron, and lead for export. **Bauxite** (**bawk**-syt) is also mined. This ore is used to make aluminum.

Many of Australia's goods are shipped from the port of Sydney. It is the best port in the country. Sydney is a major city in eastern Australia. It is also the oldest and largest city in the country. Large factories in Sydney make food, cars, and textiles. The city is a center for art and music too.

Alice Springs is a much smaller city than Sydney. It is found on the eastern edge of the Western Plateau. This is near the center of the continent. Highways and railroad lines connect Alice Springs with the northern and southern coasts. Miners and ranchers go to Alice Springs for supplies. Tourists visit in winter to enjoy the warm, dry weather. They hold a boat race called "Henly-on-the-Todd." The Todd River is always dry at race time. So people pick up the boats and carry them down the riverbed!

Sydney Opera House, Sydney, Australia

Surfers at Bondai Beach, Sydney, Australia

Water for real boating is found on the coasts of Australia and on the rivers of the southeast. Australians can enjoy water sports all year because of the mild weather. Many people enjoy soccer, golfing, cycling, and hiking.

Most students can walk or ride bicycles to school during the winter months of April through September. They attend free public schools from the age of 5 until 15. If a student works hard, he or she can also go to a fine high school and a university free.

Most Australians are descendants of English and Irish immigrants. These immigrants began to arrive in Australia about 200 years ago. Today the language and ways of life in Australia are much like those of the United States.

Section Review

Write your answers on a sheet of paper.

1. Which deserts are to the north and south of the Gibson Desert?
2. How do the Aborigines hunt in the desert?
3. Where do you think most Australians live? Why?

CHAPTER 18 Forest Regions

Bamboo forest, Honshu, Japan

Trees grow on almost every continent. They grow where it is hot and rainy. They grow where it is cold and snowy. Certain trees are the largest living things on earth.

Some plants and animals that live in forests can live nowhere else. There are even people whose way of life depends on the forest. Forests give us many things, from house materials to maple syrup.

At the end of this chapter, you should be able to:

- ○ Describe and locate the different kinds of forests.
- ○ Explain why forests are important to people and to other living things.
- ● Read a population density map.
- ○ Identify some of the products of forests.

1 Land and Climate

Different kinds of forests grow in different climates. An evergreen forest can grow in a cold climate. A deciduous forest needs a warmer climate.

The soil of a forest region also helps to determine the trees that will grow. Some forests have richer soil than others. The soil in deciduous forests is often more fertile than the soil in evergreen forests. The soil of any forest region, however, is less rich than the soil of a grassland region.

The climate and soil of a forest region determine the kinds of trees that will grow. They also influence the way of life of the people who live there.

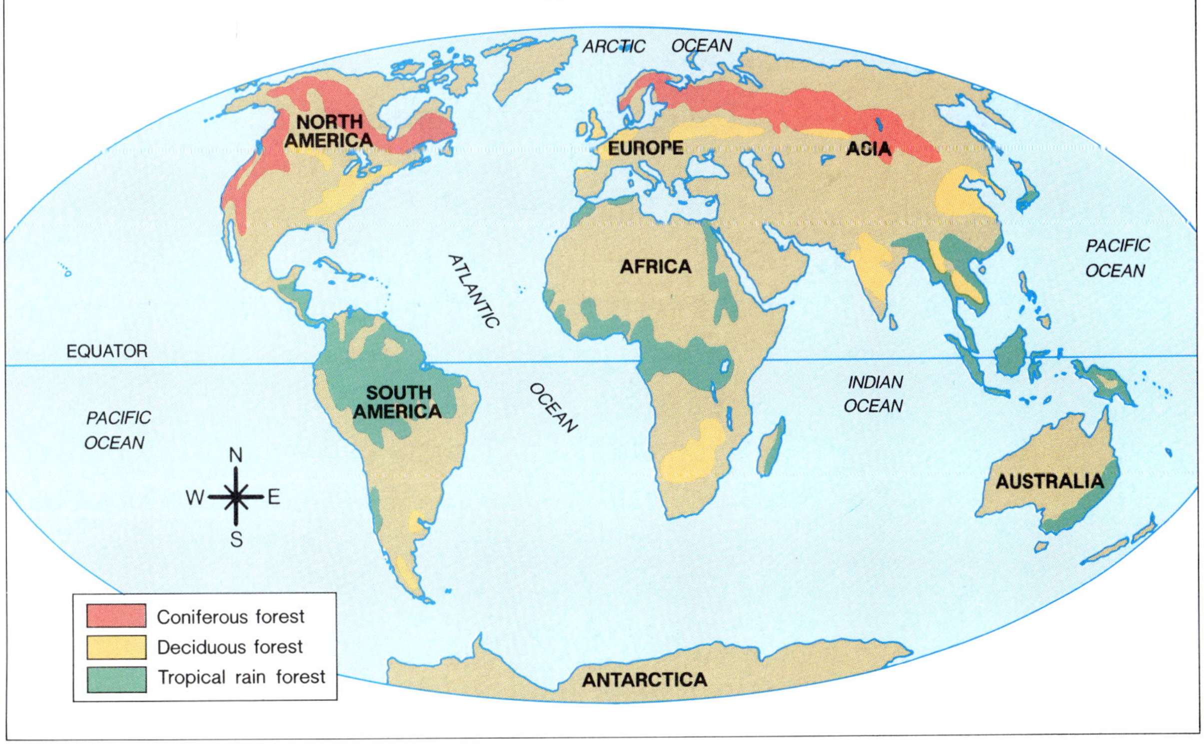

Forest Regions of the World

Near a forest of conifers, Sinkiang, China

Types of Forest Regions

Northern forests are those that grow closest to the North Pole. In a northern forest, the average high temperature is less than 0° C (32° F). Between 25 and 50 centimeters (10 and 20 inches) of rain falls in a year.

Northern forests are made up of conifers. These trees grow well in cold climates. Forests of conifers are found across the northern plains of North America, Europe, and Asia. Conifers also grow on the high mountain slopes of these continents. In the United States conifers are found in the Rocky Mountains. They also grow in the Sierra Nevada in California and the mountains of the Pacific Northwest region.

Farther south forests of deciduous trees can grow. In a deciduous forest, the average high temperature for six months of the year is at least 10° C (50° F). At least 40 centimeters (16 inches) of rain falls in a year. The richest deciduous forests in North America are found in the central Appalachian Mountains.

broadleaf tree
a tree with flat, wide leaves

Deciduous forests are sometimes called broadleaf forests. A **broadleaf tree** has flat, wide leaves. Most deciduous trees are broadleaf trees. But some broadleaf trees are evergreens. Broadleaf forests are found in Europe and Asia. Smaller broadleaf forests grow in Africa, South America, and eastern Australia.

Tropical rain forests grow mostly between $23\frac{1}{2}$° N latitude and $23\frac{1}{2}$° S latitude. Rain forest temperatures range from 20° C to 34° C (68° F to 93° F). At least 200 centimeters (79 inches) of rain falls in a year. More kinds of trees can grow in tropical rain forests than in other forests. Most of these trees are broadleaf evergreens.

Tropical rain forest, Brazil

The Amazon rain forest in South America is the largest such forest in the world. Tropical rain forests also grow in central Africa and southeast Asia.

How Forests Are Used

At one time, forests covered over half the world. Now they cover less than a third. People have always used forests. They use the trees for lumber. In many places wood has been the main fuel for cooking and heating.

Trees have also been cut and burned to make room for farmland. Cutting and burning has usually been done in broadleaf forests. The soil and climate in these forests is often good for farming. In northern forests the soil is too poor for farming. Also, the climate is not warm enough for crops to grow well.

Trees must be cut and burned to farm in a tropical rain forest. Even so, the thin soil remains fertile for only a few years. So farmers must move often. For this reason tropical rain forests can support only small populations.

Planting a pine seedling in a burned forest

When too many trees are cut or burned in one place, the soil can wash away easily. Many of the world's forests have been damaged because soil has washed away. But people are beginning to take better care of forest regions. The study of managing forest resources is called **forestry**.

forestry
the study of managing forest resources

Forests are more than a source of wood. They soak up rain and provide a source of water for streams, lakes, and wells. They also supply the earth with much of its oxygen. All animals need oxygen to breathe.

Forests provide homes for many plants and animals. And they are important places of recreation for people. Forests are valuable resources. They must be protected and used wisely.

Section Review

Write your answers on a sheet of paper.

1. What kinds of trees grow in the coldest climates?

2. Where is the world's largest tropical rain forest?

3. Why is forestry so important?

2 Plant and Animal Life

Plants other than trees grow in the forest regions of the world. They differ from one region to the next. The animal life of the forest regions also varies from place to place. A variety of plants and animals are found in nearly all parts of a forest.

Forest Plants

Forests have five different layers. The tops of the tallest trees make up the highest layer. This is where the trees have most of their leaves. Below this layer are the tops of the shorter or younger trees. The tallest trees shade this layer. Farther down is a layer of bushes and shrubs. If the forest has many trees, very little sun reaches this layer. It may contain few plants.

Grasses, ferns, flowers, and other soft-stemmed plants grow beneath the shrubs. They grow thickest where the most light can get through the top layers. Mosses grow on the forest floor. Leaves, twigs, and dead plants might also be on the forest floor.

Prairie Creek Redwoods State Park, California

Birch trees, Baxter State Park, Maine

Spruce, fir, and pine trees grow in northern forests. Giant redwoods grow along the California and Oregon coasts. These conifers form a thick upper layer. Not much light can reach the lower levels. So there are few shrubs, grasses, or flowers in northern forests. Mosses may grow on the forest floor and on the trunks and branches of trees.

Deciduous forests have many plants in their lower layers. This is because the upper layers are not as thick as they are in northern forests. In fall and winter more light can get through. Some deciduous broadleaf trees are oak, maple, hickory, ash, and beech. Broadleaf evergreens include bay, holly, live oak, and magnolia. These trees grow in the southeastern part of the United States and in Australia and New Zealand.

Most of the trees in tropical rain forests are broadleaf evergreens. Little light gets through the thick upper layers in most places. Few plants can grow in the lower layers. But in some areas of the rain forest enough light can get through for plants to grow. These places are called jungles.

Some trees in the tropical rain forest produce

food. Cashews and figs grow on rain forest trees. Balsa, brazilwood, mahogany, and rosewood trees are used to make furniture. Some plants, such as ferns, mosses, and orchids, grow on tree branches. Many vines also grow in tropical rain forests.

Forest Animals

All the layers of a forest have animal life. In northern forests squirrels and chipmunks gather nuts from cones in the top layers. Woodpeckers and small birds search for insects. Raccoons climb up and down trees looking for nuts, berries, eggs, insects, and small animals. Wolves prey on animals on the forest floor. Owls, hawks, and falcons prey from the air. Small snakes, mice, and lemmings live on the ground. A **lemming** is a small, mouselike rodent. Moose, bears, foxes, and ducks also live in northern forests.

lemming
a small, mouselike rodent

Some animals of northern forests also live in deciduous forests. These include snakes, frogs, woodpeckers, hawks, and owls. Deer, wildcats, and skunks live in these forests as well. In winter, when there are few insects, some animals eat seeds and nuts instead. Others hibernate all winter. Some birds fly to warmer regions.

Monkeys live in tropical rain forests all over the world. Some spend all their time in the tops of trees. They eat the fruits and nuts that grow there. Bats, parrots, and toucans (**too**-kanz) live in the treetops too. A **toucan** is a fruit-eating bird with a large beak. Chimpanzees and wild cats, such as tigers and leopards, spend time in trees and on the ground. Ants are found at all levels too. Bees, butterflies, moths, and termites are other forest insects.

toucan
a fruit-eating bird with a large beak

Spider monkey, Mexico

Antelopes, hogs, frogs, turtles, lizards, and snakes are other animals that live in tropical rain forests. Many eat roots, fruit, leaves, and seeds. Some eat other animals.

A tropical rain forest has many plants and animals. This is so even though these forests have only a thin layer of fertile soil. So much life is possible because of the hot, moist climate. Things grow fast. But when they die, dead plants and animals rot quickly in the moist soil. In this way the soil always has food for new plants to grow.

Section Review

Write your answers on a sheet of paper.

1. Describe the five layers of a forest.
2. What do some animals of deciduous forests eat in winter?
3. Why do tropical animals not have to hibernate?

3 The Forests of Canada

Forests cover more than a third of Canada. In the northern part of the country, these huge forests cover rugged hills, plains, and mountains. To travel from place to place, people must use narrow, winding roads over the ridges and through the tree-filled valleys. They also use the many lakes to "land" small airplanes.

Traveling through northern Alberta, Canada

Summers are short in the northern forests. Winters can last eight or nine months. Temperatures are far below freezing during this time. Deep snow makes automobile travel impossible through the long months of winter.

Yet in many small towns of the northern forests, people work all year. Lumberjacks ski or drive snowmobiles to the trees they cut. When the spring thaw comes, the logs are floated down rivers to sawmills.

In mining towns nickel, gold, and silver are dug up all year round too. Some towns are built above the mines. Workers in these towns need not travel at all during the cold season. During the winter the roads are closed. The rivers are frozen. The only contact the people have with other forest towns is by radio.

Many Canadians of the northern forests hunt deer and other animals. Still, they get much of their food from southern farms. They buy and store enough to last all winter. The Canadian government helps ship goods to the people living in the northern forests. Developing the valuable resources of this region is very important to Canada.

A Look at Canada

Canada is a country with many types of landforms. In the west there are rugged mountains and forested valleys. East of the Rocky Mountains are wide, fertile plains.

A wide plateau surrounds the lowlands along the shores of Hudson Bay. The plateau has many low, rocky hills. Most of this region is forest. To the north of the plateau are the Arctic lowlands and islands.

In eastern Canada there are fertile lowlands along the St. Lawrence River. Most of Canada's population lives here. A section of the Appalachian Mountains stretches through northeastern Canada.

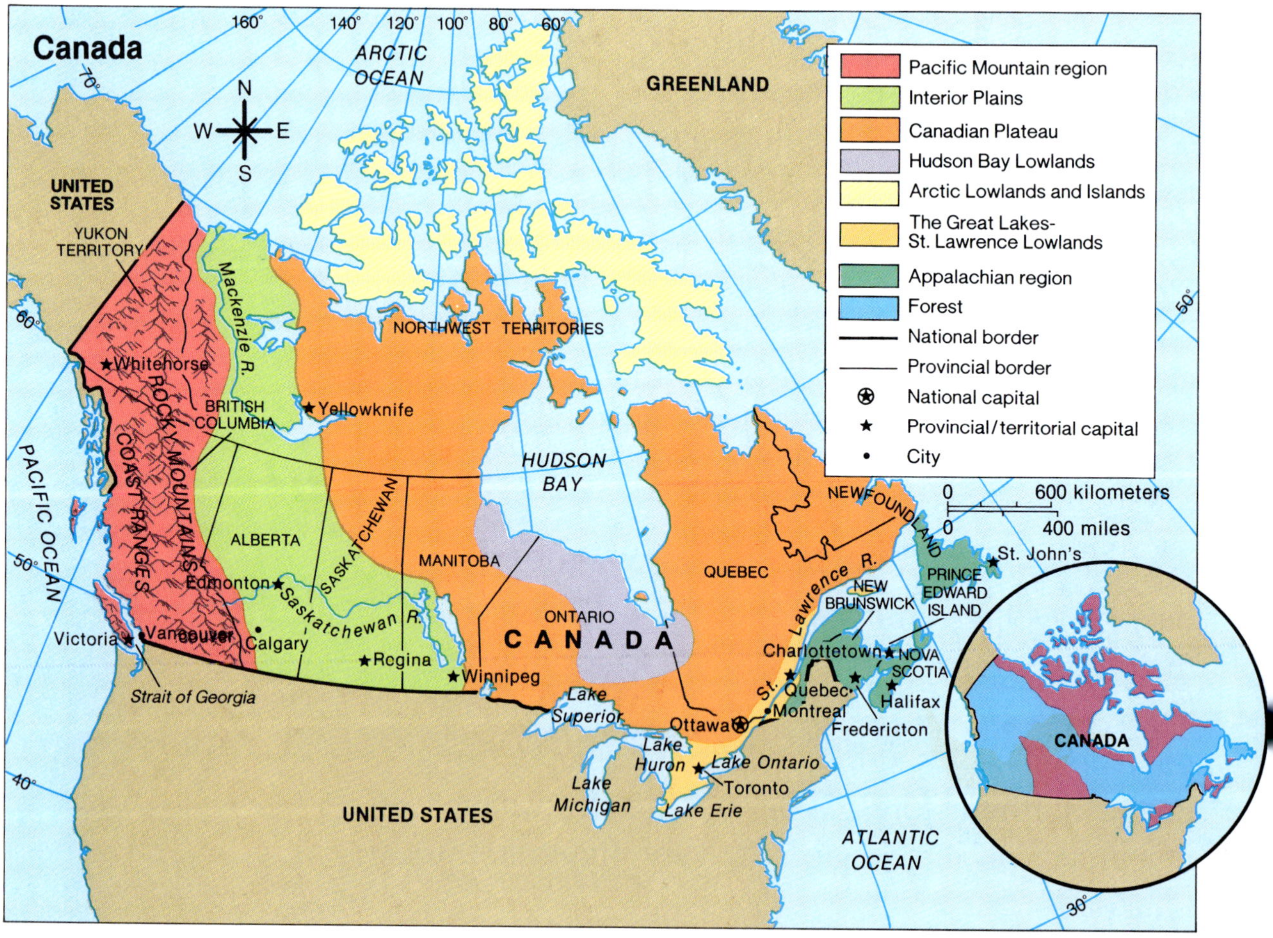

An oil well on farmland, western Canada

Canada has many lakes, rivers, and ocean harbors. Boats are the main means of transportation in many parts of the country. The largest cities are on the shores of the Great Lakes, the St. Lawrence River, and the Strait of Georgia. Mountain rivers provide these cities with hydroelectric power.

The climate is colder in most of Canada than it is in the United States. Much of Canada has long periods of frost in winter. Summers are warm but short in most of the country.

Canada's greatest resources are the good soil of the prairie farmlands and the trees of the forest lands. Canada has much more forest land than farmland. And many farms are snowed in during winter. But the farms still produce great amounts of wheat and other crops. Canada has resources under the ground too. It is rich in oil, gas, and mineral wealth. Nickel, zinc, and uranium are mined.

Old Port Park on the St. Lawrence River, Montreal, Canada

Some of the products from both the forests and the farms of Canada are shipped to Montreal. Montreal is Canada's largest city and one of its busiest ports. Many French-speaking Canadians live in this city. Advertisements and street signs may be written in both English and French.

Toronto is the second largest city in Canada. Food processing is its leading industry. Printing, publishing, and computers are also important.

In most of Canada's cities, the people live much as do people in the United States. Some groups of people keep their old traditions. French, Scottish, German, and Ukrainian people still speak the languages of their European ancestors. In the north some Inuit (**ihn**-oo-it) still follow the ways of their ancestors. The Inuit are a kind of Eskimo people.

Section Review

Write your answers on a sheet of paper.

1. How do the people of the northern forests of Canada get their food?

2. Which two languages are spoken in Montreal?

3. Why are rivers so important in Canada?

4 The Tropical Forest of Borneo

Borneo (**bawr**-nee-oh) is an island in southeastern Asia. It is the third largest island in the world. Two thirds of Borneo is covered by thick, tropical rain forests. Only small parts of the island along the coast are cleared for farmland. Parts of the northern hills have been cleared for grazing.

The forests of Borneo grow from the flat, swampy southern coast to high on the tops of mountains. These forests are kept moist by rain nearly all year round. In many places more than 380 centimeters (150 inches) of rain falls every year. The weather is as warm as it is wet because Borneo is on the equator. Only the highest mountains are cool. But snow hardly ever falls, even on the mountaintops. Frost is never seen in the lower forests. The average temperature in these forests is 27° C (80° F).

Coconut plantation, Kalimantan, Borneo

The broad tops of the trees often block almost all sunlight. Bushes and small plants cannot grow on the dark forest floor. But the birds and animals have learned to live in the sunny upper layer of the forest. More kinds of monkeys and birds live in Borneo's rain forests than in any other in the world. The people who live in the forest hunt these animals. They also gather bird eggs for food.

The trees themselves have many uses too. The wood of the teak tree is very valuable. Coconut palms have dozens of nuts. These nuts have milk inside them. The coconut meat can be eaten from the nut or can be dried. The dried meat of coconuts is called **copra** (**koh**-pruh). Sago (**say**-goh) palms are used for a kind of flour. Rattan (ruh-**tan**) palms are used for making furniture. Other trees produce spices and chemicals for making leather.

copra
the dried meat of coconuts

The forest goods of Borneo cannot be taken by car or train to be sold. Most parts of the forest do not have roads or railroads. The region has many mountains and is packed with plants. So people travel on the rivers to the coastal cities. These rivers start in the mountains of central Borneo.

Borneo—Island Under Three Flags

The island of Borneo is under the control of three countries. The largest section, Kalimantan (kal-uh-**man**-tan), is a province of Indonesia. Sarawak (suh-**rah**-wahk) and Sabah (**sahb**-ah) belong to the country of Malaysia. Only the small northern land area called Brunei (**broo**-nie) is independent.

The sections of Borneo are divided by mountain ranges. These mountains run out from the center of the island like spokes of a wheel. Find them on the map on page 363.

Swampy coastal plains surround the mountains. The largest plain is in the south. It is inland from the city of Bandjarmasin (bahn-jur-**mah**-sin). Some of the coastal plains have good soil. Others have salty soil because the ocean water floods over these plains during storms.

Many rivers flow through Borneo. They are used by the people for travel and fishing. Malay (muh-**lay**) and Indonesian people live along the rivers. The many different kinds of fish found in the rivers are their main food.

These sailing boats on the Barito River in Borneo are being loaded with lumber. The lumber will be carried to the Indonesian island of Java.

Dayak women pound rice to remove the husks.

The Dayak (**die**-ak) people live by smaller streams in the mountains of Borneo. There are many different Dayak tribes. Each has its own language and customs. Some still follow the ancient ways of their tribes.

The Dayak live in villages of 100 or more people. The people in each village all live in one long house. The house is built on stilts. This keeps it out of the moist soil. The long house is a village under one roof.

The Dayak grow rice on hillsides. They work together to grow the crops. Children over the age of 10 work alongside their parents. The Dayak are skilled at making tools and blowguns. They heat and form metal just as a blacksmith does. They can shoot birds and monkeys out of tall trees with their blowguns.

Recently some resources have been found on Borneo. These are different from those resources used by the Dayak. Diamonds and oil have been taken out of the earth by modern companies.

The Sultan's palace, Brunei

Diamonds are mined in the mountains. They are sold to wealthy merchants in the coastal cities. Oil is found along the shores of Borneo. It has made the people of some cities very wealthy.

Bandar Seri Begawan (**bun**-dur **ser**-ee buh-**gah**-wun) is a growing oil city in Brunei. Balikpapan (bahl-ik-**pahp**-ahn) and Tarakan (tahr-rah-**kahn**) in Kalimantan are also rich oil cities. Stores, theaters, and schools are found in these cities. They are much like those of Europe and the United States. But the oil refineries have brought pollution. The air of these cities is not as clear as it is over the forest homes of the Dayak.

Section Review

Write your answers on a sheet of paper.

1. How many islands on the earth are larger than Borneo?
2. Name two types of palm trees used by the forest people of Borneo.
3. How would the diamond miners in the mountains of Borneo probably take their diamonds to the coast?

SOCIAL STUDIES SKILLS

Reading a Population Density Map

population density the number of people living in each square kilometer or mile of an area

You can find out how thickly settled an area is by reading a **population density** map. Population density is how closely together people live, or how thickly settled an area is. This population density map shows how many people live in each square kilometer (or mile) of Canada.

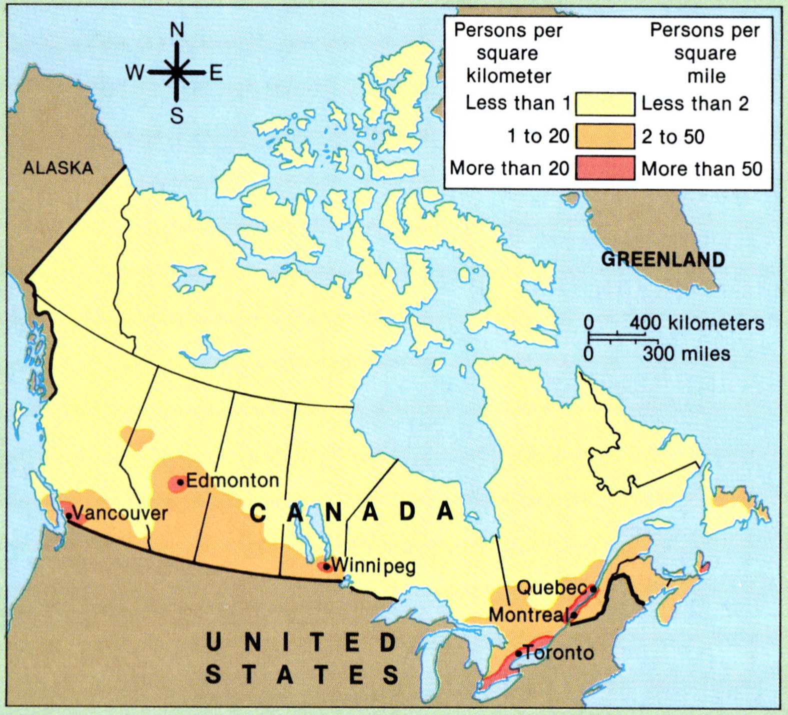

In cities and towns where people live very near their neighbors, the population density is high. In the countryside, or in mountain or desert areas, people live far apart or in small groups. These areas have a low population density.

Look at the map key. It explains what each color of the map means.

Practice Your Skills

1. How many people are there per square kilometer (or mile) in northwestern Canada?
2. Which is more thinly settled, northern or southern Canada?
3. What is the population density near Vancouver? Montreal? Toronto? Winnipeg?
4. Does most of Canada have a high or a low population density?

FAMOUS PEOPLE

Jane Goodall is famous for her work with chimpanzees in Africa. Since 1960, she has studied them in their natural homes. Goodall's work has helped us understand much more about these animals.

Jane Goodall was born in England in 1934. In 1960, she went to Tanzania (tan-zuh-**nee**-uh) in eastern Africa. She has done most of her research at the Gombe (**gum**-beh) Stream National Park.

When Goodall started her work, she had to be very patient. At first the chimpanzees were afraid of her. They hid from her in the forest. But she sat quietly, and slowly they began to trust her.

Goodall watched the chimps very carefully. She took many notes. She also wrote reports about the animals. At one time scientists believed chimpanzees ate only fruits and vegetables. But Jane Goodall learned that they also eat insects, young monkeys, and pigs. She learned that they can sometimes be violent, even toward one another.

Jane Goodall worked alone for four years. Then more people came to study and work with her. Now there is a research station at Gombe Stream National Park. She and other scientists still study the chimpanzees. They have found that these animals are more like humans than any other animals.

Close-up on

Winter Carnival in Quebec Would you stand outside to watch a parade if the temperature were below freezing? Thousands of people do this on the first and last nights of the Winter Carnival in Quebec (kwuh-**bek**). They come to see the parades. Then, to stay warm, they dance in the streets to lively French-Canadian music.

Winters are long and cold in Quebec. The people get tired of staying indoors, away from other people. So in February they have a celebration that lasts for 10 days.

Bonhomme (bun-**um**) means "good person" in French. In the Winter Carnival Bonhomme is a person dressed up as a happy snowman. He leads the parades, dances, and other events of the carnival.

Bonhomme helps to judge the famous ice-sculpture contest. Some sculptures are made by profes-

Boat race on the St. Lawrence River

the World

sional sculptors. Others are made by other people at the carnival, just for fun. The city builds an ice palace for the carnival. It is made out of several hundred tons of packed snow.

The carnival includes outdoor sports for people who can brave the cold. The Pee Wee Hockey Tournament is held for players between 10 and 12 years of age. All children can ride the giant sled run in front of the Chateau Frontenac (shah-**toh fron**-teh-nak), a large hotel in the city.

For grown-ups, a canoe race takes place on the partly frozen St. Lawrence River. The people must drag their canoes over the ice to the open water of the river.

When the first warm day of spring comes to Quebec, all of the ice and snow sculptures melt. But Bonhomme and the carnival will come back next winter!

Winter Carnival parade

The Ice Palace

UNIT REVIEW

Word Work

Write the sentences below on a sheet of paper. Fill in the blanks with the correct words from the list.

oasis dune bauxite population density

1. _____ is the number of people living in each square kilometer or mile of an area.
2. An _____ is a place in the desert where there is enough water for many plants to grow.
3. A _____ is formed when wind blows sand into a pile.
4. The ore from which aluminum is made is _____.

Knowing the Facts

Write your answers on a sheet of paper.

1. How is the climate of a desert different from the climate of a tropical rain forest?
2. What kind of work do most people in Botswana do?
3. Why do farmers in tropical rain forests have to move often?

Using What You Know

Choose one of the following activities to do. Follow the instructions given here.

1. Explain why more people live in southern Canada than in northern Canada.
2. Use an encyclopedia to make a list of products made from the different parts of trees.

Skills Practice

Use the following map to answer the questions below. Write your answers on a sheet of paper.

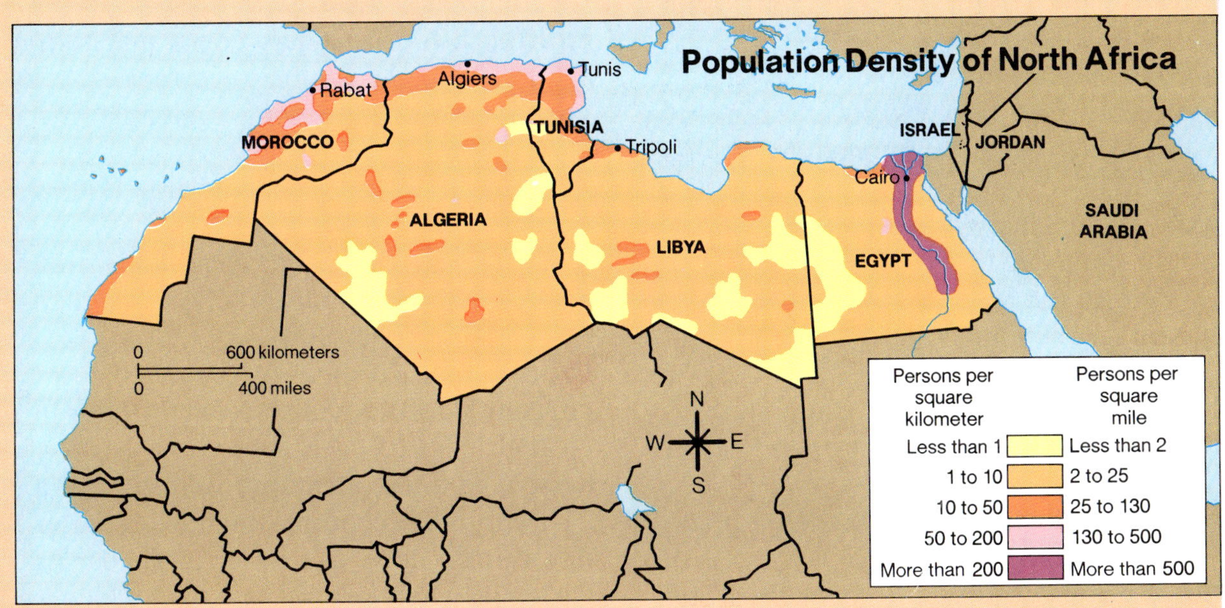

1. How many people per square kilometer (or mile) live in the area around Cairo?
2. Which is in a more densely populated area, Algiers or Tripoli?
3. Are the more densely populated areas near the coast of northern Africa or inland?
4. Does most of northern Africa have a high or low population density?

Your State

Think about the population of your state. Is your area densely populated? Why do you think the population density is high or low? Are you near any forests or deserts? If so, how does the forest or desert influence how many people live nearby?

GLOSSARY

Aborigines the first people to live in Australia
altitude the height of land above the level of the sea
arroyo a ditch formed by flood water
assembly line a way of manufacturing in which work is moved from one worker to another
axis an imaginary line that runs through the center of the earth from the North Pole to the South Pole
basin an area of land that is surrounded by higher land
bauxite ore used to make aluminum
bay a body of water having land on at least two sides
bola a rope with a ball attached to each end, used as a lasso
boomerang a curved or bent throwing stick
broadleaf tree a tree with flat, wide leaves
canal a waterway dug across land for ships to go through
canyon a deep valley with steep sides
cargo a load of products carried from one place to another
carnivorous animal an animal that eats other animals
climate the kind of weather a region has over a long period of time
colony a place settled by people from another country and still ruled by that country
combine a large machine that cuts and gathers grain
communication the sending out of ideas and information
compass rose the drawing showing the main directions of north, south, east, and west on a map
Congress the part of the United States government that makes many of our country's laws
conifer a tree that has cones and thin, needlelike leaves
conservation preserving valuable resources
continent one of the seven large bodies of land on the earth
continental divide the geographic area that separates the direction in which water currents flow
copra the dried meat of coconuts
current a fast-moving stream of water in the ocean
dam a wall-like structure built across a river to help control the flowing water
deciduous tree a tree that sheds its leaves each fall
delta an area of land at the mouth of a river
deposit a large area of a mineral deep in the earth
desert a sandy area with no trees or water
distance scale a measuring line on a map that helps to figure the distance in kilometers or miles from one place to another
double bar graph a graph that compares two sets of the same kind of information
drought a long period of time with little or no rain
dune a sandy hill formed when wind blows sand into piles
economic activity a way that people use their resources to live
equator the imaginary line that circles the middle of the earth, halfway between the North Pole and South Pole

erosion the wearing away of land by water or wind
evergreen a tree that keeps its leaves all year
export a product sent from one country to another
fertile good for growing plants and crops
fleece the coat of a sheep
food processing turning crops into food products
foot the lowest part of a mountain
forestry the study of managing forest resources
frontier land that is mostly unsettled
gaucho a South American cowhand
gem a precious stone used to make jewelry
geyser a hot spring that shoots water and steam into the air
glacier a large, thick mass of ice
globe a round model of the earth
gorge a deep, narrow passage between mountains
government a group of people who are elected to make laws and lead a community, state, or country
grain elevator a large tower for storing grain
grassland an area where grasses are the main form of plant life
grid a series of evenly spaced lines used to locate places on maps
grove a large field of trees
growing season the period of time in which the weather is warm enough for crops to grow
hemisphere half of a sphere; on a globe, a hemisphere represents one half of the earth
hibernate to spend winter or summer sleeping
highland an area of hills or mountains
High Veld the prairie land of southern Africa
homesteader a person who settles on land provided by the government
House of Representatives the branch of Congress with members elected according to the state's population
humid moist or damp
hurricane a fierce storm of wind and rain
husk the outer covering on grains such as wheat and corn
hydroelectric power energy produced by water power
import a product received by one country from another
irrigation supplying water to dry land through pipes, ditches, or canals
landform a shape of land, such as a mountain, valley, or plateau
landforms map a map that uses colors to show the height and shape of the land, such as mountains, highlands, plateaus, and plains
landmark an important thing or place that stands out from everything around it
latitude line an east-west line drawn parallel to the equator on a globe
lava hot, liquid rock
lemming a small, mouselike rodent
limestone a kind of rock used in steelmaking and in building
line graph a graph that uses lines to show information and how that information changes
longitude line a line drawn from north to south from pole to pole on a globe
lowland a low, flat area of land
magma the hot, melted rock inside the earth

manufacturing making finished goods from raw materials
map a drawing of part or all of the earth's surface that shows where things are located
map key the section that explains the symbols used on a map
merchant a business person who buys and sells goods
mestizo a person who has Spanish and Indian ancestors
mineral a material dug from the earth
mining the process of taking mineral deposits from the earth
missionary a person who teaches others about religion
moisture water or other liquids in the air or on the ground; wetness
mound a pile, or heap, of earth
mountain range a group or series of mountains
mouth the place where a river empties into a larger body of water
natural gas a light mineral often used for fuel, often found near petroleum
natural resource something from nature that people need or want, such as water, coal, soil, and forests
nomad a person who has no permanent home
North Pole the point located at the most northern place on a globe
oasis a place in the desert with enough water for many plants to grow
ocean a large body of salt water that covers much of the earth's surface
ore a mixture of rock, soil, and minerals
pampa a grassy, treeless plain of southern South America
peak the pointed top of a mountain
peninsula a body of land almost completely surrounded by water
permafrost soil that is always frozen
petrochemical a product that comes from oil or natural gas
petroleum an oily, liquid mineral
pie graph a drawing of a whole circle divided into parts
pioneer a person who tries something first and opens the way for others to follow
plain a low, flat land area
plate a section of the earth's crust
plateau an area of flat land higher than the land around it
pollution damage to air, water, or land by smoke or dust
poncho a wool cape
population all of the people who live in a particular place
population density the number of people living in each square kilometer or mile of an area
port a place where ships can load and unload goods
prairie a large area of flat land covered with tall, thick grass
preservation taking care to make sure landmarks are kept safe from damage
President the leader of the United States government
prime meridian a special longitude line that is the starting point for measuring all other lines of longitude
ptarmigan a type of bird with feathered feet, found in mountainous and cold regions
pueblo a house made of mud bricks and built into the side of a cliff
ranching raising large herds of animals such as cattle, sheep, or horses
ravine a narrow valley with steep sides
raw material a material in its natural state, used in making finished goods
refinery a factory that cleans a raw material and makes it ready for use

region an area of land

representative government a government in which lawmakers are elected by the people

reservation an area of land set aside for a certain purpose, sometimes as a homeland for American Indians

reservoir a lake or pond where water is stored for use

resource a supply of valuable or useful things, such as water, coal, soil, forests, or air

revolution the movement of the earth in a circle around the sun

rural away from cities and close to farms

savanna a grassland of tropical climates

Senate the branch of Congress in which each state elects two members called senators

shaft a deep passage dug into the earth to remove mineral ore

shearing the cutting of a sheep's wool

slave a person who is owned by another person

slurry copper ore and water ground up in a mixture

South Pole the point located at the most southern place on a globe

steppe a grassland that is drier than a prairie but not as dry as a desert

succulent a plant with thick, waxy, or leathery leaves

summit a mountain's highest peak

suspension bridge a bridge suspended from cables hung between towers

swamp a lowland area covered with shallow water

symbol something that stands for a real thing

synthetic a human-made material

temperate neither very hot nor very cold

temperature the measure of how hot or cold a place is

textile cloth made from cotton, linen, or other materials

timberline the point on a mountain above which trees cannot grow

time line a way of listing important dates or events in the order in which they happened

time zone one of 24 areas or zones of the earth in which the time is one hour earlier than the zone to its east

toucan a fruit-eating bird with a large beak

tributary a river or stream that flows into a larger body of water

tropical hot and wet

tundra a wide, treeless plain where few plants or animals live

volcano an opening in the earth's surface through which hot liquid rock and other materials are forced out

weather the condition of the air at a certain time or place

wonder something that is surprisingly beautiful, or very unusual

wood pulp ground-up wood fibers from logs

zinc a metal used in making iron and paint and also used in electric batteries

INDEX

ART CREDITS

Eric Vander Arend p. 274; Wendy Biggins p. 219; Bill Edwards p. 171; Tom Herbert pp. 62, 63, 91; Kerry Polite pp. 228, 242, 251; Pat Steiner pp. 102, 182, 240.

MAPS: General Cartography, Inc. Fine Line Illustrations, Inc. pp. 16–17

PHOTO CREDITS

UNIT 1: p. 20 Kent and Donna Dannen/Photo Researchers; p. 21 (t) Bryce Flynn/Picture Group, (b) Nicolas de Vore/Bryce Coleman; p. 22, Dick Davis/DPI; p. 23 Ron Ruhoff/Shostal Assoc.; p. 28 J. Alex Langley/DPI; p. 32 (l) HRW Photo by Jackie Curtis (r) Tom Ives; p. 34 Jonathan Wright/Bruce Coleman; p. 34 Vic Beunza/Bruce Coleman; p. 38 Focus on Sports; p. 39 (l) Georgia State Tourist Div., Dept. of Industry and Trade, (r) Lawrence Frank; p. 40 David Muench; p. 41 Shostal Assoc.; p. 42 Jeff Foott/Bruce Coleman; p. 43 Bettmann Archive; p. 46 (l) Hedrich Blessing, (r) Las Vegas News Bureau; p. 47 Photo Researchers; p. 48 Ken Lax; p. 49 Lawrence Frank; p. 50 Bettmann Archive; p. 51 (b) Mark Sherman/Bruce Coleman, (t) Free Library of Philadelphia.
UNIT 2: p. 54 Photri; p. 55 (t) A. Pierce Bounds/Uniphoto, (b) George Wilson; p. 56 M.E. Warren/Photo Researchers; p. 60 (l) Raphael Macia/Photo Researchers; (r) Michael J. Pettypool/Uniphoto; p. 65 Porterfield Chickering/Photo Researchers; p. 66 Bruce Roberts/Photo Researchers; p. 69 Metropolitan Opera Assoc.; p. 70 HRW Photo by Jackie Curtis; p. 71 Maine Historical Society; p. 72 John Hancock Mutual Life Insurance Co.; p. 73 Bettmann Archive; p. 74 Thomas Gilcrease Inst. of Am. Hist. & Art, Tulsa, Okla.; pp. 75–76 The Bettmann Archive; p. 77 Artie Grace/Sygma; p. 78 Metropolitan Opera Assoc., p. 79 (l) Alan Apardi/Blackstar, (r) HRW Photo Bank; p. 81 Owen Franken/Sygma; p. 82 Les Moore/Uniphoto; p. 84 Dick Durrance II/Woodfin Camp; p. 85 Henry Moore/DPI; p. 86 HRW Photo by Russell Dian; p. 89 Manuel Rodriguez; p. 89 Philip Jon Bailey/Picture Group; p. 90 B. Cory Kilvert, Jr./Stock Shop; p. 92–93 George Wilson.
UNIT 3: p. 96 Appel Color Photography; p. 97 (t) Charlton Photos, (b) Al Stephenson/Phelps Agency; p. 98 Hank Morgan/Phelps Agency; p. 101 Carleton Ray/Photo Researchers; p. 103 Majani/Sygma; p. 104 Bill Weems/Phelps Agency; p. 108 Gillies Peress/Magnum; p. 109 Alpha; p. 110 Katrina Thomas/Photo Researchers; p. 112 Russell Thompson; p. 113 Bettmann Archive; p. 114 Colonial Williamsburg; p. 116 Hank del Espinasse/The Image Bank; p. 117 Wide World Photos; pp. 119–121 R. Cotton Ashton/Phelps Agency; p. 122 Fred Zimmerman/Phelps Agency; p. 123 Sy Israel/Shostal Assoc.; p. 124 Tony Ray Jones/Magnum; p. 125 Mike Porter; p. 126 Jerry Cooke/Photo Researchers; p. 129 HRW Photo by Russell Dian; p. 132 (l) Abby Aldrich Rockefeller Folk Art Center, Williamsburg, (r) Baltimore Museum of Art; p. 133 Steve Payne.
UNIT 4: p. 136 Appel Color Photography; p. 137 (t) HRW Photo by Russell Dian, (b) Ewing Galloway; p. 138 Craig Aurness/Woodfin Camp.; p. 141 Bill Bridge/DPI; p. 142 E. Nagele/Alpha; p. 148 William S. Nawrocki/Click Chicago; p. 149 Ewing Galloway; p. 150 Eric Carle/Shostal Assoc.; p. 151 Bettmann Archive; p. 152 Greater Omaha Chamber of Commerce; p. 153 George Catlin, National Gallery of Art, Paul Mellon Collection; p. 155 Library of Congress; p. 156 George Catlin, National Gallery of Art, gift of Mr. and Mrs. Paul Mellon; p. 157 Francis Alexander, National Gallery of Art, gift of Edgar William and Bernice Chrysler Garbisch; p. 158 Missouri Historical Society; p. 159 UPI; p. 160 & 163 Library of Congress; p. 162 Alex Maclean/Landslides; p. 164 Robert McElroy/Woodfin Camp; p. 165 Sam C. Pierson/Photo Researchers; p. 166 Alex Maclean/Landslides; pp. 168–170 Grant Heilman; pp. 172–173 (r) Inter. Institute of Milwaukee County; p. 173 (l) John D. Anundsen.
UNIT 5: p. 176 Photo Researchers/Larry Mulvehill; p. 177 (t) Craig Aurness/Woodfin Camp; (b) Sam C. Pierson, Jr./Photo Researchers; p. 178 Tom McHugh/Photo Researchers; p. 183 Jan Halaska/Photo Researchers; p. 185 Bob Strauss/Woodfin Camp; p. 186 Texaco; p. 187 B.E. Fichte & Assoc.; p. 189 Malcolm Varon, © 1977; p. 190 Craig Aurness/Woodfin Camp; p. 191 Ronald F. Thomas/Taurus; p. 193 Institute of Texan Cultures; p. 194 University of Texas at Austin; p. 195 Thomas Ives; p. 196 (t) Margo Blair/Click Chicago, (m) J. Schweiker/Photo Researchers, (b) Baylor College of Medicine; p. 199 Sam C.

Pierson, Jr./Photo Researchers; p. 200 Leo Touchet/Woodfin Camp; p. 201 Arizona Office of Tourism; p. 202 Arizona Photographic Assoc.; p. 203 Glenn Short; p. 205 John Cooper; p. 206 American Sheep Producers Council; p. 208 Michal Heron; p. 209 (t) Elliot Erwitt/Magnum, (b) Michal Heron.

UNIT 6: p. 212 Charles E. Rotkin/Photography for Industry; p. 213 (t) Tom McHugh/Photo Researchers, (b) Convention and Visitors Bureau of Denver and Colorado; p. 214 Dennis Stock/Magnum Photos; p. 220 Bill Grange; p. 221 Charles E. Rotkin/Photography for Industry; p. 223 Colorado Historical Society; p. 224 Rollie McKenna/Photo Researchers; p. 225 Maud Davis Baker/Montana Historical Society; p. 226 John Running; p. 227 (t) Smithsonian Institution, National Anthropological Archives, (m) Montana Historical Society, (b) The Schlesinger Library, Radcliffe College; p. 229 American Heritage Center, Univ. of Wyoming; p. 230 Union Pacific Railroad; p. 231 Wyoming Travel Commission; p. 232 Colorado Department of Public Relations; p. 233 R. Rowan/Photo Researchers; p. 234 Robert Searns/Urban Edges; p. 236 R.J. Glovan; p. 237 Nicholas de Vore III/Bruce Coleman; p. 238 Charles E. Rotkin/Photography for Industry; pp. 240–241 Thomas Ives.

UNIT 7: p. 244 R.W. Kane/DPI; p. 245 (t) Keith Gunner/Bruce Coleman, (b) Werner Story/DPI; p. 246 James Randklev/Alpha; p. 249 Charles Schneider/Photophile; p. 250 Wide World; p. 252 Ned Haines/Photo Researchers; p. 254 W. G. MacDonald; p. 255 Steve Solum/Bruce Coleman; p. 257 Oregon Historical Society, Portland, Oregon; p. 258 Tony Howarth/Woodfin Camp; p. 259 American Museum of Natural History; p. 261 The Granger Collection; p. 262 Camera Hawaii; p. 263 Wide World; p. 264 (t) Wide World, (l) Courtesy of Laurel L. Bland, PhD. and AMU Press, Asian Pacific University, Anchorage, (r) Oregon Historical Society, Portland, Oregon; p. 267 Steve Meltzer/West Stock; p. 268 Marv Wolf/After Image; p. 269 Culver Pictures; p. 270 George Hall/Woodfin Camp; p. 271 Shostal Assoc.; p. 273 Shostal Assoc.; p. 274 Rocky Weldon/Leo DeWys; p. 278 (t) Tom Tracy/Alpha, (b) Bettmann Archive; p. 279 © Warner Bros., Inc., 1966.

UNIT 8: pp. 282–283 Ken Stepnell/Taurus; p. 283 (t) Ernest Braun/Image Bank, (b) Sullivan & Rogers/Bruce Coleman; p. 284 David Muench/Image Bank; p. 287 (t) F. Gohier/ Photo Researchers, (b) Owen Franken/Stock Boston; p. 288 Howard Soucerek; p. 289 Wendell Metzer/Bruce Coleman; p. 290 (l) C.B. Frith/Bruce Coleman, (r) H. Gritscher/Peter Arnold; p. 291 Nicholas de Vore III/Bruce Coleman; p. 292 (l) Stephen J. Kraseman/Photo Researchers, (r) Sullivan & Rogers/Bruce Coleman; p. 293 (l) Stuart Cohen/Stock Boston, (r) Sullivan & Rogers/Bruce Coleman; p. 295 Clyde H. Smith/Peter Arnold; p. 296 Danilo Boschung/Leo de Wys; p. 297 Erich Lessing/Magnum; p. 298 Paolo Koch/Photo Researchers; p. 300 Toby Richards/Bruce Coleman; p. 301 Arthur Lavine/Leo de Wys; p. 302 Jacques Jangoux/Peter Arnold; p. 303 Martin Gostelow/Bruce Coleman; p. 306 Robert Frerck/Odyssey Productions; p. 307 Craig Aurness/Woodfin Camp; p. 308 (l) Philip Jon Bailey/Stock Boston, (r) Frank Siteman/Stock Boston; p. 309 Burt Glinn/Magnum; p. 311 Lynn Stone/Bruce Coleman; p. 312 M.P. Kahl/Bruce Coleman; p. 313 Leonard Lee Rue III/Animals, Animals; p. 314 Marc & Evelyne Bernheim/Woodfin Camp; p. 315 John Bryson/Image Bank; p. 316 Howard Soucerek; pp. 319–320 Tass/Sovfoto; p. 322 Geog Gerster/Photo Researchers; p. 323 Jessica Ehlers/Bruce Coleman; p. 324 Bendick Associates/Monkmeyer Press; p. 325 Carl Frank/Photo Researchers; p. 325 Carl Purcell/Photo Researchers; p. 327 (l) SEF/Art Resource, (r) John Curtis/Taurus.

UNIT 9: pp. 330–331 John Shaw/Bruce Coleman; p. 331 (t) Victor Englebert/Photo Researchers, (b) Peter Ward/Bruce Coleman; p. 332 Owen Franken/Stock Boston; p. 334 Dan McCoy/Rainbow; p. 335 Burnett H. Moody/Bruce Coleman; p. 336 E. & H. Schreiber/Photo Researchers; p. 337 Joy Spurr/Bruce Coleman; p. 338 C. Haagner/Bruce Coleman; p. 339 Brake Field/Bruce Coleman; p. 340 Jen & Des Bartlett/Bruce Coleman; p. 342 Leonard Lee Rue III/Photo Researchers; p. 344 Diane Rawson/Photo Researchers; p. 345 Johan Elbers/Int'l Stock Photo; p. 347 A.B. Joyce/Photo Researchers; p. 348 Stephen Frink/Image Bank; p. 349 Rick Smolan/Woodfin Camp; p. 350 J.P. Nacivet/Leo de Wys; p. 352 Hiroji Kubota/Magnum; p. 353 Bruno Barbey/Magnum; p. 354 John Running/Stock Boston; p. 355 Chuck Place/Image Bank; p. 356 Dan Budnik/Woodfin Camp; p. 357 David Overcash/Bruce Coleman; p. 358 Fulvio Eccardi/Bruce Coleman; p. 360 Reinninger/Leo de Wys; p. 361 Dilip Mehta/Contact Press; p. 362 George Zimbel/Monkmeyer Press; pp. 364–365 Victor Englebert/Photo Researchers; p. 367 Matsumoto/Sygma; p. 369 A.P./Wide World; p. 370 Mark Antman/Image Works.